Owen McCaffe~

PI ~

Over the past twenty yea~ ~y´s plays
have been performed throu~ and have won
various awards. His work in ~anic: Scenes from
the British Wreck Commissio~ ~ Inquiry, 1912 (MAC,
Belfast); The Absence of Women (Lyric Theatre, Belfast,
and Tricycle Theatre, London); Days of Wine and Roses
(Donmar Theatre); Closing Time (National Theatre,
London); Shoot the Crow (Druid and Prime Cut
Productions, Belfast); Mojo Mickybo (Kabosh); and
Scenes from the Big Picture (National Theatre, London,
and Prime Cut Productions, Belfast), which won the
Meyer-Whitworth, John Whiting and Evening Standard
Awards: he is the only playwright to win these three
major awards in one year for the same play. In 2012,
Quietly marked his debut at the Abbey Theatre. This
production transferred to the Traverse Theatre for the
Edinburgh Festival 2013 and was awarded a Scotsman
Fringe First.

by the same author from Faber

QUIETLY
TITANIC
THE ABSENCE OF WOMEN

OWEN McCAFFERTY

Plays One

The Waiting List

Shoot the Crow

Mojo Mickybo

Closing Time

Scenes from the Big Picture

with an introduction by Mark Phelan
and a foreword by the author

faber and faber

First published in 2013
by Faber and Faber Limited
74–77 Great Russell Street, London WC1B 3DA

Typeset by Country Setting, Kingsdown, Kent CT14 8ES
Printed in England by CPI Group (UK) Ltd, Croydon CRO 4YY

2 4 6 8 10 9 7 5 3 1

For Peggy
good girl – well done

Contents

Introduction

A DAY IN THE LIFE OF . . .

*'All I've ever wanted to do is tell stories
about people who go unnoticed through life.'*

In Germany, *Scenes from the Big Picture* is known as *A Day in the Life of Frank Coin*. It's a wonderful title, not only for the way in which the prosaic limitations of literal translation are elegantly evaded, but because its eponymous elevation of the play's smallest character encapsulates the very essence of McCafferty's work: it portrays the 'insignificant' roles and relations of ordinary, everyday people.

The *dramatis personae* of this collection are not politicians or paramilitaries or powerful figures. They have little agency or authority. They are subject to historical forces, not shapers of them. Drawn from the margins of society, from the lowly ranks of those who leave no mark and make little noise, their lives and stories are placed centre stage where, in performance, they possess a moving presence and power.

This collection chronicles the evolution of McCafferty's craft: from the one-man monologue of *The Waiting List* (1994) to the Altmanesque complexity of *Scenes* (2003). It also records his continuing experimentation with the rough vernacular of Belfast speech – its rhythms, idioms, syntax and slang – shaping its spiky sounds into something altogether more lyrical. Of course, Irish dramatists have long held previous form in this field, although the voice of the characters here couldn't be more different from the mellifluous Synge-song of John Millington's wild West, or the speechifying denizens of Sean O'Casey's Dublin slums, for it's from the quotidian inarticulacies of working-class speech that McCafferty quarries the incipient poetry and musicality of his dialogue.

And yet, in spite of the playwright's fascination with language and storytelling, many of these plays, paradoxically, are concerned with the lack of meaningful communication between people; the inability – mainly of men – to express their feelings to friends and family:

> **Iggy** a've been doin all the talkin it's yer turn now
>
> **Joe** a don't like talkin

When they do talk, apropos the bickering tilers of *Shoot the Crow*, their badinage comically leads to confusion or confrontation. Even if they *do* try to communicate their deeper feelings, as when Socrates struggles to express his inner turmoil, his embarrassed workmate, Ding-Ding, struggles equally hard *not* to hear him, while Petesy later harangues Socrates for his 'snivellin poncy cryin' as it violates 'the first rule' among working men. Such issues around men's identities, anxieties and inability to express themselves, which ultimately unravel their lives and relationships, are marbled throughout McCafferty's work.

Language and masculinity are not the only themes that can be mined from this collection: class, alcoholism, loneliness and the loss of innocence form equally rich seams. The latter is explored in *The Waiting List*'s rueful recollection of the explicit and invidious ways in which children growing up in Belfast are exposed to, and conditioned by, sectarian violence. The same theme is devastatingly explored in *Mojo Mickybo* and holds true, too, for the older characters of *Closing Time*, regarding the lives and relationships Alec, Robbie, Vera and Joe enjoyed before they are violated by the 'Troubles'.

THE TROUBLES WITH THE TROUBLES

There has long been an expectation that playwrights from the North of Ireland are *required* to address the political conflict here. It's an obligation that has inspired and enervated in equal measure, with authors sometimes relying on, and resorting to, hackneyed forms and hidebound themes. The Troubles have provided plentiful material for thrillers and tragedies, melodramas and farce, soaps and soapboxes. Indeed the clichéd figures of the star-crossed-lovers-across-the-barricades are still in service today as sentimental allegories for political reconciliation. However, these forms and themes are exhausted, and are all too often inadequate in capturing the complexities, contradictions and ambivalences of life in post-conflict Northern Ireland.

McCafferty's work, however, represents something different. It is distinguished by the way in which the conflict is handled obliquely, for his drama is never concerned with *acts* of violence, but in their *aftermath*. The Troubles are almost always in the background; offstage, where gunmen remain shadows in the darkness of the wings.

That's not to say that the conflict is ignored or avoided, for many of his characters have had their lives indelibly affected by political violence. It suddenly shatters the relationship between Mojo and Mickybo, traumatically signalling the end of their childhoods. It similarly devastates the lives of the drinkers in *Closing Time*, leaving them in a purgatorial state of paralysis that's shared, too, by Dave and Theresa Black, the grieving parents of one of the 'Disappeared' in *Scenes*.

Significantly, the victims (and perpetrators) of paramilitary violence aren't identified in terms of their political or religious provenance, for apart from the perforce revelation of *Mojo Mickybo* we rarely know if characters are Catholic or Protestant, nationalist or unionist. McCafferty deliberately denies us such convenient categories and classifications, forcing us to focus instead on their shared humanity. For it is the grey areas in between – rather than the Orange and the Green – that interest McCafferty and which are explored in his work. Moreover, his elevation of the personal over the political enables these plays to transcend any tribal or territorial fealties, so that they touch upon universal themes of birth, death, work, love, loss, suffering, salvation, hope and despair.

In this way, the clichéd conventions, narratives and stereotypes of 'Troubles drama', so brilliantly parodied in 'The Burning Balaclava' – the play-within-a-play of Frank McGuinness's *Carthaginians* (1988) – are conspicuously absent here. The author instead offers a very different perspective of a place that's long been over-determined by images of the Troubles; revealing a much more complex picture of a city and a community that's emerging out of conflict.

One of the most distinctive, if debilitating, features of our otherwise successful peace process in Northern Ireland is the fact that we've no state mechanism or apparatus in place for dealing with the past, or to undertake any form of truth recovery, an issue that has been handled in a deliberately desultory fashion. It was not part of the 1998 Good Friday Agreement and there is still precious little political consensus as to how best to deal with the legacies of violence and sectarian division. The vacuum resulting from this political failure means that artists have an enormously important role to play in our ongoing processes of conflict transformation, especially in theatre, given that its public and participatory nature makes it the most political of all art forms.

Against this background, Owen McCafferty is the most important 'post-conflict' playwright to have emerged from the North – a claim that may seem strange given his aversion to dealing directly with the Troubles and his antipathy

towards overtly political or polemical drama. Neverthe-
less, his work does provide a voice for victims, survivors
and those collaterally caught up in the Troubles, though
this is handled without any didactic message, but deftly, in
a dolorously understated manner. No matter how sub-
dued this voice is, it's still important given the lack of
formal recognition or redress of victims of the conflict,
whose stories and experiences have been egregiously
sidelined and silenced for the sake of political expediency
throughout the peace process.

McCafferty's importance as a post-conflict playwright
also lies in the fact that he writes about those who played
no part in the conflict; whose stories have no place in the
metanarrative of the Troubles; whose lives are remarkable
only for the fact that they were ordinary people living in
extraordinary circumstances. He also adroitly records the
deeply ambivalent responses of those who've experienced
no palpable 'peace dividend' in the past decade; those for
whom the material conditions of their lives have changed
little, in spite of all the corporate rhetoric of urban regeneration and rehabilitation that has accompanied so much
of the peace process:

> **Robbie** belfast's changin isn't it – the keep sayin it's
> changin – so it must be fuckin changin – this place is
> changin – places down the road are fuckin kips – this
> place be like the way it was before . . .
>
> **Vera** how's it goin t'be different this time
>
> **Robbie** different times that's why

BELFAST: BOOM TOWN

*'Why would one place break your heart
more than any other.'*

Almost all McCafferty's plays, like those of Stewart Parker before him, are set in his native city, where he's lived in the Ormeau Road area since the early 1970s. Throughout the Troubles this stretch of road was segregated on sectarian lines, with the largely Catholic, nationalist lower Ormeau separated from the mainly Protestant, loyalist upper Ormeau by a bridge over the river Lagan that (dis)connected both communities. This is the sectarian border so blithely transgressed by the protagonists of *Mojo Mickybo*, who hail from 'up the road' and 'over the bridge'. Similarly, the setting of his most recent play, *Quietly* (2012), is modelled on a bar on the lower Ormeau, and the actor Patrick O'Kane, a mainstay of McCafferty's work who hails from the Ormeau area, even suggests that the playwright captures the speech of this particular part of the city.

Consequently, Belfast is more than merely the *mise en scène* for all five plays in this collection; it's almost a character in itself. And yet, no matter how profoundly Belfast informs and inflects these plays, their imaginative geography is never circumscribed by the city's limits. Indeed, their local roots are transcended, as the global routes of recent productions of McCafferty's work can so eloquently testify. His plays have been translated and performed in Japan, Germany, Chile, France, America and Australia; while in the past twelve months *Mojo Mickybo* – whose machine-gun dialogue of stylised Belfast speech is perhaps the most challenging – has been translated into French and Brazilian Portuguese. Locale and dialect, it seems, are not insurmountable obstacles for actors and audiences beyond these islands . . .

In Ireland, however, we too often view the local in pejorative terms; something that's parochial and parish pump. On the other hand, we've been equally guilty of considering (Irish) theatre almost exclusively in national terms; in relation to theatre institutions, histories, canons, tours and traditions. Such frames, however, occlude something fundamental: theatre is *always local*, as it's performed live in an evanescent present that's fleetingly shared by actors and audiences, night after night after night. Tellingly, Irish theatre's most internationally acclaimed playwright, Brian Friel, sets his work within the confined imaginary borders of Baile Beag; a salutary reminder as to how the local, national and global converge in performance and how 'small town' can be experientially understood by audiences wherever it is translated. It's an appeal that's equally true for urban artists like McCafferty, whose work is local without ever being parochial.

*

Commissioned by Point Fields Theatre Company and performed a few months before the IRA ceasefire, *The Waiting List* (1994) was one of four monologues comprising *Angels with Split Voices*. As an early piece that was part of a project explicitly exploring 'identity and place', *The Waiting List* does deal more directly with the Troubles in its autobiographically informed monologue relaying the thoughts of a young father and his reminiscences of childhood. This is no clichéd invocation of innocence, however, but a disturbing evocation of the damaging effects sectarian violence has had on children. His experiences are emblematic in many ways of an entire generation who have been deprived of the innocence of childhood; their lives circumscribed by territorial boundaries and parental admonitions: 'don't go here, don't go there, watch who you play with, be in before dark'.

One memory of cycling freely around the city with his friends in the hot summer of 1971 vividly captures how children encounter (and enforce) the sectarian geography of the city. When he and his friends accidentally stray into a playground in 'enemy territory' they are immediately interrogated by other children:

> where you from
> what school do you go to
> what football team do you support
> say the alphabet
> sing the sash
>
> . . . smack

Another significant memory is the murder of his 'hip' history teacher, a 'community worker, hands across the divide type', who 'took a shine to me' and gets him involved in a local youth club where one night:

> bang, bang, bang, bang . . . a hole in the head – thick
> purple blood on a cord jacket – a smart man with
> brains hanging out of him – the ante had just been
> upped – men steal lives while boys play games

This last line hauntingly distils the essence of *Mojo Mickybo* while the incident itself is based on McCafferty's memory of the murder of his history teacher, to whom he dedicated the play in 2002. A precursor to *Mojo Mickybo*, *The Waiting List* reveals the invidious processes through which children are acculturated to violence and conditioned to sectarianism and segregation.

Angels with Split Voices borrowed its name from a painting by Gerald Dillon, a Falls Road artist who learned his trade while working as an apprentice painter, decorator and labourer in London. It provides a rather curious connection to the milieu of McCafferty's 1997 play *Shoot the Crow* which, like Jimmy Murphy's *Brothers of the*

Brush (1993), relates a day in the life of working-class men on a building site.

First performed by Galway's Druid Theatre Company, *Shoot the Crow* features four Belfast tilers working on a shift that will be sixty-five-year-old Ding-Ding's last day of work. Worried about life after retirement, Ding-Ding intends to keep working as a window cleaner but needs 'readies' to buy out someone's round, whilst nineteen-year-old Randolph is also saving 'readies' to buy a motorbike as he dreams of travelling abroad. Their fellow tilers, Socrates and Petesy, are also financially hard-pressed; the former has failed to pay maintenance to his separated wife and son, while Petesy cannot afford to pay for his daughter's school trip to France. Consequently, both sets of men concoct separate schemes to steal and sell a pallet of tiles which comically unravel.

Shoot the Crow's vivid dialogue and use of dramatic irony as the tilers' deceive each other with conflicting schemes and shifting allegiances make the play a great comic vehicle for actors. Its levity is also shot through with gravity for it touches, too, on the unfulfilled aspirations and ambitions of workers who have few options open to them, 'yous think yous are something an yes are nothing – just three fuckin tilers that have nothing – are going nowhere – an lead empty fuckin lives'.

Empty lives are very far from the subject of McCafferty's 1998 play, *Mojo Mickybo,* which marked a major milestone in his career. This roisterous two-hander relays the story of Mojo and Mickybo, two kids who strike up a friendship in the hot summer of 1970 as the world all around them is on the brink of tumultuous change. As they act out the roles of Butch Cassidy and the Sundance Kid, fending off restless natives in the form of local bullies, and fantasising about their favourite superheroes, both remain innocently oblivious to the dangers of an adult world disintegrating around them. They're also equally ignorant of the sectarian divisions between them that, ineluctably, drive them apart, and with sudden savagery as Mickybo returns home to find his father has been shot dead: a traumatic discovery that destroys their friendship, 'orange bastard – yas killed my da – yas dirty fuckin orange bastard'.

Mojo Mickybo demands dynamic physical performances from its two actors who must play seventeen different characters, often alternating between them, and each other, at great speed. These frenetic human etch-a-sketch performances generate tremendous kinetic energy on the stage that brilliantly captures the effervescence and innocence of children's imaginations. Irish audiences throughout the 1990s were presented with an extraordinary number of two-hander plays, many of which, like Patrick McCabe's *Frank Pig Says Hello* (1992) and Enda Walsh's *Disco Pigs* (1996), featured the perspectives of psychopathic young people. However, what distinguishes *Mojo Mickybo* is the innocence of its protagonists even as they play amidst a landscape of violence, where sticks from bonfires, petrol bombs and plastic bullets are playthings as they ponder what happens to other wee boys who've had their legs blown off by bombs and how they can escape being 'murdered in their beds'.

Mojo Mickybo portrays the inexorable process whereby this playful innocence is lost. In performance it is poignantly effective, for the audience is always aware that these children's roles are played by adult actors whose mature voice and bodies incarnate the very story of how Mojo and Mickybo grow up in Belfast to be men who, when they happen to meet later in life, 'pretend we didn't know each other'.

Set in the decrepit hotel bar that was once the 'best run' boozer on the street, but is now on the brink of collapse, *Closing Time* (2002) evokes the material and metaphorical condition of both the pub and its punters. The hotel itself was bombed thirteen years earlier, a traumatic event that has profoundly affected the lives of Joe, Vera and Robbie. Robbie has drunk away the compensation money for the hotel and destroyed his marriage in the process, while Joe's wife, who had been caught in the bombing, never recovered from the atrocity and later flees, leaving her grief-struck, guilt-ridden husband unable to return home. And so, ever since, he has slept in the hotel though his home is only across the street. Alec, a brain-damaged handyman employed by Robbie to help out at the hotel, is perhaps the most poignant figure of all:

Iggy he always like that

Robbie what ya mean from birth or what

Iggy aye

Robbie no – postman was he – milkman

Joe somethin like that – delivery or somethin – don't know

Robbie doin his roun's – this is away at the start like – twenty years an more

Joe would be that

Robbie jumped out a car they did – shot 'im in the head an away – not right since – slowed 'im up y' know – couldn't repair whatever damage was done – said it wasn't him they were lookin for to – alec had taken somebody elses shift or somethin – no good t'him that

McCafferty never clarifies whether the gunmen are republican or loyalist or if Alec is Catholic or Protestant: these details are of no importance.

Throughout the play, references are made to political progress and developments on the news, and to radical changes taking place in the city. Such regeneration and progress cruelly contrast with the paralysis of their own lives. However, as is characteristic of McCafferty's drama, the prospect of redemption, change and hope are ever present, albeit in the pyromaniac intent of Alec as he sets forth for Joe's house 't'burn the place t'the groun'.

This collection concludes with what is, arguably, the greatest play written by an Irish playwright in the past twenty years. Joycean in its prismatic perspective, *Scenes from the Big Picture* (2003) presents twenty-one characters in a twenty-four-hour period so that its eponymous 'big picture' of modern life in the city is produced in a kaleidoscopic series of vignettes. The setting is Belfast, but not as it's ever been staged before, for this could almost be any other major city in the world as McCafferty deliberately decontextualises Belfast, decoupling it from the clichéd images and caricatures that characterise its usual (re)presentation as he seeks to show, in his own words, how the setting 'could have as easily been Leeds as Belfast'.

This strategy is embodied in a beautifully understated gesture in one of the shortest scenes in the play. Elderly widower Frank Coin is tying his shoelaces and listening to the radio in the background when a newsreader announces: 'the political talks continue although all parties involved have agreed they have reached an impasse'. The rest of the report is abruptly cut short as Frank turns the radio off, before bracing himself once more to face the world without his beloved wife, with whom he still converses, 'another day ahead of us elsie – go out here and stretch my legs'. For McCafferty, this is the 'big picture': the personal stories of ordinary people who live their lives here amidst the *backdrop* of the Troubles, as opposed to the conflict being the story in itself, as is par for the course in media representations and popular perceptions of Belfast.

These assorted vignettes are eventually woven into an epic narrative as, in an Altman-like fashion, the play unspools the stories of more than a score of characters whose lives intricately coincide and converge, creating a communal image of Belfast utterly unlike any other representation of this city to create what one critic hailed as 'a more or less perfect play'.

And yet, the Troubles casts its shadows of gunmen on *Scenes*: a cache of weapons buried in an allotment serves as a dirty metaphor for the legacies of the past; a drug dealer is kneecapped; and at the very heart of the play is the devastating portrayal of a middle-aged couple whose son was 'disappeared'. No details are provided as to why this happened or who was responsible, or its relation to the unfolding peace process – all of which effectively accentuates the audience's attention on the anguish experienced by the family and their desperate need for closure: 'we need to bury him so that the fuckers that shot him don't have the last say'. As the excavations eventually yield up the body of their missing boy, the expiation of their grief is utterly devastating; and a potent indictment of the peace process's abject failure to represent or redress the victims of violence for fear of endangering its 'progress'.

If the last scene of *Scenes* is the shortest in modern Irish drama, it's also one of the most moving. Just prior to it, we've learned from Frank Coin, the elderly flâneur of the play who flits in and out of scenes and barely speaks, that he lost his wife to cancer more than a decade ago, and he mentions in passing that he recently heard 'a fella on this programme . . . about space' on the radio:

he said that when we talk – the sound we make travels up into space and goes on forever – it never goes away . . . listenin to it a had this thought y'know – wouldn't it be good to think that if there was somebody ya could no longer talk to – that if ya said somethin to them that yer words would travel up into space and that the might meet up with words that that person had once said to you – wouldn't that be a nice thing

Then, in the final scene, while the nocturnal sounds of the city crescendo as the noise from traffic, babies crying, church bells, music, machinery, sirens, shots and shouts commingle before a sudden meteorite storm brilliantly bathes the stage in light, Frank, walking home from the pub, stops in the street and, as the stage starts to darken, looks up to the sky and says: 'i miss you elsie'.

*

This little act, offered up before the vastness of the heavens seems so innocuous, so insignificant . . . and yet, as an expression of love and loss, it's epic and elemental; an act that is registered and reverberates in the heavens. So as the play stunningly segues from the terrestrial to the celestial and the sounds of sirens and shots slowly subside; the earthly world slips away, and the city (and its Troubles), are transcended. This, for McCafferty, is the cosmic big picture as he reminds us all of the importance of the everyday lives of ordinary people: those whose lived experiences may rarely be recorded or represented. But they *matter*.

DR MARK PHELAN
Lecturer in Drama, Queen's University Belfast
July 2013

Foreword

Peggy and I always noticed them when we were in the car on our way to do the weekly shop. They looked too well-dressed and elegant to walk anywhere and yet this man and woman we never talked to always walked to and from the shops. Rather than going to the big Tesco's once a week they preferred to shop daily at the smaller Tesco Express. We didn't see them every day but enough to say 'There's that couple again'. We played a game – see who could spot them first. Sometimes pulling out of the drive we were already looking for them. Saying 'There's that couple again' always made us smile. They looked like the kind of older couple you would like to grow into. Their faces had character. They knew how to carry themselves. We never made contact with them. It wasn't that type of relationship. We admired them from afar. They had no need to know that.

A few months ago we were pulling out of the drive and we spotted the woman walking to the shops. We were both about to say 'There's that couple again', but then realised she was on her own. The next time we spotted her she was on her own again and the time after that. At first we said 'He's probably in hospital' but the more often we spotted her alone the more often we said 'Maybe he's dead'.

I had to go into town this day for a meeting and decided to take the bus rather than get Peggy to drive me. The well-dressed elegant woman was at the bus stop on her own. She stood near the kerb. I sat behind her in the shelter. It was the first time I had been that close to either of them. I was going to phone Peggy and tell her I was only feet away from the 'there's that couple again' woman whose husband might be dead and that I might say something to her. I didn't phone. She had that look. You can see it in people who have lost someone. That look that says their life is missing part of itself. I thought I should speak to her. I wanted to say to her, 'You don't know me – but I just want you to know – that my wife and I used to spot you and your husband walking to the shops – and I need you to know that just by watching you I know you loved each other – we could see it in you – it was spotted.' I sat and looked at her. The bus pulled up and she got on. I stood behind her while she scanned her bus pass. She sat near the front downstairs. I sat upstairs thinking 'I should walk down the stairs now and speak to her – I mightn't be this close again.' I sat and looked out the window. She got off the bus before I did. I was never going to speak to her. I don't. I write about it. And change it.

OWEN McCAFFERTY
July 2013

THE WAITING LIST

The Waiting List was first staged at the Old Museum Arts Centre, Belfast, on 18 April 1994.

The performer was Lalor Roddy

Directed by David Grant
Produced by Point Fields Theatre Company

An empty stage except for the frame of a pram. The actor should be in his mid-thirties and wearing either a dressing gown or pyjamas.

a big sherman tank of a pram jammed against the front door – prams – to keep children in and bad boys out – they have a list – a shopping list for taigs fenians popeheads pan-nationalists republicans catholics – not two hundred yards and two weeks away this fella's in the sack with his girlfriend

night night dear
night night dear

door kicked in – bang bang bang bang – end of story

now there's a list – and you never know i might be a desirable commodity – on sales as it were – lingering in the bargain basement so to speak – i'd rather be past my sell by date but i'm not even half way to my allotted three score and ten – plus i'm not working at the moment which means your waiting time's doubled or seems like it cause i've nothing to do except paint the house a shitty yellow colour and push the youngsters – in the sherman tank – through this mixed – but not completely integrated area – mixed only in the sense that i couldn't put a flag out or douse petrol over mountains of wood in the middle of the street and get a spark from two flints to make it whoosh – singing fuck this and fuck that – while scribbling down misspelt names on the back of a feg box with a well chewed biro stolen from the bookies – mixed in that sense – not that i'd ever want to do those things

you understand but you never know – that's the problem
round here you never know – a wee bit of fear keeps you
on your toes – never quite at ease – just slightly edgy – i
could always ask i suppose – next time i'm doing the
shopping and i see one of the lads poncing round dunnes
stores with his dark glasses pot belly chunky gold
jewellery fat wife and snattery children

excuse me am i on your list – in between everything you
need for an ulster fry in one pack and a slimy bag of
frozen chips – five per cent less fat of course – i would
like to know – it would help me in my capacity as
decision maker if i knew i was going to be around to
view the consequences of my decisions

it's hard to say kid
he whispers out the side of his mouth while – one of his
snattery skinhead kids claws at his ma's taut bulging mini
skirt for a toy machine gun – (they learn early) – with
real imitation bullets flashing lights and noises just like
the one rambo has sewn in between his muscular thighs –
as he beats a track through the jungle blasting the shit
out of the dirty gooks

it's open season you see kid – it's difficult to tell – it's a
lottery – your number's in the hat what more can i say –
after the shopping i always give her one on the sofa – do
you wanna watch

so i'm waiting here – night after night – pram against the
door – looking across the street to the house i was brought
up in – thinking – musing – playing with the idea – why
would it be me – am i on the list

tock tick tock tick tock tick

football in the entry – twenty aside – dogshit everywhere –
use it for goal posts – i'm geordie best – dribble dribble
swerve faint swerve dribble dribble – looks up – (sign of a

good player always looks up) – whack – and it rattles the
net – the crowd go mad – geordie geordie geordie –
united thirty-seven chelsea sixteen – stick insects sliding
in the shit and dreaming of wembley – (not croke park)

goal
off side
your ma
aye your ma

dawn to dusk – a big boy appears on the scene – hair
down to his arse jeans up to his arse and boots gleaming –
shined by his loving mother four times a day

he's a scout sent by matt busby i've seen him in the park

the stick insects gather round – ears pricked – eyes like
saucers – minds agog

are you a scout
aye sort of – (ha ha ha) – you you and you

whisper whisper

my da told me some guy gets over a hundred quid a week
and he only plays for spurs
jesus
bollocks
what'd he say
who you playing for
will your ma let you go
fuck up fenian bastard

smack smack kick kick – a bloody nose and me geordie
best too – football jerseys off tartan scarves on –
mcdonald mcdougall mcclaymore mckingbilly the clan of
robbie burns – who gives a fuck – and me i'm still geordie
boy and sure a good kicking never does you any harm
anyway – demarcation lines are drawn – whatever they
are

don't go here don't go there watch who you play with be
in before dark

father
the boy should take up boxing – good clean sport –
discipline the mind – defend yourself
mother
it'll ruin his good looks – look at your fid you ugly wee
bugger

high cheek bones – i should have been a movie star but
was never spotted – not by anyone from hollywood
anyway – just keep playing and it'll all go away that's the
trick – failed the quallie that year – couldn't believe it –
einstein i was – got a bike for being a failure – a gobi
desert summer – ulster 71 in full swing – dodgems helter
skelter waltzers big wheel – a quick thrill to unite the
warring tribes – i'm on my bike – peddle peddle peddle –
everywhere everyday – after wembley that big race in
france was getting a turn – three of us this day – a biking
gang – the ton-up boys – get lost and end up in some –
get a damp cockroach infested flat on the nineteenth floor
for your demob suit estate – not like the entry – no dog
shit anywhere – a bit of greenery and a playground –
swings see-saw roundabout climbing frame – all good
stuff – the ton-up boys

where you from
what school do you go to
what football team do you support
say the alphabet
sing the sash

should have taken up boxing looks as if the cheek bones
are going to get a burl anyway
push faster faster faster – faster you fenian bastard – need
a rest sit on the grass – feel your mate's dick

smack

feel it you fruity fucker – this one's a fruit and a fenian

punch – dr martens – kick kick kick – children can be
cruel bastards they're like adults that way – i'm starting
to get the hang of this now – i'm a taig and they're
orangemen – what could be simpler – things are starting
to hot up – houses and petrol bombs – hand in hand –
made for each other – there's nothing like a bit of heat on
a cold night when you're watching crossroads – the place
was never the same after sandy bit the dust – that's what
brought meg's bad headaches on you know – a mate of
mine left his dog to guard the house – whoof – the
orangemen called him hot-dog – made him crazy –
nothing like a bit of humour – the parish priest after
having a yarn with the almighty formed a stop dogs
going whoof in the dark of night vigilante group –
patrolling the streets with hurls and bin lids – all dogs
can sleep safe in their kennels – it's their owners who do
the tossing and turning – myself i'm doing a bit more of
the former than the latter

there's a wee girl fancies you two streets away – she's a
protestant
what do you think lads
get in there you're a cert thing
all orangewomen do it
do you see the diddies on her she didn't get them sitting
by the fire

seven o'clock next night up the entry – find a patch with
no patch shit – (ha ha) – talk talk talk – lumber lumber
lumber – feelie feelie feelie

let's do this on a regular basis
why not you're such a nice guy

floating on air – tiptoeing from cloud to cloud – i'm in
love – i'm in lust – i'm in deep shit – next day skipping

down the corridors of knowledge pulled – three hard
men – the ra – boy's version – shiny oxfords bald heads
earrings short parallels black socks – the uniform

we've been told you're seeing an orangewoman – please
refrain from this anti-social activity
but you don't understand men – (men) – feelie feelie the
diddies and the bliff

smack – just to clear the wax from my ears

her brother's inside for murder – put your country before
your dick or we'll beat the shit out of you

silence silence silence – lumber lumber lumber – feelie
feelie feelie – it's all over-flow as the plumber said to his
girl

why
i'm frightened
oh
well men how'd i do – the republican cause will never die
while i'm alive sure it won't

blah blah blah – school – halcyon days

homework boy late boy hair boy earring boy cursing boy

blackboard compass – whack whack whack – the inside
of a tractor tyre cut to shape – whack whack whack –
best years of your life – there was one guy though –
history teacher – always talking about sun yat-sen and his
wee merry men – community worker hands across the
divide type – big moustache no tie long hair cord jacket
desert boots – a hip guy – he took a shine to me – used to
tell me dirty jokes and let me smoke in the store room –
me and him him and me – brought me to the youth club –
got me interested in table tennis – he used to bring me
home when the tartans were on the hunt – sun yat-sen
and his wee merry men – i'm standing in the gym this

night – not half a brick's throw away from the table
tennis room – watching fellas with low cheekbones beat
the shit out of each other – bang bang bang bang – you
see there was a pane of glass missing from one of the
windows in the table tennis room – and if you had a
mind to – if you put yourself out a bit you could have
climbed over the front wall crawled through the long
grass on your elbows and knees like a commando aimed
a gun through the missing pane and . . . – if you had a
mind to – a hole in the head – thick purple blood on a
cord jacket – a smart man with brains hanging out of
him – the ante had just been upped – men steal lives while
boys play games – skip teak stick ra hey man no prob

let's join up
i will if you will

ten pence a week – funds – football teams written in a
black book – all code you know – i'm arsenal – the
gunners – (ha ha ha) – no readies forthcoming and it's
smack smack smack – even revolutionaries must think in
commercial terms – education officer that's me – lectures
in someone's da's garage that smelt of car oil and home
brew – padraig pearce wolfe tone robert emmet henry joy
mccracken – matinee and evening performances all
repeated

who didn't pay their divvies this week – goody goody

stage one – this is a gun this is how you clean a gun this
is how you hold a gun this is how you hide a gun – stage
two – when being chased while carrying a gun fall to the
ground roll head over heels or arse over bollocks stand
upright and confront the enemy – stage three – scout
uniforms and drill – march march march left right left
right turn left turn right attention at ease fart belch spit
scratch your nuts – all in irish – big day – march down
some street in some area to commemorate some guy who

was murdered some time ago – baden powell gear on a
pair of shades and away we go – up and down and down
and up up and down and down and up – what a boyo i
am – is this worth the price of four singles a week or
what – can yous all see me – up and down and down and
up and away we go – la la la la la . . . – spotted –
informed on – someone out of my da's work – shout
shout shout – bawl bawl bawl – clip round the ear – one
less volunteer in the struggle for freedom

i want to leave
you'll have to get a kicking
don't worry i'm getting used to it

took up gaelic football after that – a bit of culture in the
sporting arena

and it's colm mcalarney over the bar

agricultural sports – it's a game for close knit
communities who breathe fresh air and there's me
alienated and likes the smell of petrol fumes – maybe i
just didn't have the bottle for it – i was walking down the
road one night after training when i was pulled by the –
why don't you go out and catch some terrorists mob

who are you – where you coming from – where you
going to – how do you spell your name

all the time spread-eagled – normal practice – the boys
are full of jungle juice – laughing and joking – rifle barrel
in the middle of my back

why don't you play soccer you fucker – republican
fucking sport – we know where you live you bastard

still laughing as i ran home – fuck this for a game of
darts – have to get out of here find myself – the big old
u s of a is the place for that – bring a dram of irish
whiskey and a piece of linen in case you bump into an

old sod for the old sod – i met this thirty stone homosexual
drug pusher – ate everything from a bag of coal to a
hamburger – just like the movies it was – heat wave old
folk in dallas dropping like flies and there's tomatoes the
size of your fist – wake up go to the beach worship the
sun god get stoned eat fist like tomatoes get stoned
couple of beers get stoned go to bed – bliss – ireland
never heard of the place

you've a lovely voice – your vocal patterns are so lyrical –
it sounds like you're singing all the time it's really
beautiful
fuck up and pass the joint
have a shot – all harps drink whiskey – god bless the ole
sod – four green fields

all crying their lamps out

the british are mother fuckers – protestants are mother
fuckers – niggers yids pollacks spicks wops chinks gooks
ruskies and those no good low down bastards who
kicked custer's ass – all mother fuckers – i'd love to see
the place – my granny's from leeson street do you know
that – a civil war – jees that must be great – do you have
fish in ireland

eyes opened – mind broadened – time to go

say hi to your folks – have a nice journey man

i travelled – i broke free – now i'm an enlightened person
unaffected by my hideous surroundings – i am above the
humdrum – aloft and aloof – education – back to school –
grind grind grind – swot swot swot – university –
philosophy – a higher plane – socrates plato aristotle
heidegger sartre epistemology phenomenology
metaphysics logic – nationalists loyalists – bollocks –
communists – shoulder to shoulder with your fellow man
or woman – sorry person – human – sweat of the brow –

the common good – solicitors digging holes binmen
performing heart surgery that's the business – invited to a
meeting i was – oh aye – walked into this bar – hole in
my jacket to look the part – full of ole lads society didn't
give a toss about and the place reeked of piss – brilliant

no i'm afraid we're upstairs

a log fire woolly jumpers beards and pints of guinness –
everyone babbling about the mating habits of wood
pigeons and obscure french film directors in between
giving the capitalist lackies a verbal pasting

when i was younger my history teacher was shot dead –
why do things like that happen
after mating the male sits on the eggs – wood pigeons
share their parental responsibilities – wood pigeons have
a lot to teach us if only we would listen
why don't we move downstairs it's a bit too cosy up here
i think we're just fine here – you can enlighten them
without mixing with them – god you're so naïve

and some guy in the corner wearing a save whale sperm
t-shirt picks his horses from the guardian and rips a hole
in his new denims – on the jukebox they're playing – give
peace a chance – give my friggin head peace – i never
went back – not that i was missed – wood pigeons were
never my thing

then i met a girl – by chance – at a dance – not that i ever
do – unless i'm drunk and then i can't

i love you
i love you too

ding dong ding dong – wedding bells – went to spain for
our honeymoon – all sun sand and sangria – just like the
brochure said – met up with this crowd from – belfast

it's great to be away

why can't belfast be like this
i've no problems loving my neighbour
why can't we live together

reaching for my second crate of san miguel and reflecting
on the moral decline of the western world i said

it seems to me or shall i say it is my considered opinion
that communism – on paper at least – is indeed the best
system under which humans can live
commie bastard

you can't win can you – holidays out children in – it's
time to settle down – philosopher's don't earn much
readies – it's understandable there's no real need for it in
these parts – then someone says to me – you look like a
tiler – and i thought maybe i do – mix a bucket of stuff
fire it on the floor fire it on the wall get the tiles slap them
on grout it all up and there you go – bathrooms kitchens
and the odd en suite – life couldn't be better – there's a
bit of money coming in the kids have new uniforms and
i'm too old to be chased – i'm thinking this place isn't so
bad so long as you stick to a routine – (which you can't
really help doing cause that's the way things are) – and
ignore everything around you (which is what we all do
anyway) – happy days – i even brought the kids down to
see the tall ships – i mean to say – it's like you can be here
and not really live here – you look but don't see – you
hear but don't listen – and you think but don't question –
it's great – then my slumber is interrupted – i'm standing
in a bathroom this day slapping on some nearly expensive
wouldn't have them in my own house pink tiles – i broke
about four of them on the trot – (had to get rid of them
quick in case i was sued for negligence) – semi-detached
car caravan motor bike two children and a good looking
wife – (i lingered on her for a while it must be the seven
year itch) – who doesn't need to work – this guy worked

in mackies and when things were going bad shifted and
earned his crust in shorts – mobility – good if you can get
it – the job's finished – everyone's happy – a cup of tea
put some paper on the sofa before you sit and some
chocolate bickies

will you take a cheque
certainly we're here to accommodate you the customer

his writing was like my wee lad's and he couldn't spell my
name – now here's me sometimes working sometimes not
sometimes money sometimes potless – and there's him
flitting from place to place gathering a pile of goodies on
the way – sure it's not his fault – if you've a seat reserved
on the gravy train you're hardly going to hang around
the station are you – why don't i ever cop on – you see
whenever i'm pushing the kids round these streets in the
sherman tank i keep thinking to myself – this is where
i've lived all my life – this is my community – but it's not –
i don't feel at ease here – my whole life hemmed in – jesus
what a waste

and now there's a list

SHOOT THE CROW

Shoot the Crow was first staged by the Druid Theatre Company, Galway, on 26 February 1997. The cast was as follows:

Socrates David Ganley
Petesy Anthony Brophy
Ding-Ding Patrick Waldron
Randolph Fergal McElherran

Director David Parnell
Designer Paul McCavley
Lighting Designer Tina MacHugh

Characters

Ding-Ding
sixty-five

Socrates
thirty-nine

Petesy
thirty-six

Randolph
nineteen

The play takes place during the working day of four tilers on a building site in Belfast. They are tiling adjoining rooms – a public toilet and a shower area.

The stage is divided in two. There is a door leading to 'on-site' (i.e., offstage) and another between the two rooms. It is Friday, the end of the working week.

Mid-morning tea break. Ding-Ding is asleep. Randolph enters from on site carrying two cups of tea and a magazine.

Randolph petesy an socrates are stayin down in the other room – talkin a lotta shite – here's yer tea – don't mind me now – just you have a wee kip there an i'll run about like a blue arsed fly gettin you fuckin tea – tea in the special cup – (*He sets the cup down and circles it.*) – don't touch the cup – ding-ding's special cup – the cup – fuck you an yer cup – have a kip aye just you welt away there we'll all work roun ye – who needs cups when ya have bikin magazines that's what i say – (*He sits and opens his magazine.*) vroom fuckin vroom (*Ding-Ding wakes.*) look at that – a large set a wheels with some wee doll wrapped roun ye – is that the business or what – i get the readies t'gether that's me on the bike an off ski – long y'reckon it take t'do that – save for a bike – did a tell ye that's what i'm doin savin for a bike – long – couldn't take that long like – a few squid every week – a few squid – join a club an that – have 'm – like christmas clubs only for motor bikes – long d'ya reckon – need a licence first like – that'll not be a problem – me an ma mate been practisin on push bikes – same type a crack like innit – not as heavy or as fast but it's the same neck a the woods like – cuppla a shillins every week – licence – bike – an then it's the get yer philias fogg gear on ye an away we go – except i'd have some wee doll with me instead a that dopey french geezer he has knockin about with him – plus i'd be on a bike all the time instead a that

23

trains steamers an balloon chats – wanna see the ones in
the magazine i have – magic – wanna see the wee dolls
innit fuckin unbelievable – big three wheel efforts – just
lie back an sally on – big money they are like – big
readies – take more than a few quid there every week – a
wee one do me – so long as y'can fit two on it – go through
that tunnel dixie a cuppla hours it's all pernod and
distilled water an bung us another clatter a them frogs
legs – a wee doll on the back a the bike wingin yer way
through france – an yous boys fucked – slappin shit
coloured tiles on some wee oul doll's wall – d'ya reckon
that ding-ding – what d'ya reckon

Ding-Ding ya know fuck all – y'know that – fuck all
about fuck all

Randolph i'll be whistlin dixie with the camels roun the
kazbah – no sweat about it – vroom vroom

Ding-Ding aye vroom vroom

Randolph aye – what – i've just told ye what i'm gonna
do regardin me an the world an the big picture – what's
the problem here – ya have t'make plans don't ye – isn't
that what we're all about – makin plans an that – gettin
the stuff ahead a ye sorted out

Ding-Ding make plans – what for

Randolph what for – what does that mean what for – the
future – that's the crack – ya do shit now so ya can sort
yerself out for the future – there's no point in graftin an
that if it's not gonna help ye paddle yer own dixie later in
life is there

Ding-Ding that right – what's that

Randolph what d'ya mean what is it it's a letter – a letter

Ding-Ding correct a letter – who's it from

Randolph c'mon til

Ding-Ding heavy hole – it's a letter from heavy hole – fucker

Randolph didn't send me one

Ding-Ding no he didn't send you one – it's a thank you letter – not typed now hand written – the personal touch – he's thankin me for my time – doesn't say that but that's what it means – the time i spent helpin him t'get wherever he's goin – fuck'im – a lifetime spent graftin an ya end up with a thank you note – hand written – we mustn't forget that – today's the day randolph kid – today's the day

Randolph thought ya weren't retirin til next week

Ding-Ding no – today

Randolph did he drop ye anythin – sort ya out for a few extra squid

Ding-Ding ya only get what's comin t'ye in this world son – in my case that adds up t'fuck all squared

Randolph fuck'im

Ding-Ding correct fuck'im

Randolph no more graftin for ye – yer home on a boat that way – feet up in front a the dixie – few bets eye the gee gees cuppla swallys in the afternoon – fuckin landed ya are

Ding-Ding that's what a mean randolph son – that's what i'm tellin ye – ya know fuck all about fuck all – see that letter – that's what all yer plans amount til – fuck all

Randolph a few quid away a week – i know what am at – i'll not be hangin aroun for any fuckin letter from some geezer who wouldn't recognise yer coupin if he passed ye in the street – fuck at

Ding-Ding go now – do it now – see if ya don't yer goose an ducked – longer ya spend doin this tighter the noose gets round yer fuckin neck – an after a while it's you that tightens it cause ye get used to the feel a the rope – do it now – get the bike now an go now

Randolph what with – a need t'earn some readies t'get it don't a

Ding-Ding fuckin steal it if ya have to – do whatever ya have t'do – all i'm sayin is don't let fuck all pass ya by – thinkin about somethin unless ya do it does nothin but fuck ye up

Randolph a work – a earn readies – a get the bike – that's it there's nothin else to it – simple

Ding-Ding work – work – ya know what work is – it's a fuckin con – work lets ye think ya can sprint like a gazelle then it straps fuckin lead boots roun yer plates a meat – i've a few shillins in ma sky rocket look at me i'm a king – only problems is son the few shillins is never enough to buy yerself a fuckin crown – ya always think the crowns on the cards though – it must be other people wear them – until one day yer standin in some shit hole talkin t'some kid with a hand written letter in yer pocket sayin thank you for yer trouble – it's a fuckin con – an know what the real beauty about all that is – the real sting in the tail – ya can't do without it – cause if ya don't have it yer napper goes – no work an the head's away

Randolph stop givin me grief ding-ding will ye

Ding-Ding i'm tryin t'help ye here – what is it the bike means t'ye – escape – freedom – gettin t'fuck out – doin yer own thing bein yer own man – that what it means – i'll help ye get it

Randolph you a big sackfull a readies planked somewhere
aye

Ding-Ding there's a pallet a tiles lyin roun the front there
right

Randolph aye

Ding-Ding we'll steal them

Randolph get t'fuck – what an get nathered like that
plumber fella the other day

Ding-Ding fuck him

Randolph nothin t'do with him – it's t'do with gettin
caught

Ding-Ding ya want the bike don't ye – this is a way a
gettin it – the only way a gettin it – i'll help ye out

Randolph how you helpin me out i didn't suggest it –
helpin yerself out – gettin back at heavy hole or somethin

Ding-Ding fuck all t'do with heavy hole

Randolph what

Ding-Ding what what

Randolph what's in it for you besides that deep inner
feelin of warmth ya get from helpin a work mate – that
ya didn't much give a fuck about before

Ding-Ding d'ya want it or don't ye

Randolph what do you want

Ding-Ding same as you

Randolph what's that

Ding-Ding not t'be trapped – not t'wake up in the
mornin an wish ya had some other punter's life cause
yer's isn't the shit ya thought it was cracked up t'be

Randolph after t'day you can do that can't ye – no pressure on ye – do whatever ya want – ye've time t'do that now – isn't that what it's all about retirin an that – time t'ease off or whatever

Ding-Ding a don't want time that's the fuckin point – time's no good to ye when ye've been used t'not havin any – it fucks ya up – a don't want that

Randolph what then – what

Ding-Ding a winda cleaner – i'm gonna be a winda cleaner

Randolph get t'fuck – winda cleaner – aye winda cleaner – a know aye

Ding-Ding somethin wrong with that – it's not gonna make me rockafella but it'll get me a few shillins every week an give me somethin t'do – that's all i'm lookin a few shillins an somethin t'do

Randolph yer gonna steal like so ya can be a winda cleaner

Ding-Ding correct

Randolph this might seem like an obvious question to you ding-ding – cause at the moment ya seem t'be workin on a different type of a fuckin level from the rest of us – but why do ya need a chunk a readies in order t'become a fuckin winda cleaner – ya gonna buy a gold plated bucket aye

Ding-Ding a have t'buy somebody else's roun off them that's why – a was panickin about this retirement chat then somethin happened an i thought that'll do me – there's this oul lad lives two doors down from me – oul lad – that's fuckin good – fella's only two years older than me – he's a winda cleaner – cuppla weeks back he couped

off the ladder an fucked his leg up – can't clean windas
no more – i met him limpin his way roun for a few pints –
sittin with other fuckers like himself all hatin each other
for bein there – i'm talkin to him he's tellin me about his
leg an that – i kept thinkin t'myself he's fucked – ya could
see it in his lamps – dead – empty – no fuckin spark in
them y'know – nothin t'fill his time with ya see – his
napper's gone he's fucked – that can't happen t'me
randolph son – they'll find that oul lad in six months'
time sittin in his chair stiff as a board – cold as ice – dead
for four days an no fucker know about it – that's not on
randolph kid – that's no way for any human t'end up –
he's sellin his roun – first come first served – if i get in
there now i'm in business

Randolph i don't get that – that doesn't make any sense
t'me – somethin ye like doin aye – a can understan that –
but where's the pleasure in standin half way up a ladder –
wet – monkeys – wipin the suds of some fucker's window
– a don't get that – the thinkin behind that's all up the left

Ding-Ding fuck all that – what i'm doin has got fuck all
t'do with you right – this is about you – you want readies
towards yer bikin fund – well this is an opportunity –
that's all you gotta concern yerself with – fuck all else

Randolph what about petesy an socrates – say anythin
t'them – what about them

Ding-Ding just me an you – nothin t'do with them it's
just me an you

Randolph say fuck all

Ding-Ding say fuck all – between me an you – nobody
else's business

Randolph they were involved ya'd have t'split it four
ways then wouldn't ye

Ding-Ding ya would

Randolph fuck that

Ding-Ding half better than a quarter

Randolph ya got all the gear then

Ding-Ding what gear

Randolph the black gear – ya got all the black gear

Ding-Ding black gear

Randolph tights – jumpers – gloves – those woolly chats ya pull over yer napper

Ding-Ding ropes an pulleys

Randolph aye

Ding-Ding helicopter be handy

Randolph helicopter

Ding-Ding we're shiftin tiles into a van at lunch time we're not stormin the fuckin embassy

Randolph lunchtime – lunchtime– that's fuckin daylight that is

Ding-Ding correct – we'll not need fuckin torches then either will wa – place is empty at lunch time – no hassle – fire the tiles in til the van – shift them plank them – get back t'them later

Randolph that all like – nothin else no

Ding-Ding what

Randolph i don't know – just seems very normal like – very ordinary or somethin

Ding-Ding we're just stealin tiles randolph son – if tilers are gonna steal somethin tiles seems like the obvious

thing y'know – if we worked down a diamond mine now
that be a different matter – but things bein what they are
we're stuck with the fuckin tiles

Randolph talk me through it again

Ding-Ding a just fuckin said

Randolph talk me through it

Ding-Ding lunch – tiles – van – shift – plank – sell – bingo

Randolph not need masks then

Ding-Ding don't fuck me about boy

Randolph a wanna wear a mask – i want it t'be at night –
cut the fence gear with them big clunky scissors – drug
the guard dogs with meat an pills an shit – a robbery
y'know like a real robbery – pity a didn't have the bike –
quick get away – off ski

   Ding-Ding grabs Randolph by the throat.

Ding-Ding this isn't a joke – i can't have ya fuckin things
up for me y'understand – ya can't fuck things up

Randolph yer hurtin me

Ding-Ding either yer doin it or yer not – but don't think
ya can fuckin mess me about on this

Randolph i'm not

   Ding-Ding lets go.

Ding-Ding if ya don't wanna do it just say so – if you
want somethin badly enough ya take risks to get it – do
you want it or don't ye

Randolph a don't know – what do you think – i don't
know

31

Ding-Ding i'm not tellin ye what t'do ya make yer own decisions – know yer own mind an do what ye think's best

Randolph if we're caught i'm fucked

Ding-Ding an if we're not

Randolph if we're not i'm half way there

Ding-Ding vroom vroom – randolph – vroom vroom

Randolph lunchtime

Ding-Ding lunchtime

Socrates and Petesy enter other room from on site.

Petesy if it's not in the other room it has t'be here – or there

Socrates aye whatever – do ya understan what i'm sayin about this – it's like ya were on a journey an yer lookin at the scenery an shit as ye go along – then ya arrive where yer meant t'be at – but if somebody was to say t'ye what road did ye take – how'd ye get here – ya wouldn't be able t'fuckin say – that's the type a thing i'm talkin about – understan what i'm sayin

Petesy you have a look for it i'll check on these two

Socrates yer not listenin t'me

Petesy just have a jeff juke about the place will ye

Socrates aye

Petesy (*enters other room*) he's doin my fuckin napper in again

Ding-Ding his head's gone

Petesy we're on journeys now that have no roads or somethin – doin my fuckin napper in – come in t'do a day's graft – ya end up slappin on tiles with one a them fuckin tibetan chats that sit on their jam roll an do their nappers in with thinkin

Ding-Ding his head's gone

Petesy aye

Ding-Ding aye

Petesy what's the crack in here ya's weltin away at this or what

Ding-Ding finished up there aye

Petesy bit a groutin just – have t'be red up t'day now

Ding-Ding aye

Petesy ya gettin plenty a work outta him ding-ding aye

Randolph i'm alright

Petesy just you keep cleanin the buckets – never enough clean buckets – always need clean buckets ding-ding don't ye

Ding-Ding oh aye – clean buckets

Petesy got one dipped in bronze do ye for yer retirement chat

Ding-Ding aye

Petesy no more graftin – pig in shit wha

Ding-Ding aye

Petesy aye – yous two see a delivery note lyin about no

Ding-Ding what ya want it for

Petesy check the adhesive on the job

Ding-Ding nah

Petesy if he's nothin t'do ding-ding fire him in with us

Ding-Ding aye

Randolph plenty t'do

Petesy day's work kill ye

Randolph aye a know

Petesy away back in here t'talk to the oracle

Ding-Ding his head's away

Petesy exits next door. Randolph makes masturbatory gestures after him.

Petesy two tossers – ya find that

Socrates wha

Petesy what d'ya mean what – a said to ye have a butcher's for the deliver note

Socrates fuck the delivery note

Petesy it's important a wanna see if these tiles are on it or not

Socrates fuck the tiles

Petesy fuck the delivery note – fuck the tiles – we'll all just sit here with our heads jammed up our onion will wa

Socrates delivery note – that it like – that where we are – aye

Petesy yes

Socrates i'm tryin t'make sense of somethin here – understan what i'm sayin – i'm tryin to throw a curve ball – have a look at things from a different dixie – a different perspective – know what a mean

Petesy (*looking for delivery note*) no

Socrates tilt the beam of light that's fuckin dixin down on us at a different angle y'know

34

Petesy aye

Socrates i'm standin at a bus stop other mornin –
monday mornin early – this guy a know from when a
was a kid stanin across the way – there's two winos
waitin t'get their starter for the day – he queues up with
them – i'm thinkin he's goin in for a packet a smokes on
his way t'work – he's a plumber or somethin fucked like
that – the place opens an the three a them are like
greyhounds out a the trap – he didn't get smokes he
bought a carry out – couldn't even be bothered fuckin
puttin it in a bag – four tins a that rocket fuel gear in his
hand – doesn't give a fuck who sees him cause his head's
fixed on the gargle – i used t'kick football with this guy
now he's millin four tins of piss yer begs gear t'wake him
up – t'get him sorted out – it frightened me y'know –
lookin at him fucked me up

Petesy some fella ya played headers with turned into a
wino – what

Socrates what happened t'that guy – how'd he arrive
where he's at – what happened between bein a kid an
doin all that shit and millin tins up an entry on a fuckin
monday morning – what happened

Petesy ya gonna help me look for this

Socrates know what a realised when a was lookin at this
guy – he had his own life – i still thought of him as the
wee lad kickin football – but he wasn't – he was there
living out his own life – that meant i was living out my
life but i'd never fuckin noticed that before – know what
i'm sayin – i wasn't aware of my own life

Petesy look under the tool box

Socrates fuck the delivery note – i'm not interested

Petesy look under the tool box

35

Socrates fuck the delivery note – fuck the box – if yer not aware of yer own life it means that ye haven't really participated in the shit that happens t'ye – so ya end up at a certain point thinkin how the fuck did i get here – like there was no control over it y'know – i'm doin this i'm doin that – i'm separated – i haven't seen her and the wee lad for a cuppla months – what's all that about – how'd that happen – was it always gonna happen – could i have stopped it from happenin – what does shit like that mean

Petesy i can't find it – no delivery note – the tiles don't exist – happy days

Socrates what d'ya reckon – it's like do we live our own lives or do we live them through other people or what – what d'ya think

Petesy don't know – the don't exist – a told ye – nobody knows about them – didn't a tell ya that

Socrates are ya listenin t'me – d'ya have any thoughts on shit like this – is it just me or we all like that or what – what d'ya think

Petesy socrates stop it – just fuckin stop it – i have no room for this gear y'understan – i've other stuff in my life t'sort out – practical shit y'know – the real world – mortgages – bills – work – that world – understand – the don't exist – right – all we gotta do is fire them in the van

Socrates so that's it – nothin else – that's it – all we're about is stealing tiles is it

Petesy correct a mundo – twenty minutes gets them in the van nobody's any the wiser

Socrates the real world – the practical world

Petesy real – practical – yes

Socrates one a the plumbers got caught tea leafin the other day – he's banjaxed – that practical enough

Petesy an what

Socrates he's out – we get caught we're out

Petesy a heard nothin about that – what plumber

Socrates what plumber – what plumber – the plumber plumber

Petesy there's two plumbers

Socrates the big fat geezer

Petesy they're both big fat geezers

Socrates the one that kicked a hole in an alsation's throat – that one

Petesy a doberman – an the fella ripped its lugs off

Socrates ripped its lugs off – what for – you talk a lotta balls y'know that

Petesy wasn't it goin after one of his kids or somethin – another thing too it was a spark not a plumber – know the wee small one with the big napper an the goat beard – him

Socrates him – sure he's not married

Petesy maybe the dog was goin for him then i don't know

Socrates what would he rip the ears off it for

Petesy to fuckin stop it

Socrates how would that stop it

Petesy rippin its lugs off wouldn't stop it

Socrates no – that just piss the dog off – kickin a hole in its throat's a different matter – can't do any damage if it's a chelsea boot stuck in its throat

37

Petesy oh – neither of the plumbers wear chelsea boots – the spark does though

Socrates that's not right now cause they all wear trainers – in case they get a shock

Petesy ya couldn't kick a hole in a dog's throat if ya were wearin trainers anyway

Socrates why not

Petesy why not – what's wrong with you why not – cause they're made for runnin not kickin holes in the throats of mad fuckin dogs

Socrates chelsea boots are – are the

Petesy well there's certainly a bit more fuckin wear an tear in them isn't there

Socrates kicked a hole in yer head

Petesy doberman – no ears – spark

Socrates whatever – fuck that – the fat plumber one with the beard

Petesy him aye

Socrates banjaxed

Petesy what's that gotta do with us

Socrates heavy hole'll be on the look out now

Petesy no delivery note – so the don't exist

Socrates they're not ours know what a mean – the don't belong t'us

Petesy things that you tea leaf don't normally belong to you else there'd be no point in fuckin stealing them

Socrates aye but we know heavy hole – we know him – that makes it personal

Petesy fuck heavy hole – what's he ever done for us

Socrates that's not the point

Petesy that's precisely the point – he ever invite ye up til his house – no – ya ever go out for a swally with him – no – you on his christmas card list – fuckin no – we don't know him he employs us that's it – he's a businessman an we graft for him – fuck all personal about that

Socrates what that mean we're entitled to steal off him

Petesy accordin to the rules i live by yes – he's a lot more than i'll ever have an i helped him get it so fuck'im

Socrates aye a know fuck'im – but ya know what a mean – there's a principle involved here – like it or not he's part of our world isn't he – it be like stealin from yer own – morally it's not right

Petesy tell me this well – is it morally right that we only get paid enough readies – on purpose by the way don't forget that on purpose – that we only get paid enough readies t'keep our heads a cuppla inches above the shit heap – is that morally right

Socrates ya get paid the worth of what ya do – fuckin market forces an all that gear dictate that don't the – that's fuck all to do with heavy hole – economics – supply an demand – that's what that's all about

Petesy look all them things are a con – they're there t'make sure that people who haven't a pot t'piss in remain without a pot t'piss in – i don't go by those rules – i go by rules that suit me not someone else

Socrates it's difficult isn't it – makin up yer mind about stuff – havin problems about decidin about things at the moment y'know

Petesy it's not life an death shit socrates we're only stealin a pallet of fuckin tiles – look – heavy hole's insured we steal the tiles he claims the readies back – what's fairer than that

Socrates that's true now – hadn't thought about that one – that illuminates the whole proceedins a touch – what about the other two

Petesy fuck'em

Socrates fuck'em

Petesy nothin t'do with them – they're t'know nothin about it – it's between me an you

Socrates just me an you

Petesy just me an you – sixty-forty split

Socrates sixty-forty

Petesy aye – i get the biggest share cause it was my idea

Socrates how d'ya know i wasn't thinkin about it

Petesy didn't ya just give me all that right an wrong shite

Socrates might've been lyin – could've been thinkin about it all along

Petesy ya said fuck all well

Socrates a wanted t'see how the land lay – what yer tellin me here is you get extra readies for speakin

Petesy how the fuckin land lay – right – alright – were ya thinkin about it

Socrates no

Petesy what the fuck then

Socrates sixty forty – if we're caught aren't we both goose an ducked – so what's this sixty-forty business

Petesy just for the sake of argument ya were thinkin about it – ya didn't give it any of the verbals so there's no point in it – i thought it and spoke it – so i started the whole process off – that's why sixty-forty – anyway it's me that has the contacts

Socrates who

Petesy if a tell ye you'll know then

Socrates correct – who

Petesy jimmy blow

Socrates jimmy blow – jimmy fuckin blow – the whole site knows that

Petesy aye but ya said fuck all – it's the same thing

Socrates sixty forty behave yerself (*Ding-Ding enters from the other room.*) that's not on y'know

Petesy alright in there ding-ding aye

Ding-Ding aye – need another pair a snips spring's gone in mine

Petesy in the tool box

Socrates sixty fuckin forty

Petesy sixty forty listen t'him will ye – we're tryin t'work out ding-ding – what the percentage split would be between – fruit an sugar in a pot a jam – i reckon sixty forty

Ding-Ding sounds right to me

Socrates it's not well – i'm tellin ye it's not

Petesy aye – ya get the snips ding-ding

Ding-Ding aye – find the delivery note did ye

Petesy no – doesn't matter i'll count the buckets or somethin

Ding-Ding if ya come across it give us a shout

Petesy what for

Ding-Ding i wanna check somethin on it

Petesy check what

Ding-Ding somethin

Petesy aye but what

Ding-Ding nothin

Petesy somethin – nothin – what

Ding-Ding a think we're a box a spacers short – if a had the note a could check it y'know

Petesy if a come across it sure i'll fire it in t'ye

Ding-Ding aye – sixty forty sounds right t'me socrates

Socrates not in my book it's not

Petesy cook book ding-ding wha

Ding-Ding exits to other room.

Petesy what's wrong with you – they're not t'know nothin about this – say nothin

Socrates a don't know about all this

Petesy ya can't back out now it's all up an runnin

Socrates i didn't declare my hand either way – we're just talkin – all we're doin is talkin

Petesy a can't do it on my swanny it's a two man effort

Socrates a fifty fifty effort

Petesy puttin me under pressure now

Socrates i'm just sayin what's fair that's all

Petesy what's fair

Socrates aye

Petesy scrub it – forget it – we'll not do it that's fair

Socrates aye

Petesy aye

Socrates you positive now – it's clear it's sorted out in yer head – the war's over regardin this

Petesy not doin it

Socrates i've a suggestion well

Petesy what

Socrates see the pallet a tiles out there nobody knows about we'll steal them

Petesy away an fuck

Socrates if we agree t'steal them i get a bigger whack cause it was my idea

Petesy my idea

Socrates that was a different idea which you've just knocked on the head – this is a new idea – my idea

Petesy who's yer contact

Socrates jimmy blow

Petesy fuck off

Socrates my idea – my contact – what's the problem

Petesy i need the readies

Socrates who am i the fuckin aga khan

Petesy a need it for somethin definite – it has t'be got – everythin else is shit right forget about all that this is the reason right

Socrates what – what is it

Petesy ya gonna let me explain – this is personal shit a don't like doin this – i'm forcin myself t'tell ye y'know

Socrates welt away

Petesy thank you

Socrates it's a pleasure

Petesy one a the kids – the eldest wee girl – really bright kid y'know – fuckin frighten ye sometimes the crack she comes off with – intellectual gear i have problems gettin my head round y'know – me an her ma sittin there half the time with blank coupons just listenin til her – she's top trick in school an all that business – anyway her school's doing this exchange dixie extended holiday type a thing t'france – an she's been picked to go – there's grant money available from somewhere – which is fine – but you've gotta fork out a big whack of it yerself – the readies has t'be in next week – haven't got it understan – in a way i'm thinkin fuck it it's only a holiday she doesn't go it's not the end a the world for her – but in the back a my mind i keep thinkin this an opportunity for the kid – experience stuff i didn't experience – go t'places i've never been – somethin might come of it y'know – all this shit here it's good enough for me it's what i'm used to – but if somethin better can happen for her why shouldn't it happen – an even if it didn't it would be somethin to look back on y'know – that's it – that's the reason

Socrates i don't believe you just told me that

Petesy i didn't wanna say – didn't a say a didn't wanna say

Socrates ya fuckin did though

Petesy no sixty forty fifty fifty

Socrates very good that's very good petesy

Petesy what

Socrates i take any type a cut a look like a complete bastard now don't a

Petesy are ya in or out

Socrates hobson's fuckin choice

Petesy forget a told ye

Socrates aye

Petesy i'm serious forget about it – yer either in or out

Socrates what if a say no – you be happy with that

Petesy ya say no ya say no – are ya sayin no

Socrates i'm not happy about this petesy – emotional fuckin blackmail y'know – i'm not happy about that – made me responsible for shit that i'm not responsible for

Petesy responsible for fuck all – if ya don't wanna do it then don't do it – makin me feel like i'm beggin ye here – fuck off – my family i'll look after them – a don't need you or no other fucker – emotional blackmail – a business deal that's what yer bein offered – a fuckin business deal – don't think yer doin me any favours – it's a business deal an nothin else

Socrates right alright sixty forty

Petesy no fifty fifty i want fuck all from ye

Socrates a don't mind if

Petesy a don't give a fuck what ya mind – this is a business deal – fifty fifty or nothin

Socrates don't be gettin all fuckin heavy here

Petesy i'm not i'm calm – yes or no

Socrates alright

Petesy ya sure now

Socrates d'ya want me t'sign somethin – i've said alright haven't a

Petesy have t'be at lunch time

Socrates aye

Petesy just need t'get ridda them other two – say we'll meet them for a swally roun the corner – celebrate ding-ding's good night irene trick

Socrates aye

Petesy i take the wee lad roun now clean the van – get it ready

Socrates aye

Petesy everything sound

Socrates aye

Petesy bit silent on it y'know

Socrates i'm agreein with ye – aye means i'm agreein with ye

Petesy you be alright here on yer own – get everythin squared up

Socrates aye

Petesy in the name of fuck (*Enters other room.*) you be alright on your todd ding-ding

Ding-Ding aye

Petesy c'mon randolph me an yous going to clean the van out

Randolph why

Petesy what does it matter to you why we're just doin it – so c'mon – fancy a cuppla gargles at lunchtime ding-ding – all head roun the corner bit of a celebration an that

Ding-Ding lunch time

Petesy aye

Ding-Ding i've a cuppla things t'get sorted out

Petesy yer last day y'know can't let it go without an oul swally an that

Ding-Ding we'll see

Petesy c'mon you

Petesy and Randolph exit to on site.

Socrates no talk about nothin just words – no talk

Makes an attempt to go back to work.

I can't be arsed with all this

He enters other room where Ding-Ding is working.

ya busy

Ding-Ding enough t'keep me goin

Socrates aye

Socrates sits down and watches Ding-Ding work.

Ding-Ding ya finished in there

Socrates nah

Ding-Ding much a do

Socrates nah

Ding-Ding adhesive's shite – too dry – lyin too long

Socrates d'ye ever cry ding-ding – ye ever just sit down an cry

Ding-Ding no

Socrates i did the other day – a worked somethin out for myself an cause a realised the truth about somethin it made me cry – it's like it had been there all along an it was slowly workin its way out y'know – somethin locked inside me waitin to be worked out – d'ya ever get that – ever feel like there's shit locked away deep down or whatever tryin t'bust out or somethin

Ding-Ding no

Socrates it was to do with my da – him as a person y'know – d'ye ever do that – think about what type of person yer da was really like y'know – get rid a all that sentimental fuckin gear an just have a look – d'ya ever do that

Ding-Ding no – give us over them snips

Socrates (*he does*) everybody thought my da was a great fella y'know a character – yer da's a character – always remember people sayin that – dead now like – yer brown bread doesn't matter a fuck what ya were does it – yer oul lad dead aye

Ding-Ding a lifetime – retirement fucked 'im

Socrates my oul lad was a hero t'me – when i was a kid a used t'think that if everybody respected me the way people respected my da that yer life would be worthwhile y'know – somethin worth livin – his funeral was fuckin massive – all weepin – there'll not be another one like yer da – if yer half the man yer da was you'll do alright son – ya never understand shit that's goin on aroun ye til after it's over sure ye don't – bright man never made anything of himself y'know – spent all his life graftin – digging – liftin – sweatin – that fucked him up – took to the gargle an that's when everybody thought he was a great fella – on friday's i had t'go roun t'the bar an get money off him for my ma y'know – i can see him sittin there crowd round him drink flyin an him holdin court – used to bring me into the middle of them y'know – cause i was his son that made me a great fella too – a hero my hero – y'know what i worked out ding-ding – the thing that made me cry – i worked out that there's difference between bein a character and havin character – my da was a small insignificant little person who gave a fuck about nobody but himself – he thought more about gettin a slap on the back for bein a great fella by some other useless fucker than he did about the people that should've mattered to him – his family his wife his kids – when i was fifteen he fucked off – gave me some bullshit speech about how his life was a failure an how he was a burden on us all an then he fucked off – left me ma with five kids – still a character of course – still gettin the slaps on the back – no bottle – the man had no fuckin bottle – rather than live a decent life he wanted to be a character in a story – fuck'im

Socrates cries, not openly but with resistance. Ding-Ding continues to work. Socrates stops crying. Silence.

Socrates i'm sorry

Ding-Ding aye

Socrates i'm sorry ding-ding – i'm sorry

Ding-Ding aye – that united's a bad lot aren't the – watched them the other night – gettin fuckin hammered the were end up winnin one t'nil – jammie bastards – other team must've hit the bar four times – wee lad rattled it from about thirty yards – like a fuckin bullet it was keeper didn't smell it – jammie bastards – ya see it – must've been thirty fuckin yards

Socrates nah

Ding-Ding good game – jammie bastards thirty yards like

Socrates aye – things happen in cycles like don't the – same shit keeps comin roun again an again

Ding-Ding that's right – same match last year same shit happened – jammie bastards

Socrates a don't mean that – that's not what i'm talkin about – why the fuck would a wanna talk about that

Ding-Ding what then

Socrates the same shit happens – my da fucks off – i end up fuckin off – a haven't seen her or my wee lad for months now – that's what i'm talkin about – that's what a mean

Ding-Ding oh that – right

Socrates aye that – not whether some pimply gobbed overpaid little runt can kick a fuckin ball or not – that – my life – that

Ding-Ding aye

Socrates a should go roun an see them shouldn't a – what d'ye think should i go round an see them

Ding-Ding i don't know – when

Socrates now – go roun an see them now – do it now

Ding-Ding aye now – if it's in yer head do it now

Socrates talk to them

Ding-Ding aye talk to them – stay there for a while have lunch i'll cover for ye

Socrates maybe arrange t'bring them out for dinner or somethin – bring them out t'night – just the three of us – talk to them

Ding-Ding i'll cover for ye – dinner tonight's a good idea

Socrates you say t'petesy – tell him – tell him i'll be back soon

Ding-Ding never mind about that – fuck that i'll sort that out

Socrates aye now – now'd be the best time

Ding-Ding aye

> *Socrates exits to on site.*

> *Petesy and Randolph enter from on site.*

Petesy (*to Randolph*) start sortin out that crap in the corner (*To Ding-Ding.*) where's heart on his sleeve away – saw him beltin out the gate there

Ding-Ding away roun t'see his fork an knife an wee lad

Petesy ya serious

Ding-Ding his head's away – one minute he's slabberin about his da or somethin next thing he's up an away – somethin not right with him

Petesy he say how long like – what – gonna be away long or what

Ding-Ding he just up an scarpered – i don't know

Petesy he said nothin

Ding-Ding somethin about lunch

Petesy back before lunch

Ding-Ding gonna have lunch with them he said

Petesy lunch when – lunch when we're havin lunch – lunch then or lunch some other time

Ding-Ding lunch he said – fuck i don't know – ya eat lunch at lunch time don't ye – talkin about dinner as well

Petesy not lunch then dinner – is that what he said dinner

Ding-Ding both – must be hank marvin

Petesy let me get this straight here – he's not comin back that it

Ding-Ding look petesy i don't know his head's done – he's talkin about his da then he's on about his fork an knife an wee lad then he's talkin about meals then he's up an away

Petesy fuck'im – said nothin like just away – fuck'im

Ding-Ding there's somethin not right with him i'm tellin ye

Petesy a know that

Ding-Ding i'm graftin away he's spouttin some cleavers in my ear about discoverin somethin about his da or somethin – next thing he's gurnin away like a child – mad man know what i'm sayin – name a fuck ya can't be at that crack – that's not on – ya can't be at that

Petesy a know that – a know that – fuck'im

Ding-Ding all the years i've been graftin never witnessed the like a that – i've seen men go through some serious shit but a mean it never got outta order – just burst into tears – a don't know what the fuck he was expectin me t'do – not equipped t'handle that gear like am a

Petesy who the fuck is – that's the problem too he's puttin it on to us – he should know better like shouldn't he

Ding-Ding correct – know better that's right

Petesy you listenin to this randolph – this is important listen to what's bein said here

Randolph what

Petesy when yer workin with other men right in a situation like this – see all the emotional shit that ya get elsewhere keep it til yerself – cause once ya start givin it the verbals yer napper goes – men yer workin with don't want that – always gotta keep the napper straight

Ding-Ding fuckin embarrassin that's what it is – embarrassin other people yer are

Petesy man's right – not only are ye fuckin about with the relationships between you an yer workmates yer embarrassin people as well – first rule of work – if it's not within the chat that we work within ye say fuck all – remember that – fuck all

Randolph got ye – fuck all

Ding-Ding tried to steer him away from it too havin none of it he was – he's givin it the weepin trick i piped in with what ya think about the match the other night

Petesy that's a good one – sound bet – football's always a sound bet

Ding-Ding fucker let on he hadn't seen the match

Petesy he had an opportunity – ya give him an opportunity

Ding-Ding practically told me to shut up – fuckin head's gone

Petesy a know that – see the one yer wee man hit from thirty yards – fuckin doosey

Ding-Ding jammie bastards – a kept sayin that

Randolph same wee lad hit one like that the other week too

Ding-Ding a saw it – fuckin belter

Petesy hit them with both feet he can

Ding-Ding if the put that wee lad up for sale ya couldn't buy him – some a them third world chats wouldn't have enough national fuckin income to pay for that wee lad

Petesy he's good

Ding-Ding star he is

Petesy he's not comin back then – fuck'im

Ding-Ding lunchtime – after lunch – i don't know

Petesy just up an away – fuck'im – i'm away here

He exits to other room.

Randolph i reckon ya get ten million for that wee lad – he'll not stay with them that type a readies floatin about – ya think he'll stay with them

Ding-Ding don't give a fuck what he does son – that's socrates away durin lunch – all we gotta do now is get rid of shit for brains there

Randolph aye

Ding-Ding what was all that crack about cleanin the van out

Randolph nothin just said it looked like a shit heap

Ding-Ding save us doin it

Randolph i did do it

Ding-Ding save me doin it

Randolph aye

Petesy (*other room – thinking aloud*) swannin off – no reason like – can't trust a man at that crack – can't say what he's thinkin – fuck that (*Pause.*) randolph mere a minute

Randolph (*enters other room*) what

Petesy shut the door behind ye

Randolph what

Petesy that cryin trick fucked ding-ding up didn't it – he's alright ding-ding isn't he – soun man

Randolph aye

Petesy i was just thinkin about somethin there – just between me an you now – ya understan that

Randolph aye

Petesy that's good – socrates' a bit dodgy at the moment y'know – ya get the feelin from him he'd drop tools an do a bunk on ye if it suited him – that's not a good situation work wise an with ding-ding packin it in it's all a bit up in the air y'know – could get somebody else in for ding-ding but then we mightn't hit if off with the guy or whatever y'know – an that would fuck the whole show up – might be a better idea if you took over from ding-ding

Randolph ya serious – that'd be brilliant petesy – a need the extra readies y'know an that would help me

Petesy slow down there tonto nothin's sorted yet – normally take two or three months but i could bend heavy hole's ear about it – maybe speed the thing up – tell him yer sound get him on yer side y'know – think that be a good idea – would ya be up to it ye reckon

Randolph certainly no sweat about it petesy i'd be sound

Petesy few extra shillins in yer sky rocket of course come the end a the week

Randolph that'd be great – i'm savin to buy a motorbike y'know – have t'put money away in a club an that y'know

Petesy are ye – that's good – extra responsibilities as a said – bit of decision makin

Randolph i can handle that

Petesy i think ya could

Randolph when ya gonna say t'heavy hole soon like – next week or what – when ya sayin til him

Petesy that depends on you

Randolph what way

Petesy fuck all for fuck all – i do somethin for you you do somethin for me

Randolph what – anything name it

Petesy pallet a tiles lyin out the front there – a want ya t'help me steal them

Randolph shit

Petesy there's nothing to it kid – just fire them into the back a the van at lunchtime – shift them – that's it

Randolph pallet a tiles roun the front – lunchtime

Petesy aye –fuck all to it plus there's a few quid there for ye

Randolph lunchtime

Petesy friday lunchtime everyone fucks off – place til ourselves – happy days – tell ding ding meet him roun the bar for a swally – weigh in late

Randolph what if i knock ya back

Petesy ya gonna knock me back

Randolph don't know

Petesy put it like this – no good word to heavy hole plus i can make life shit for ye y'know

Randolph it is already

Petesy more shit then – i need ye t'do this for me

Randolph why

Petesy got fuck all to do with you why – y'understand – nothin – all you need know is i need someone t'give me a hand – that's all – workmates helpin each other out – isn't that the way the world should be

Randolph aye work mates helpin each other out

Petesy just look upon it as a business deal that works to both our benefits – you get what you want i get what i want – nobody's any the wiser no harm done

Randolph aye

Petesy away back in there give him a hand – oul fucker probably sleepin by now

Randolph aye

Petesy ya get nothin for nothin kid

Randolph aye

Randolph enters other room.

Ding-Ding what shit for brains want

Randolph nothin

Ding-Ding nothin

Randolph aye nothin (*Pause.* Randolph *starts scratching his arms.*) fuckin arms goin mad with itch

Ding-Ding grout dust – drop a soap an water sort that out

Randolph it's not that

Ding-Ding what

Randolph a didn't want t'say anythin to ye about it

His head starts to twitch.

there's that away now too

Scratching – twitching – his body jerks.

the jerkin now – it only happens at certain times – it's stress related – first happened when we were kids just about t'raid an orky an this started – first the scratching then the other gear

Ding-Ding i've heard of it – (*Scratching.*) it can be serious (*Twitching/jerking.*) has been know to stay with people for years

Randolph stop fuckin about

Ding-Ding maybe it's contagious

Randolph the stress comes from a reaction to the notion of gettin caught – my lamps will start to swell up soon then a go temporarily blind

Ding-Ding (*stops*) nothin wrong with a bit a nerves randolph son

Randolph no joke

Ding-Ding don't fuck me about – a told ye that

Randolph (*stops*) we'll leave it til monday tiles still here then it's a bog cert they're nobody's

Ding-Ding this job's finished today – i'm leavin today – we're doin it – today (*Arm around Randolph's shoulder.*) think about the motorbike – ya see it – just you keep that picture in yer head

Randolph but ding-ding it's not

Ding-Ding (*pulls Randolph close-tight*) a commitment been made – there's nothing else t'be said – (*Smiling.*) don't panic son – there's no need to panic

Randolph i'm not i'm not i'm sound – just havin a bit of a laugh y'know – just a bit of an oul laugh – ease the tension a bit ding-ding that's all – nothin t'worry about where i'm concerned

Ding-Ding we're sound then

Randolph alright if i go for a dander for five minutes – just want t'walk about the place check everything's alright y'know

Ding-Ding you do that you do that son

Randolph exits to on site.

Ding-Ding temporary fuckin blindness – wha

Petesy working in one room Ding-Ding in the other.

Socrates enters from on site to room Ding-Ding is in.

Socrates thank you for covering for me – you are a man of good character an outstanding and upstanding individual whose worth – like all real martyrs – will only be realised when you bite the big one and take your rightful place amongst the gods

Ding-Ding i thought

Socrates don't think do – the foundation of all human endeavour

He exits to other room.

Ding-Ding fuck him

Petesy where the fuck where you

Socrates this another lover's tiff honey – not jealous were you

Petesy where were ye

Socrates i had an idea – a thought – i acted on it and from that some good has burst onto the scene – now the world's a happier place

Petesy happier fuckin place – aye – ding-ding's said ya were away for lunch – lunch that's what he told me – just up'ed an fucked off – that's what he said

Socrates aren't a here now – had t'come back for the pilfering chats didn't a

Petesy i was thinkin about that – it might be better if

Socrates all systems are go – know what happened t'me there – something small but something good which makes it probably something big doesn't it

Petesy socrates about the other – thing there's somethin

Socrates howl on a minute this is important a need to speak this out y'know – i'd worked out y'see that my da didn't treat his kids an wife well – an it looked like i was goin that way – so a said fuck it i'm goin roun t'see them – bit iffy at the start – so a thought i'll be honest here fuck it – i'll be honest – i'm confused i said – i'm lonely an i just wanted t'see you an the wee lad – she smiled – brilliant – first time i was ever honest with her an she smiled – wanted t'bring the two a them out tonight for a meal – special dixie y'know just the three of us – just spendin time together talkin that's all – she wasn't keen on the idea – a smile doesn't wipe the past out i understand that – the wee lad says he wants t'go to the pictures – she says why don't you take him – i'm takin my wee lad to the pictures tonight – him an me – a boys' night out – ya could see it in his smile – me an my da are goin to the pictures

Petesy good – good – about this other thing

Socrates what

Petesy the tiles

Socrates aye everything's sound lunchtime

Petesy a don't know – hearing about the plumber gettin maclatched an that – it's thrown me a bit y'know

Socrates fuck all t'do with us that's what ya said – ya said that didn't ye

Petesy a know a know that – it's just maybe this is a bad idea at the moment – maybe we should leave it for now y'know – let the dust settle – give it a few days

Socrates it's bein done now we decided that – no need for any more thinkin about it

Petesy i know what we decided – all i'm sayin is it might be a bit dodgy

Socrates she says to me in passin like that she was skint –
i've been givin her fuck all for a while y'know – i said til
her don't worry about that that's alright i'll get ye a
chunk a readies – it has t'be done – the woman has bills
to pay an shit – y'know

Petesy leave it til monday or later next week even – now
seems like a bad time that's all

Socrates i've already said – i've made a commitment here
y'know – i can't go back on that – she's happy about the
situation understand what i'm sayin

Petesy i'm just not sure

Socrates fuck not bein sure – ya put me in a corner
earlier on – you were sure enough then

Petesy put in fuck all corner – ya made yer own decision
nothin else involved there – nothin

Socrates you were on ma back an ya know it – made me
feel like the wee girl's trip an everythin was beat out if
i didn't come on board

Petesy a business deal that's all – a don't wanna hear
anything about that – a said t'ye an that's it

Socrates ya gonna let me speak here – i've somethin t'say
y'know

Petesy don't be gettin all fuckin

Socrates can i speak here (*Pause*.) you had yer reasons –
ya told me them – i understood the were important t'ye –
so instead of tellin ye t'go an fuck yerself a came on
board – all i'm doin now is the same thing – i'm tellin
you this is important to me – it's not just doin somethin
cause it's there t'be done – there's a reason an the readies
are important to me

Randolph enters from on site.

Randolph is there any chance

Socrates we're talkin here randolph

Randolph a just wanted t'see if

Socrates a don't give a fuck what ya want i've told ye we're talkin here – go in with ding-ding – whenever we're finished ya can do all the talkin ya want – go on – go

Randolph exits to other room.

Socrates ya understand what i'm sayin here – you asked me to do somethin an i went along with it – now i'm askin you to do something an i want you t'go along with it

Petesy right

Socrates right what

Petesy right right

Socrates good – i'm just gonna nip out an get some flowers – be a nice gesture that wouldn't it – a nice gesture

Petesy be a nice gesture t'do some fuckin work – i think that would be a nice gesture

Socrates it's nearly lunchtime aren't ya only gonna sweep up

Petesy a was but if yer doin fuck all i'm doin fuck all

Socrates whatever – i've a good feeling about today – feels like the start a somethin – somethin different – a don't know

Socrates exits to on site.

Petesy fuck it

Ding-Ding and Randolph in other room.

Ding-Ding did ya count them then

Randolph no

Ding-Ding no

Randolph aye – no

Ding-Ding why didn't ye count them

Randolph ya never mentioned countin them

Ding-Ding be a handy piece a information t'know

Randolph aye

Ding-Ding i'll do it will a – seein it needs t'be done an you didn't do it i'll do it

Randolph aye

Ding-Ding might nip roun an see if a can get yer man about the george formby dixie

Randolph what

Ding-Ding when i'm cleanin – forget it

Randolph aye

Ding-Ding exits to on site.

Socrates enters from on site carrying a bunch of flowers.

Socrates smell them – fill yer snazzle with that aroma

Petesy aye lovely

Socrates from now on any job we're on all bring in a bunch of flowers – put them in vase chats leave'em about the place – instead a all this buildin concrete shite – bit a colour about the place

Petesy aye

Socrates i'm tellin ye – whenever ya feel a bit dankers an that have a butchers at the flowers – then go over an snort their beauty up intil yer napper – make ya feel at one with the universe – make ya feel glad to be alive boy

Petesy ya reckon

Socrates a do – what's the crack here – lunchtime – sit around for a few minutes – get them out t'fuck – go an do the business meet them roun for a swally

Petesy aye

Ding-Ding enters other room from on site.

Ding-Ding a hundred and forty four boxes – plenty – got that other chat sorted out too – wee man's happy enough – drop him roun the readies over the weekend – fucked he is – had a get him up outta his scratcher – no life for a person that – go in here chew the fat with these two get them outta the road do what we have t'do meet up with them later for a swally

Randolph aye

Work.

Petesy (*from the other room*) nose bag time

Lunchtime.

Randolph and Ding-Ding enter other room. There are four buckets turned upside down. They all sit and have tea from a flask – mid conversation.

Petesy that's what ya said – ya said that – didn't he say that – ya said everythin

Ding-Ding ya did ya said everythin

Socrates aye an what

Petesy no i'm not havin that – there must be some kind a dividin line some type a demarcation y'know

Ding-Ding man's right cause somebody says somethin doesn't make it true – it's like yer man in the paper that geezer who put the dead sheep or somethin in that glass tank chat

Petesy hearst

Ding-Ding aye him – that's not art no matter what that fucker says t'me it's not art

Socrates that's my point if ya accept any of it ya have t'accept the lot of it

Randolph that wall that we've tiled ship it over to the tate aye

Socrates ya could aye why not

Petesy right howl on here – say a person makes their own clothes

Socrates that's art – do ya not think that's art

Petesy ya gonna let me finish – ya never let anyone finish – a person makes their own clothes – the have t'wash them don't the – nobody wants glad rags art or otherwise that are fuckin abraham lincoln – the wash them an the put them on the line – no better still the wash them it's rainin outside so they hang them on the radiator t'dry – you go roun to their house t'visit an ye see the clothes dryin – is that an exhibition

Socrates clothes are meant t'be worn aren't the – anyway if the hang them for a purpose yes

Petesy bollicks – and the were hung for a purpose – t'dry

Ding-Ding socrates that purpose chat doesn't matter cause the person lookin at them doesn't know what the crack is

Socrates what's that gotta do with it – it's the person who's hangin them not the one lookin at them

Ding-Ding on the way roun to the house ya get soaked – ya take yer clothes off hang them beside the other ones – somebody else comes in has a jeff juke at the radiator – are yer clothes part of a exhibition now

Socrates i didn't make my clothes

Ding-Ding same crack as before they don't know that

Randolph (*to Petesy*) lend us yer cup

Petesy no

Socrates (*to Ding-Ding*) what does that matter

Ding-Ding petesy said it earlier on – art an all that fuckin gear has t'do with the geezer lookin at it not with the geezer who made it

Petesy correct – thank you ding-ding

Socrates it's one a them unanswerable ones like isn't it

Petesy how's it unanswerable if we've answered it

Randolph (*to Petesy*) you've finished yer tea lend us yer cup

Petesy no – a keep tellin ya this – no

Randolph yer finished

Petesy is he deaf – are you deaf

Socrates give the wee lad the cup – fella's allowed a mouthful a tea

Petesy no – he does this all the time no

Randolph do what all the time

Petesy where's yer own cup

Randolph what ya askin that for – why's he askin that – a don't have a cup ya know a don't have a cup

Socrates it's unanswerable – it is it's unanswerable

Petesy me an ding-ding wouldn't be allowed t'get it right sure we wouldn't

Ding-Ding we answer the unanswerable – that's us

Randolph am i invisible here

Petesy might as well be yer not gettin the fuckin cup – this is my cup where's yer cup

Randolph i don't have a cup

Socrates petesy just give him the fuckin cup

Petesy give him yers

Socrates i'm not finished yer finished give him the cup

Petesy no – he has t'learn this is work he's responsible for his own stuff – not havin his own cup means he's not takin the thing seriously

Socrates takin what seriously

Petesy work

Socrates he doesn't take work seriously cause he doesn't bring a cup

Petesy not any cup his own cup – an yes

Randolph a don't want yer cup stick it

Petesy a will

Socrates i don't understan that – a cup like

Petesy ya don't understand what

Socrates yer argument – the thinkin behind what yer sayin – it's all up the fuckin left

Petesy what – there can't be logic t'normal things like – we can't have our own logic no – you only understand the logic of the loftier head firmly up yer jam roll world – we're not allowed logic

Socrates settle yerself

Petesy aye a know – but a mean it's not always up there some of it's down fuckin here y'know

Ding-Ding ya can have my cup

Randolph yer cup

Petesy (*to Ding-Ding*) yer gonna lend him yer cup

Socrates no one touches yer cup – it's a rule – we all thought the thing must've been handed down t'ye from moses

Ding-Ding (*to Randolph*) do ya want a cup of tea or not

Randolph aye but there's no way i'm usin yer cup – that's the cup – ya don't touch the cup even i know that – say a broke it – a don't want a lend of it no

Ding-Ding i'm not lending ye it i'm givin ya it

Socrates yer frightenin us ding-ding

Petesy yer givin him yer cup the cup that no one can touch

Ding-Ding when i first started a bought the cup – now i'm leavin might as well give it t'the wee lad

Socrates yer passin him on a cup

Randolph yer passin me on a cup

Ding-Ding aye

Randolph what am i gonna do with it

Ding-Ding drink yer fuckin tea out a it

Randolph no – that's serious shit that – like puttin a curse on me

Ding-Ding it's only a cup

Randolph it's not it's the cup – it's ding-ding's cup – a workin man's cup – all that gear – couldn't drink outta that

Ding-Ding suit yerself

Socrates use mine

Randolph fill it up there (*To Petesy.*) what

Petesy no tea left

Socrates time for a swally anyway

Ding-Ding we headin roun aye

Petesy aye

Randolph headin roun

 Nobody moves.

Ding-Ding sure petesy why don't you an socrates welt on roun there – we'll meet ye for a swally later

Petesy meet us

Ding-Ding aye me an randolph has somethin t'sort out

Petesy what

Ding-Ding what

Petesy aye what

Ding-Ding what – funny as fuck sometimes the way ya just forget somethin when somebody asks ye – the head's a weird fuckin gadget like isn't it – randolph what is it – it's just not comin t'me – can you remember

Randolph no

Ding-Ding no

Randolph no

Petesy can't be too important can it

Ding-Ding important alright – a have to – ah – have t'let the dog out – the dog has t'get out y'know

Socrates what dog – you don't have a dog

Ding-Ding a don't no that's right – the wee woman beside me though – wee woman beside me has a dog – she's away – i told here i'd do the business y'know – bring the wee lad with me y'know

Socrates bring him – what for

Ding-Ding big fuckin dog – huge big fucker – take the two of us y'know – big beast of a thing

Randolph sure why don't me an petesy meet yous roun there – an socrates can go roun with ye let the dog out – socrates likes dogs

Socrates i like dogs

Randolph aye – yer always talkin about them aren't ya

Socrates no – hate the fuckers hate all animals

Randolph i thought you like dogs – sure yous two go roun anyway – didn't ye want me for somethin petesy

Ding-Ding socrates can't go the dog'll do its nut

Socrates i'm not goin anywhere – why would the dog do its nut

Ding-Ding funny fuckin animal

Randolph haven't me an you t'sort somethin out petesy – a tile slipped or somethin roun the other room

Petesy that's alright i sorted that out

Socrates sure the dog wouldn't know me

Ding-Ding that's it ya see hates people he doesn't know – anti social bastard

Randolph it's something else then it's not that – what is it petesy somethin else isn't it

Petesy no nothin else

Socrates do you know the dog randolph

Randolph what dog

Socrates the fuckin dog

Randolph no – are ya sure petesy

Petesy positive

Randolph right – that dog – ding-ding's dog – aye a know that one – big fuckin dog that – i'll go roun with ye ding-ding give ya a hand will a

Ding-Ding yer comin roun t' help me with the dog

Randolph oh aye

Ding-Ding sure about that

Randolph must be starvin by now

Ding-Ding hank marvin – so we'll meet yous two roun there then

Socrates aye

Petesy aye

Ding-Ding an what – are yous headin roun there now or what

Petesy hang on here for a while (*To Socrates.*) you wanna hang on here for a while

Socrates hang aroun for a while aye

Ding-Ding welt roun now an get a seat for us all – don't wanna be standin fuck that caper – we don't wanna be standin

Petesy place is empty it's always empty

Ding-Ding aye that place that place is empty – we're not goin there goin roun the other place

Socrates other place'll be bunged

Ding-Ding that's why i'm sayin t'welt roun now an get a seat

Petesy i'm not goin there – what would ya want t'go there for can't get movin in it – you hate that place anyway – always sayin it's full a shite hawks

Ding-Ding a thought it be nice today – last day celebration – bit more up market y'know

Petesy up market fuck that

Socrates aye fuck that

Ding-Ding what one do you wanna go to randolph

Randolph the one ya need t'rush roun now an get a seat in

Petesy (*to Ding-Ding*) is that where you wanna go

73

Ding-Ding aye – be better – fuck that other place

Petesy we'll go there then

Ding-Ding yous better motor then – get a good seat one near the winda

Socrates all the seats be away by now (*To Petesy.*) all be away by now

Petesy long ago – ya couldn't get a seat in it now for love nor money

Ding-Ding i'm tellin ye if ya welt roun ya will

Petesy all gone now – we'll stand sure – i don't mind standin (*To Socrates.*) d'you mind standin

Socrates no – standin's alright

Ding-Ding i'm not standin

Petesy go to the normal place then

Ding-Ding aye – other place is a fuckin kip anyway

Socrates thought it was up market

Ding-Ding it's a fuckin kip

Petesy so we'll see yous roun there then – better pints anyway

Randolph yous headin now

Socrates too early

Ding-Ding you'll miss the stew

Petesy fuck the stew

Socrates better get roun an sort that dog out – have its own leg chewed off by now

Ding-Ding fuck the dog

Socrates ya can't leave it with no grub

Ding-Ding what d'you care sure you hate animals nature all that shite

Socrates a know that but a wouldn't leave a dog with no grub

Ding-Ding fuck the dog

Petesy not goin roun then

Ding-Ding a just said fuck the dog – fuck the dog means i'm not goin roun

Petesy the two a yous headin on roun then – roun to the other place

Ding-Ding no

Socrates you'll miss the stew

Ding-Ding i don't like stew

Socrates i've seen ye eat stew before

Ding-Ding no ya haven't

Socrates a have

Petesy i've seen ye

Randolph so have i

Ding-Ding (*to Randolph*) you've seen me eat stew have ye

Randolph thought a did – must've been – soup – what was it soup

Ding-Ding aye soup – an that's shite roun there too

Socrates food is shite roun there

Petesy good pints though

Randolph the do – the do good pints

Ding-Ding aye

Petesy just sit here for a while then

Ding-Ding looks like it

They sit in silence.

the notion for a gargle's wore off me

Randolph me too

Ding-Ding if yous two wanna

Petesy i'm not that keen myself

Ding-Ding aye

They sit in silence.

ya sure now – i don't mind like – a know it's my leavin dixie an that but a mean if yous wanna welt on that's alright

Petesy nah – a couldn't be arsed now

They sit in silence.

Socrates fuck this – there's a problem here that needs t'be solved – honesty that's the thing – honesty

Petesy socrates

Socrates it's alright it's sound – my experience t'day has taught me that the only truth that the – that the best way forward in any situation is to open yerself up – to be honest

Petesy sure about that

Socrates hundred percent – because of circumstances outside our normal work situation petesy and i have been forced into a situation we would not normally find ourselves in – the role of tea leafs – there's a pallet a tiles outside that we have planned to steal – i now realise that not lettin you two know our plans was a mistake – and i apologise as workmates and people we have known for some time – we should've treated you better and informed you of what we were plannin to do – which is what i am doin now (*Pause.*) so as this operation needs to be completed during lunch time petesy and i will now take our leave to do the dirty deed – unless of course you have something to say about the situation – in which case i would appreciate it if you would keep yer comments brief – as time is of the essence

Petesy (*applauding*) yer good – yer very good – i have something t'say

Socrates you do

Petesy oh yes – where the fuck do you get off telling people my business – who the fuck give you permission t'speak on my behalf

Socrates a thought

Petesy ya didn't think – what ya did was open yer gob an speak – the one thing ya didn't do was fuckin think

Ding-Ding may i intervene in this spirit of openness

Petesy oh fuck aye intervene away

Randolph ding-ding i don't

Ding-Ding i'm speakin for both of us – this situation involves us an what i'm doin is speakin for us – understan

Petesy what

Ding-Ding me an the wee lad had planned t'steal the tiles too

Petesy you an him

Ding-Ding didn't a just say that

Socrates this is good – i like this – ya see now if we hadda been up front about this the situation

Petesy shut up a minute

Socrates i'm just sayin

Petesy keep quiet – stop talkin a minute – you an him – when did you an him decide this

Ding-Ding what does that matter

Petesy when

Ding-Ding this mornin – not that that's got fuck all t'do with you

> *Petesy hits Randolph. Socrates and Ding-Ding restrain him.*

Socrates what the fuck are ya at

Petesy let fuckin go of me let go

Ding-Ding what ya hit him for he's a wee lad – what ya hit him for

Petesy i don't like being made a fucker of – let go a me let fuckin go

Ding-Ding ya gonna calm down – get yer head clear here

Petesy i'm calm – i'm sound – just let go

> *They let go.*

Socrates ya sound

Petesy i'm sound

Socrates you alright kid (*To Petesy.*) what the fuck you at

Petesy (*to Randolph*) there was a problem ya should've fuckin said – stood up like a man an said face t'face – i'm there tryin a do the right thing by ye yer makin a fuckin eejit outta me – ya had somehin t'say ya should a fuckin said it – fucker ye

Randolph lifts a hammer.

Ding-Ding put the hammer down – yer outta order – put the hammer down

Petesy what ya gonna do with that – ya gonna use it

Randolph c'mon – c'mon – i'll put it through yer fuckin face

Ding-Ding yer on yer own kid – there's rules y'know – there's rules – ya lift a hammer yer on yer own

Randolph fuck him

Socrates we gonna calm down here a minute

Petesy ya gonna use that – c'mon – ya wanna use it fuckin use it – c'mon

Socrates calm down will ye

Petesy fuck up nothin t'do with you so fuck up

Socrates ya gonna start on me now

Petesy if that's what ya want

Socrates up t'yerself – ya wanna go that way we can go that way

Randolph ya can't treat me like shit – ya hear me – ya can't treat me like fuckin shit (*To Petesy.*) fuck you an the tiles – fuck you

Ding-Ding what he got a do with you an the tiles

Randolph (*to Ding-Ding*) fuck you too – wanna grab me by the throat now – ya wanna have a go at that now do ye – fuck the two a yous

Socrates what's goin on here

Randolph the two a them – don't say that – don't say this – just me an you – just me an you – i'm stuck in the middle – doin me a favour – fuckin usin me

Socrates (*to Petesy*) you ask him

Petesy (*to Randolph*) ya had a spoke yer mind situation wouldn't a come up

Ding-Ding (*to Randolph*) you agreed with him after ya agreed with me

Socrates you ask him

Petesy aye i asked him

Randolph he thinks yer fuckin crazy – that's why he asked me you can't be trusted yer fuckin crazy

Socrates you say that

Ding-Ding (*to Randolph*) ya wee bastard ya ungrateful wee bastard

Randolph lookin after yer fuckin self that's what ya were doin

Socrates (*to Randolph*) shut up – fuck you an fuck him (*To Petesy.*) did you say i was crazy

Petesy ya are fuckin crazy – talkin a lotta shite all the time – yer fuckin head's away with it

Ding-Ding (*to Socrates*) what you just say to me there

Socrates (*to Ding-Ding*) fuck you you heard fuck you – i'm not interested in anythin to do with you alright – fuck you

Ding-Ding grabs Socrates by the jumper.

Socrates get yer hand off me (*To Petesy.*) i was just tellin you how i felt what i was thinkin – i'm not crazy

Petesy yer fuckin crazy

Ding-Ding (*to Socrates*) you don't talk to me like that

Socrates (*to Ding-Ding*) this is nothing to do with you – i'm warnin ye now get yer fuckin hand away from me

Petesy yer fuckin crazy

Socrates (*grabs Petesy by the jumper*) say it one more time i'm gonna put yer head through the fuckin wall

Petesy (*grabs Socrates by the jumper*) any time yer ready fella – any fuckin time

Socrates breaks free.

Socrates this is the wrong way t'go about this – we're goin t'do it we'll do it fuckin right (*Moves to Randolph.*) put the hammer down – nobody's gonna touch ye just put the hammer down (*Shouts.*) put it down

Randolph puts the hammer down.

we right now – we ready t'go – i hate work – i hate bein here day in an day out with you fuckers – i hate talkin t'ye – i hate listenin t'ye – i hate bein in yer fuckin company – yous are ruinin my life an i fuckin hate yous for it

Silence.

Petesy i don't like doin this

Socrates you rather we went t'war

Petesy (*to Socrates*) yer a whingin gurnin bastard – a wimp – a snivellin poncy cryin fucker – who makes the

81

rest of us listen to the dribblin shite that pours outta yer thin lipped no backbone whingy wee fuckin mouth – i hate the sight of ye – i'm ashamed t'be in the same room as ye – you other two – yer just lazy bastards

Silence.

Randolph i – i

Socrates go ahead

Randolph i look at you three an all a see are three no good slabberin fuckers who have done nothin with their lives – yous tell me what t'do an none of yous is worth spit – yous think yous are somethin an yes are nothing – just three fuckin tilers that have nothin – are goin nowhere – an lead empty fuckin lives

Silence.

Socrates ding-ding (*Silence.*) ding-ding

Ding-Ding i don't give a fuck about any of yous – yous mean nothin t'me – i've spent most a my time with yous an yous mean nothin t' me – i don't know who any of yous are

He takes a hanky from his pocket and wipes his eyes.

Socrates that it – we finished

Petesy looks like it

Socrates it's been said – it's done – back t' normal now right

Petesy ya think so

Socrates has t'be – this is our livelihood we have t' work together it's as simple as that

Ding-Ding it's my last day

Socrates have you somethin t'say about that

Ding-Ding no

Socrates that's it finished then

Ding-Ding finished

They all sit. Silence.

that united's a shower of jammie bastards aren't the

Petesy they've the referees bribed and everything for fuck sake

Socrates stop talkin nonsense

Ding-Ding certainly the have

Randolph i think the have

Work.

It's nearly the end of the day.

Both rooms are tiled and cleaned. The pallet of tiles is now on stage. Petesy and Socrates enter from on site carrying two boxes of tiles each. They set them with the others.

Socrates this is fuckin stupid – we should've just fired them in the van

Petesy they're better here – after work when the site's empty then we'll fire them in the van

Socrates i can't be hangin about here – ya understan that – do whatever we have t'do an shoot the crow

Petesy it'll take as long as it takes

Socrates can't be late for the wee lad this pictures thing's important – can't be late – don't wanna be messin the wee lad about – wanna show him i'm dependable – don't want him goin through life thinkin i'm lettin him down all the time – that's all i'm sayin

Petesy i wanna get home to y'know – sort this shit out then a can tell the wee girl i've got the readies for her for france – a wanna do that – i don't wanna be hangin aroun either

Socrates ya get the readies t'night – if ya get it t'night i can give it t'her t'night – wee lad to the pictures give her the readies – it would help create a nice type of a feelin about the place y'know

Petesy t'night's difficult – t'morrow

Socrates t'morrow

Petesy aye – jimmy blow be on the gargle t'night – ya not get him have t'be t'morrow

Socrates positive now – a can tell her it's on its way

Petesy aye tell her

Socrates ya sure

Petesy a fuckin said didn't a – didn't a just say it

Socrates right – know what the wee lad wants t'see – i thought this was fuckin brilliant

Petesy what

Socrates thunderbirds – when i was a kid i lived breathed and shite that show – anything he wants t'know he just has t'ask his da – thunderbirds was the business – thunderbirds are go – only one a didn't reckon was number five – know that chat up in space – that wee lad never got home – i always felt that was a bit outta order

Petesy did the not shift him aroun – i thought the did – the did the shifted him aroun – a few episodes in space

then back t'the island for a rest – cuppla gargles scratch
his cleavers beside the pool

Socrates alan ya called him

Petesy aye

Socrates ya reckon he got shore leave

Petesy certainly he did

Socrates might a done alright – makes sense like doesn't
it – go gaga in space on yer lonesome

Petesy aye

Socrates could never work out that wee girl – know the
wee ethnic minority chat – couldn't work out what the
fuck she was at

Petesy she was the maid – wasn't she the maid – aye she
was the maid

Socrates maid – the had a fuckin maid

Petesy aye – she was always carryin gargle aroun on
trays wasn't she – i always thought she was the maid

Socrates adopted daughter maybe – could a been both

Petesy how the fuck could she have been both – she was
a skivvy – the treated her like a skivvy that means she
was on the payroll – you adopt someone ya don't treat
them like a skivvy do ye

Socrates that's true

Petesy i never liked that show anyway – joe ninety was a
better show

Socrates get t'fuck – lady penelope parker that big pink
fuckin roller – behave yerself

Petesy joe ninety

Socrates away an fuck – joe ninety – puttin them dopey testicles on him

Petesy couldn't've been any dopier than the ones brains wore – the had special powers those blue chats had special powers – once he put them on an got into that other chat that spinnin cage message ya knew the world was a safe place – nobody fucked with joe ninety – wee lad used t'eat dynamite for fuck sake

Socrates guff – fuckin nazi he was

Petesy who

Socrates blonde hair blue eyes an his granny was a german or somethin – fuckin nazi

Petesy behave yerself

Socrates alright mightn't been a nazi but he was definitely gay – never once saw him with a wee girl – not once

Petesy he was only a kid what ya talkin about gay – wee lad was savin the world no time for that sexual chat anyway – thunderbirds heap a shite

Socrates doesn't matter t'me one way or the other just good t'be takin the wee lad out that's all

Randolph enters carrying two boxes of tiles. Puts them with the rest.

Socrates (*to Randolph*) he thinks joe ninety's better than thunderbirds

Randolph what's he talkin about

Petesy nothin – shootin the shit – passin the time – nothin – that the last a them

Randolph aye

Socrates joe ninety – yer fuckin head's away with it

86

Petesy (*to Randolph*) ya sure now – none lyin about out there ya checked

Randolph none lyin about – a checked – that's the last of them

Socrates (*looking at tiles*) doesn't look like much does it

Petesy looks like a pallet a tiles – what ya want it t'look like

Socrates i know it looks like a pallet a tiles – that's cause it is a pallet a tiles

Petesy einstein

Socrates i mean the bit a hassle an that it caused – doesn't look like much like

Petesy look better if there were more a them that's true

Randolph doesn't matter what it looks like – gettin us what we want isn't it

Petesy shouldn't have t'fuckin steal t'get what ya want though should ye

Socrates where's ding-ding

Randolph way roun t'buy a bucket

Petesy bucket a what

Randolph winda cleanin – a winda cleaner's bucket

Petesy (*to Socrates*) that's what we've t'work with (*To Randolph.*) what the fuck are you talkin about

Randolph did he not say to ye

Petesy if he said would we be askin

Randolph a thought he said t'ye when we all agreed about the tiles an that – did he not say

87

Petesy he didn't say

Randolph that's what he's doin with his share of the poppy

Socrates buyin buckets

Randolph winda cleanin – some oul lad he knows sellin his round – ding-ding's buyin it off him

Socrates aye

Randolph i'm tellin ye that's what he said – reckons it's gonna stop him from dyin or somethin

Socrates winda cleanin stop him from dyin

Randolph somethin like that

Socrates winda cleanin

Randolph i'm only tellin ye what the man said – i don't know maybe he reckons winda cleaners don't die or somethin – i don't know

Petesy fair play til him

Socrates yer right – fair play til him's right – winda cleanin wouldn't be my preferred occupation – good luck til him though

Randolph somethin wrong with his head

Socrates nothin wrong with his head – man's allowed t'work on – wants t'do that that's up t'himself – oh no he's allowed t'do that

Petesy man's showin a bit a enterprise isn't he – nobody tellin him what t'do – out on his own – that's alright – that's sound

   Ding-Ding enters from on site carrying a bucket.

Socrates fuck it's george formby

88

Petesy when i'm cleaning dixies ding-ding wha – i've an oul shammie an a string vest in the house – that type a object would be of use t'ya now a imagine

Ding-Ding (*to Randolph*) that was nobody's business – ya understan – you do too much talkin wee lad

Randolph i thought you'd already said i didn't know

Socrates no now ding-ding that not right don't be blamin the wee lad here – we're allowed t'know that now c'mon til

Petesy if ya were gonna say nothin how were ya gonna explain the bucket

Ding-Ding explain what it's just a bucket

Petesy ya buy them all the time do ye

Ding-Ding if ya had a asked me about the bucket i'd've told ye to fuck off

Petesy that's lovely talk that from a winda cleaner – can ya picture him half way up the ladder some wee woman says t'him want yer bucket filled mister – away an fuck yerself

Socrates ya can't be at that now ding-ding – when yer a winda cleaner ya can't be talkin like a tiler

Ding-Ding away an fuck yerself

Petesy and Socrates laugh, then Randolph and eventually Ding-Ding.

Socrates what was that

Petesy that's tiler speak for thank you for expressing your opinion but on this occasion i feel i must beg to differ

Petesy and Socrates laugh harder.

Socrates / Petesy away an fuck yerself

Petesy member the day we were standin in the kitchen wee woman says t'him (*Ding-Ding.*) do you think (*Laughter.*) do you think the patterns should be randomised or uniform – how the fuck would i know

They are all in a giggling fit.

Socrates wee woman says – i don't think there's any need for that language

Socrates/Petesy away an fuck yerself

Ding-Ding oh aye very good aye a know

Petesy the other one – the white or the blue tiles – up t'yerself dear – you are the tiler – am i fuck

Socrates what about – attention

Ding-Ding member that – she had lost it – something not right with that wee woman's napper

Randolph what – what was that

Petesy you not with us then no

Socrates no – sure it must've been a good two years ago – wee woman we were workin for had the hots for him (*Ding-Ding*) – definitely some type a sexual thing goin on

Ding-Ding that's not right now – don't listen t'him – that's not right

Petesy didn't she keep givin ya apples

Ding-Ding she wasn't right in the napper that's why

Petesy she didn't give me an him any

Socrates she did not

Petesy she says to us – what's wrong with yer friend he doesn't smile a lot is he unhappy – socrates says til her (*To Socrates.*) what was it shrapnel – a bullet

Socrates no a metal plate in his head

Petesy aye – he says that ding-ding suffered some serious shit durin the war an he had t'get a metal plate in his head which was fuckin him up

Socrates no – i said t'her that yer head was divided into a happy part an a sad part an the plate was stoppin the blood gettin t'his happy part – wee woman was away with the fairies like – this got her talkin about the war an she was askin what battalion ding-ding was in

Randolph you in the war

Ding-Ding no – fuck

Socrates askin a whole lotta stuff – so me an him made it up – group squadron fuck i don't know whatever it was – she was really gettin into it – she was in the army an all (*Starts giggling.*)

Petesy she left right – it was near lunchtime – we're in the bathroom or somethin

   Ding-Ding's giggling

talkin away – bullshit – waitin on lunch – she bursts in the door an she had all the gear on her – her army uniform y'know – (*Laughing.*) – fuck – she had an apple in her hand for ding-ding – fuck – she shouted out attention here's an apple for you soldier – we're all lookin at her didn't know what t'say – lookin at ding-ding – an apple for ya soldier – he says put it on the plate (*Laughter.*) she salutes marches over an puts the apple on his head

   Mobile phone rings. Petesy answers it.

Socrates william fuckin tell

Ding-Ding attention soldier

Petesy (*on phone*) yes john how are ya – no no – just a bit of a laugh – aye oul story – all red up aye just about to – aye – what – but ya can't – a know – john ya can't expect – no – i understand that – there's no need for – right – i understand that but jesus john y'know – no i'm not – no i'm not saying that – right – right – that's extra – yes aye – it'll be – finished yes – he's here do ye wanna – no right – aye right (*Phone down.*)

Randolph attention

Petesy fuck up

Socrates what

> *Petesy walks to tiles puts his hand under the pallet and take out a delivery note and hands it to Socrates.*

deliver note – an what

Petesy ya not fuckin read – the tiles are on it – can ya not see that – it's fuckin plain enough isn't it

Socrates the tiles are on it

Petesy randolph go out to the van an get the tool box back in

Socrates for what – what ya need the tool box for

Petesy to work – what d'ya normally fuckin need it for

Socrates we're finished

Petesy the tiles are for here – there's another room t'be done an it's t'be done t'night (*To Randolph.*) did i tell you t'go an do somethin – well go an fuckin do it

Randolph exits to on site.

Socrates i don't get this – a don't understan

Petesy simple enough – we've more fuckin work t'do an we're gonna fuckin do it – what the fuck don't ya understand about that

Socrates ya didn't say anything to him why didn't ye say anything to him

Petesy like what

Ding-Ding what room

Petesy what room what

Ding-Ding what room we workin in

Petesy room – one down the bottom a the corridor

Socrates ya should've said somethin

Ding-Ding lifts two boxes of tiles and exits to on site.

Petesy we're doin it – what else is there to say

Socrates tell him no

Petesy he'll get another squad in – that's us out

Socrates fat bastard – he can't do that – fuck'im

Petesy he's done it – there is no he can't do that – he's fuckin done it

Socrates you should've said somethin

Petesy don't say that again – there was fuck all i could say – ya understan – fuck all

Randolph enters with tool box.

other room

Randolph exits to on site.

Socrates all night

Petesy four or five hours i'd say

Socrates that's it like – ya make plans – have other business in the world t'sort out – all of that means fuck all though – work fucks all that up – yer told what t'do an ya do it

Petesy it's no different for me socrates i had plans too

Socrates fuck'im

Petesy correct

Socrates four t'five hours

Petesy aye

Socrates positive

Petesy aye

Socrates have t'let the wee lad down – try t'make amends now i've t'fuckin let him down again

Petesy better start bringin these roun here – sooner we start sooner we're finished

They lift two boxes of tiles each. Exiting to on site. Socrates stops. He puts the tiles back.

Socrates i am finished

Randolph enters from on site.

i'm not doin it – i've made my mind up – i'm not doin it

Petesy don't start socrates just lift the fuckin things an c'mon

Socrates no

94

Petesy i'm tired i wanna get t'fuck outta here – can we just get this finished

Socrates no – there's more important things in the world than this – i'm bringin the wee lad to the pictures – mightn't seem like much – mightn't seem important but that's what i'm doin

Petesy yer just gonna fuck off an leave the rest of us – doesn't matter that it'll take us twice as long or fuck all – just you like worry about gettin yer world sorted out an fuck the rest of us

Socrates you can do what ya want

Petesy no i can't – i've responsibilities – i need work i need t'earn – that's what a have t'fuckin do – there's no choice here

Socrates i'm bringin the wee lad to the pictures

Petesy i'm not coverin for ya – do whatever ya like but i'm not coverin for ye – an if heavy hole asks me i'm tellin him the truth – ya fucked off – he'll sack ye ya know that

Socrates you do what ya have t'do that's yer business – i'm just tellin ye what i'm doin (*Puts his coat on and lifts the flowers.*)

Petesy i'm not coverin for ye

Socrates i'll maybe see ya on monday

    Socrates exits on site.

Petesy you'll not be here on fuckin monday – queuing up at the fuckin brew without a pot t'piss in that's where you'll be (*Pause.*) bastard

Randolph what we doin about his overtime

Petesy what

Randolph we could all do with the extra readies an if we're doin his work we should split the readies he was goin' t'get – fuck'im – we've earned it he hasn't

Petesy he gets whatever's due t'him for t'night plus we cover for him – an if heavy hole asks anythin he went home sick

Randolph but you just said

Petesy doesn't matter what the fuck i said – that's between me an him – all you need to know is we're coverin for him an that's it

Randolph why

Petesy you know fuck all do ye – why – cause the fella's right that's why – he's doin the right thing

Randolph that's not right

Petesy that's what's happenin

Randolph i'm not doin it

Petesy (*up close to Randolph*) you do what i tell you t'fuckin do – an don't think i've forgotten what ya said earlier cause i haven't – goin nowhere – that what ya think – i'll tell ya somethin kid yer gonna be the exact fuckin same – start bringin the tiles down to the other room

    Randolph lifts two boxes of tiles and exits on site.

Petesy (*on mobile phone*) i'm gonna be late – i just am that's why – i'm workin

    Late evening.

    Empty wooden pallet on stage. Randolph is sitting on pallet drinking tea and flicking through his magazine.

96

Ding-Ding sleeping.

Randolph what d'ya think ding-ding red or black – i think black myself – there's somethin classy about a black number – what ya reckon – how the fuck do you do that one minute yer talkin next yer dead to the world – a big black one that's what i reckon – wanna hear the shit i'd to take from petesy there – fuck'im – no mention a the job either – that's that banjaxed – fuck'im – all a did was speak my mind like – that was the crack like wasn't it – be like the rest of yous – i don't think so – save the readies get the bike i'm away (*Accidentally knocks his tea over.*) fuck that – i was enjoyin that – have a wee sip of yers ding-ding wha – you just sleep away there (*He drinks from Ding-Ding's cup.*) better sayin fuck all like aren't ye – just keep yer nose down an say fuck all – he's gonna give me a lotta shit like now – fuck'im – i'm goin roun t'morrow an joinin that bikin club effort – drop them a few shillin's – tenner or somethin that'll get the ball rollin – pity there wasn't a winda cleanin club goin ya could have a crack at that ding-ding – it's fucked that like innit – thinkin yer gettin somethin an endin up with fuck all – what about blue – aye blue be alright wouldn't it

Petesy (*offstage*) randolph c'mon til

Randolph right – might say t'him about the job – aye – leave the bikin club thing until he gives me the wire about the job – fuck'im – c'mon ding-ding son – sooner we get this finished sooner we get home

Randolph nudges Ding-Ding. Ding-Ding slumps over.

MOJO MICKYBO

Mojo Mickybo was first staged at Andrews Lane Studio, Dublin, on 14 October 1998. The cast was as follows:

Mojo/Narrator Niall Shanahan
Mickybo Fergal McElherron

Director Karl Wallace
Designer Terry Loane
Lighting John Riddell
Sound Stephen Handson
Produced by Kabosh Productions

Characters

Mojo

Mickybo

Mojo Mickybo is a play for two actors.
The actors should divide the characters as follows:

Mojo	**Mickybo**
Narrator	Fuckface
Gank the Wank	First Woman
Mickybo's Ma	Second Woman
Mickybo's Da	Mojo's Ma
Busman	Mojo's Da
Box Office Woman	Icecream Woman
Torch Woman	The Major
	Uncle Sidney

If possible, the actors should be
in their late thirties/early forties.

Mojo mojo

Mickybo mickybo

Mojo mickybo mojo

Mickybo mojo mickybo

Mickybo is heading a football against the wall.

Narrator belfast – the summer of 1970 – the heat's meltin the tarmac on the street the buses are burnin bright an punters are drinkin petrol outta milk bottles – this is where mojo an mickybo used to play

Mojo yer a header mickybo

Mickybo gonna bate the record

Mojo bate it in yer granny's trunks

Mickybo yer granny's trunks – mickybo's the man – bate five hundred an twenty-nine – roun to gank the wank an spit in his eye

Mojo dig ye he will

Mickybo bate that gank – spit in his big rubber eye

Mojo many ya done

Mickybo a hundred an twenty-three – twenty-four – twenty-five . . .

Mojo mickybo flat head

Mickybo onion dome

Mojo barney rip the balls comes out you'll be onion dome

Mickybo comes near me i'll boot his cat up the hole

Mojo would ye

Mickybo aye – big hairy boot right up the hole an into the lagan

Mojo get ye with that big knife cut the gizzard outta ye

Mickybo i'll cut the gizzard outta him – see when he's lyin there with no gizzard i'll spit in his good eye an gliss his chops

Mojo he comes out that door you'll shit yerself

Mickybo you'll shit yerself – you always shit yerself

Mojo you do

Mickybo you do

Mojo kack the breeks

Mickybo shit the trunks

Narrator mojo mickybo – thick as two small thieves – the greatest lads god ever pumped breath into – the day they met was the hottest ever in the whole of christendom – the sweats drippin from the trees an dogs are jumpin off bridges in the hope they can fly – the world draggin itself along like it was out of breath – a belter

Mojo many ya done now mickybo

Mickybo three hundred an twenty-four – twenty-five – twenty-six . . .

Mojo yer arse is in america

Mickybo ganko the wanko over an outo

Mojo barneyo ripo the ballso

Mickybo barneyo no gizzardo

Narrator that day wee mojo was on his own – an empty type of a day – the type a day you'd kick stones an chalk yer name on a wall rather than listen to yer ma an da spittin bullets at each other – that type of a day – know what a mean

Mojo many now mickybo

Mickybo four hundred an thirty-six – thirty-seven – thirty-eight – mojo

Mojo wha

Mickybo how d'ya stop a biafran from drownin

Narrator throw him a polo mint

Mickybo throw him a polo mint

Mojo polo mints are catmalogion

Mickybo catmalogion – sherbert dips

Mojo weeker

Mickybo weeker

Narrator after danderin here there an nowhere mojo foun himself in the park – an for the want of somethin to do he just lay on his back an looked up at the sky thinkin to himself – that if he were a giant that ate clouds he'd starve on days like this – an the only place they could bury him would be the park

Mojo ya done yet mickybo

Mickybo five hundred an thirty (*He stops heading.*) told ye told ye told ye – gank the wank bate by mickybo – five hundred an thirty headers – the bo – the lad – barney rip the balls' backdoor

Narrator kick kick kick – blatter blatter blatter

Mickybo barney rip the balls picks his arse with a big fishbone – yer cat's a dead man – offski

Narrator so we're there – the first day – mojo an mickybo – mickybo's sittin on the groun under a big dead tree diggin a hole in the dirt with a stick – mojo's standin lookin

Mickybo what ya lookin at

Mojo nothin

Mickybo i'm diggin a hole with a stick – might find somethin

Mojo like wha

Mickybo don't know haven't foun it yet – treasure maybe – i'm hidin as well like – you hidim

Mojo nah – rollin down the hill

Mickybo weeker – i'm hidin from gank the wank an fuckface – ya see em

Mojo nah don't know em

Mickybo i hate them – ugly bastards – stole my bike – a chopper – gears an everythin it had – said they didn't but the did – know barney rip the balls

Mojo nah

Mickybo everybody knows rip the balls – he puts black boot polish in his hair an doesn't wear no socks – an my da says he pisses in the sink cause he couldn't be fucked to go out to the yard – nobody's ever saw im but me – i saw im buryin dead rats over the timbers – wanna dig with the stick

Mojo aye

Mickybo if yer ball goes into his yard he slits it with a big knife an ya never get it back – i kicked fuckface's ball into his yard cause he stole my bike – big knife in fuckface's ball – now they're after me – if ya sat here all summer ya could dig yer way to australia

Mojo aye – or china

Mickybo what's yer name

Mojo mojo

Mickybo i'm mickybo – mojo mickybo mickybo mojo – sounds like a gang – where ya from

Mojo up the road – where you from

Mickybo over the bridge – you go to school up the road

Mojo aye

Mickybo i hate school – gank an fuckface always get their gang to chase me roun the yard

Mojo school's wick – except lunchtime – go over the brickies an have sand fights

Mickybo can ya fight

Mojo i kicked applegoat up the balls once cause he farted in my face – hairy dan slapped me

Mickybo me an you could be against gank the wank an fuckface – you could kick em up the balls

Mojo are the big

Mickybo ugly big bastards – me an you bate them though – get them one at a time kick em up the balls

Mojo aye – alright

Mickybo you'll have to swear on it

Mojo i swear on my granny's eyes i'm the enemy of gank the wank an fuckface

Mickybo if ya break the swear her eyes'll explode

Mojo aye

Mickybo ya wanna roll down the hill

Mojo rollin down the hill's weeker

Mickybo last to the bottom stinks a shite

Narrator the lads rolled down the hill for two days an then went to the pictures – the saturday mornin club

Mojo / Mickybo good morning uncle sidney

Uncle Sidney (*showman*) good morning children

Mojo / Mickybo big smiles for yer uncle sidney

Uncle Sidney get yer smelly kebs off that seat or i'll bust yer fuckin arse

Mojo / Mickybo sorry uncle sidney

Mojo where ya goin mickybo

Mickybo crawl under the seats up to the front an fire cola cubes up at batman's head

Mojo torchwoman'll get ye – tell yer ma

Mickybo i'll use the anti-torchwoman bat gun

Mojo hollygwaockamoly batman not the anti-torchwoman bat gun

Mickybo it's the only way robin – it's either that or bate her with the torch

Torchwoman (*speaks slowly and chews gum*) uncle sidney they're messin in the back stalls an they've their smelly kebs up on the good seats

Mickybo her light is blindin me boy wonder – fire the anti-torchwoman bat gun

Mojo (*fires the gun*) the gas is everywhere escape to the batcave

Torchwoman come back here ya wee toerags – uncle sidney uncle sidney they're torturin me uncle sidney – they have ma head turned

Mickybo the fat bitch is still alive robin hit her with a nailbomb

Mojo (*throws a nailbomb*) the light shines no more

Torchwoman (*raising her hand*) i'll swing for ye's ye's wee buggers (*Smooths her skirt.*) yes uncle sidney comin now big boy

Uncle Sidney (*unzips his trousers*) uncle sidney loves the saturday morning club – put that torch out

Mickybo the batcave boy wonder

Narrator the batcave – that would be the place to be alright – god's fear never crossin the door an every livin dead thing killed usin nothin more than a bag of cola cubes – the type of place ya could hold yer own spit forever

> *Cheeks bloated. Mickybo indicates they should bend over the balcony and empty their spit on the people below. They do this and then quickly pull back and sit in their seats.*

Mickybo i had more spit than you

Mojo no ya didn't

Mickybo aye a did

Mojo no ya didn't

Mickybo aye a did

Narrator back in the sunlight – sittin on the curb outside the pictures – watchin the soldiers stoppin cars an chewin the rest of the cola cubes

Mojo the sun makin yer sweets stick together

Mickybo aye

Mojo i like em like that

Mickybo weeker – i ate the paper on em

Mojo on everythin

Mickybo except chews – ya couldn't ate chew paper – ever go to the flicktures at night

Mojo wouldn't let ye in

Mickybo aye the would

Mojo no the wouldn't

Mickybo go tonight

Mojo to see wha

Mickybo that

> *A poster. They take up the positions of Butch Cassidy and the Sundance Kid on the poster, i.e. running forward, guns blazing*

butch cassidy an the sundance kid – cowboys

> *They circle each other as gunfighters.*

Mickybo where ya from mister

Mojo i'm a stranger in these parts boy

Mickybo i know that ya geek ye

They giggle.

Mojo i'm from outta town

Mickybo we don't like outta towners – you gotta name
stranger

Mojo banana trunks

Mickybo you ever hear of a gunslinger called pele –
banana trunks – that's me

Mojo you wanna draw pele banana trunks

They burst out laughing.

Mickybo draw pele banana trunks

Mojo sharpen yer crayon banana trunks

Still laughing, Mickybo fires shots into the air.

Narrator butch cassidy an the sundance kid – a fine
feelin it must be to be a cowboy – money in yer pocket a
horse on yer arse an a gun in yer holster – but times are
hard – there's no ham for the sandwiches an torchwoman
is in the box office payin her dues – a wee dab behind the
ears of the da's aftershave for mojo and mickbyo – just to
smell the part

They push each other forward.

Mickybo no you

Mojo no you

*They straighten up to look older and take on deep
voices.*

Mickybo two tickets for the frontstalls to see the cowboy
movie butch cassidy an the sundance kid – thank you

Box Office Woman they're back again uncle sidney – the wee friggers are back again

Mickybo two tickets for the frontstalls to see the cowboy movie butch cassidy an the sundance kid – thank you

Box Office Woman uncle sidney they're torturin me – slap the lugs off them for me

Mickybo look missus see if we don't get in i'm gonna stand outside an tell everyone we saw ye lumberin uncle sidney

Mojo (*exaggerated kissing*) we spied ye

Box Office Woman a woman's allowed a wee bitta comfort in the world – ya don't know what it's like – my man's mean an stinkin – go up to the front circle (*Angry.*) sidney get yer fat sweaty arse over here

They watch the movie and eat sweets. Big smiles.

Narrator (*sings*) don't ever hit your granny with a shovel – it leaves a dull impression on her mind – what happens mickybo when ya hit yer granny with a shovel

Mickybo her eyes pop out an her face goes like that (*Grimace.*)

Narrator butch an sundance blazin a trail – no finer men

Mickybo no finer men

Narrator glued to the screen – fightin every battle – shootin every shot – an always rootin for the good guys

Mickybo don't go up the mountain butch they get ye if ya go up the mountain (*Fires a gun.*)

Narrator half time – back to the real world – decisions have to be made – important decisions that would give a book a headache – who's who an what's what

Mickybo yer sundance i'm butch

Mojo why

Mickybo just

Mojo just why

Mickybo just cause

Mojo just cause why

Mickybo just cause i say so

Mojo i baggsie Butch

Mickybo ya can't

Mojo a can

Mickybo i'll buy ya an icecream

Mojo anythin you say butch

Mickybo fine with me sundance

Narrator icecream in bake gun in mit an we're sailin back into the wild west – a place where there's no traffic lights – men drink beer from buckets – an nobody gives a tuppenny fig if horses shite in the street

> *They sit and watch. Eyes wide open. They react to every shot fired on the screen without leaving their seats.*

Mickybo that was fuckin weeker

Narrator the war's over an now butch an sundance have to stand for the queen

> *Mickybo twirls his guns and fires them in the air. Mojo stands to attention. They make funny faces and wave bye-bye.*

Mickybo bye bye uncle sidney (*Exaggerated kissing.*)

Mojo uncle sidney lumbers big seven bellies (*Firing guns.*)

Mickybo mcmanus luiga riva

Mojo s o s dannybobo

Mickybo don del a vista

Narrator from the dim light into the dark night an straight into gank the wank an fuckface

Mickybo gank – fuckface

Fuckface you owe me a ball mickybo

Mickybo where's my bike fuckface

Fuckface we haven't got yer smelly bike

Mickybo aye ya have – it had gears an everything

Fuckface we got his bike gank

Gank didn't touch it fuckface

Fuckface my da bate me cause the ball was lost – didn't he bate me gank

Gank the tubes right outta ye fuckface

Fuckface i get another ball or i'm gonna dig ye – it was the same one the used in the world cup

Gank except it was plastic fuckface

  Fuckface slaps Gank.

Fuckface they used them in the world cup

Gank world cup fuckface

Fuckface who's yer mate

Mickybo mojo

Fuckface where ya from

Mickybo leave im alone – nothin to do with you where he's from

Fuckface where ya from

Gank aye where ya from

Mickybo say nothin mojo

Fuckface fuck up – ya hear me – where ya from

Mojo up the road

Fuckface up the road where

Mojo up the road up the road

Fuckface funny fucker are ye

Mojo no

Fuckface me an my da chases the ones up the road – afeared of us they are – i don't like you – do you like him gank

Gank no fuckface

Fuckface any odds – give us yer odds or ya have to fight us

Mickybo kick im up the balls mojo (*No one moves.*) go on mojo kick im up the balls

Fuckface come on

Mickybo mcmanus luigi riva – don del a vista – flamenco – bingo

Narrator mojo an mickybo (*Bat wings fluttering.*) down the road like bats out a hell

Mickybo the stopped chasin us

Mojo aye (*Gun out.*) butch

Mickybo wha

Mojo who are those guys

Mickybo who are those guys

Mojo i was gonna kick im up the balls mickybo a was

Mickybo i was gonna stick ma fingers in his ears pull im down an boot im up the hole – we'll do them the next time – next time we'll do them

Mojo aye up the balls an the hole – s o s danny bobo

Mickybo don del a vista – member

Mojo wha

Mickybo see if ya hit yer granny with a shovel (*Grimace.*)

Narrator mojo galloped back up the road thinkin mickybo was a geg (*Sings.*) rain drops keep fallin on my head – because i'm free nothin worrin me – mojo lifts a stick from the bonfire at the top of his street – can i move i'm better when i move – bang bang bang bang – the women at the top of his street – fluffy slippers wee legs tight skits an big fegs – big moustaches – all dead as doornails

Mojo yous are dead – i'm the sundance kid an yous are dead

> *The two women continuously smoke. One inhales the other exhales.*

First Woman wee mojo – yer a duck egg for yer da – isn't he a duck egg for his da

Second Woman duck egg

Mojo i'm not wee mojo i'm the sundance kid an yous are dead – bang bang bang bang – i was at the flicktures and saw the cowboy movie butch cassidy an the sundance kid – ever been to the flicktures

First Woman oh uncle sidney

Second Woman big uncle sidney

First Woman member uncle sidney

Second Woman he was the boy alright

First Woman good mornin uncle sidney

Second Woman night night uncle sidney

Mojo uncle sidney's a tube – me an mickybo shot him dead – we're real cowboys

First Woman yer like my man he's a real cowboy

Second Woman all men are cowboys

Mojo like butch an sundance

First Woman aye but not as good lookin

Second Woman we need good lookin cowboys mojo – ya know any

First Woman you could be our good lookin cowboy mojo – we could all live on a big ranch – it would be lovely

Mojo i'm not mojo i'm the sundance kid an yous are dead – bang bang bang bang – have to go now have to see ma ma

First Woman if ya see any good lookin cowboys won't ya tell us

Mojo bang bang bang bang – alright ma – anythin to eat ma

Mojo's Ma there's a tin a pineapple chunks in the cupboard

Mojo i'm the sundance kid ma

Mojo's Ma are ya that's good

Mojo pineapple chunks for the sundance kid – the women up the street ma say all men are cowboys – is my da a cowboy ma – me an him could be cowboys together couldn't we ma

Mojo's Ma aye son

Mojo do ya want pineapple chunks ma

Mojo's Ma no son

Mojo where's my da ma

Mojo's Ma in there gettin ready to go out

Mojo i'm the best shot in the wild west ma – throw yer feg up in the air an i'll shoot it ma

Mojo's Ma away into the house mojo

Mojo you lookin up at the sky ma – the sky all red ma – why's the sky all red ma

Mojo's Ma something's burnin

Mojo what's burnin ma

Mojo's Ma i don't know

Mojo call me sundance ma

Mojo's Ma away into the house sundance

Mojo sundance is away in to ate his pineapple chunks ma (*Eating from a tin.*) – pineapple chunks da

Mojo's Da no son a don't want any pineapple chunks

Mojo you goin out da

Mojo's Da aye son i'm goin out

Mojo where ya goin – ya goin dancin again da

Mojo's Da aye i'm goin dancin

Mojo ya must like dancin da – do you like dancin da

Mojo's Da aye son i like dancin

Mojo do ya dance on yer on da – ya always go dancin on yer own

Mojo's Da yer ma doesn't like dancin that's why

Mojo my ma likes smokin da

Mojo's Da aye

Mojo me an mickybo are butch cassidy an the sundance kid da – mickybo's my new mate da

Mojo's Da is he that's good

Mojo the women up the street da say all men are cowboys da – me you an mickybo are three cowboys

Mojo's Da cowboys – aye

Mojo can i go dancin with ya da

Mojo's Da no son dancin's only for big people

Mojo the men does the dancin an the wee lads ate the pineapple chunks – that right da

Mojo's Da aye

Narrator a lot a smokin a wee bit a jivin an there's sad songs in the air – the ring is round the church is square i drank the giro why weren't you there – enough of that says mojo – mickybo's house – blatter blatter blatter – is mickybo in mickybo's ma

Mickybo's Ma no son he's not – he's gone – it's a sad bad thing but we had to do it there was no way out of it – i was cooking a big pot of stew for us all – a big pot the size of a buffalo's head – enough stew to do us for a

121

month and a day – i was stirring the stew with the shaft
of a brush and the gas went out – panic hit the air – the
man i love header and all as he is mickybo's da had a
thirst on him that stretched the length and breadth of
ireland – and god bless the weak and distraught man that
he is in a fit of madness due to the sun had blew the last
few shillings we had on bad drink – drink so bad that it
made his feet stink and his eyes roll about in his head like
they were lost – what can ya do when yer man needs fed
an him that would ate a large child's arse through a small
rope chair – and you couldn't hand him half cooked stew
for fear of him choking on the hard bits – him not bein
able to chew that well – just in the nick a time a gypsy
man called to the door wantin to sell me some carpet – i
told him we didn't need carpet we needed money for the
gas – how much for the youngster he said – enough to let
me finish cooking the stew i said – it broke my heart but
what has to be done has to be done – i sold wee mickybo
to the gypsies so i could cook a pot of stew

Mojo's mouth open – agog.

Mojo yer a geg mickybo's ma – mickybo yer ma's a geg

Mickybo she's a tube

Mickybo's Ma my wee honeybun (*She ruffles Mickybo's
hair.*)

Mickybo wise up ma will ye – give us some money ma

Mickybo's Ma the man i love header and all as he is has
all the money son – away up an rob him

Narrator butch an sundance mossied up the street an
straight into the saloon

They push saloon doors open.

Mickybo ma ma says you've to give us some money

Mickybo's Da money is it – what makes ya think i've any money

Mickybo ya need money to buy beer

Mickybo's Da talk's cheap but ya need readies to buy gargle

Mickybo we're cowboys da

Mickybo's Da cowboys is it – an where are the cowboys for today

Mickybo bolivia

Mickybo's Da that would be the place to go alright – anywhere but this kip – what about australia – gooday gooday gooday digga

Mickybo butch an sundance were gonna go to australia but then they got shot so they didn't go

Mickybo's Da gooday gooday gooday digga – yer ma has a brother out there – an eejit like but doin alright for himself – australia – be better than this fuckin kip – what do ya think son – think we should all go to australia

Mickybo can mojo go

Mickybo's Da aye why not we'll all fuck off to australia – gooday gooday gooday digga

Mickybo wanna go to australia mojo

Mojo i'll have to ask ma ma – ma me an mickybo's goin to australia – mickybo's da's takin us – mickybo's ma has a brother out there – he's an eejit but he's doin alright for himself

Mojo's Ma (*smoking*) that's great son just make sure yer back before tea

Mickybo ma

Mickybo's Ma my wee honeybun

Mickybo ma da says we're all goin to australia ma

Mickybo's Ma yer da says more than his prayers son

Mickybo do you say more than yer prayers da

Mickybo's Da (*drunk*) she'd fuckin know wouldn't she – knows fuck all about fuck all – i'll get us there alright – me on ma swanny – i'll fuckin do it alright – don't you worry about that – no sweat about it

Mickybo no sweat about it da

Mickybo's Da no sweat about it is right an don't you think any fuckin different – i don't need no fucker to tell me or help me or fuck all else – brother in australia fuck im – he was a wanker when he was here an he's a wanker out there – it's not meant to be like this son – sort everythin out – fuck away off out a this kip – ya understan that do ye

Mickybo no da a don't

Mickybo's Da no da a don't – aye well ya should

Mickybo will a understan when we're in australia da

Mickybo's Da fuck australia an everyone in it – what the fuck would they know

Mickybo gooday gooday gooday digga da

Mickybo's Da gooday ma ballix (*Collapses.*)

Mojo mickybo yer da's a geg

Mickybo aye he's a geg – mon we'll poke sticks into barney rip the balls' cat

Mojo here pussy pussy – here pussy pussy

Mickybo pish wish wish wish wish wish wish – i heard he carries a knife the length of a monkey's arm

Mojo a monkey's arm

Mickybo aye – puss puss puss – i heard he keeps the cat in a box an only lets it out to ate rats

Mojo ever see his cat

Mickybo nah – do ya think he's ate it

Mojo ate his own cat

Mickybo aye

Mojo is that him up at the winda

Mickybo (*shouts*) ate the cat – barny rip the balls ate the cat

Mojo (*shouts*) ate the pussy rip the balls

Mickybo butch an sundance offski – there's gank on his own mon we'll get im

Mojo mcmanus luigi riva

Mickybo where's my bike gank

Gank i don't know nothin about yer smelly bike

Mickybo where's fuckface

Gank over at the launderette doin his ma's washin

Mickybo doin yer ma's washin means yer a tube – yer our prisoner so ya do as we say or mojo'll kick ya up the balls an i'll bout ya up the hole – give us somethin

Gank i have nothin

Mickybo stan a hoke

   Mickybo searches Gank.

fegs mojo

Mojo fegs mickybo

Gank there fuckface's fegs he'll kill me

Mojo hardwire Gank

Mickybo hardwire gank – tell im butch an sundance took his fegs an if he wants to know where to get us we'll be in bolivia

Mojo or australia

Mickybo or australia – go an tell im tell im when he's finished he can do my ma's washin

Gank nobody likes you mickybo and yer da's full a mad dog's keek

He spits at Mickybo then runs away.

Mickybo will we ran after him or have a smoke

Mojo have a smoke

They check all is clear and then light up.

Mickybo you ever smoke before

Mojo nah

They cough.

Mickybo magic

Mojo weeker

They blow smoke into the air.

Mickybo t'morrow we'll go roun to square head mcguckian's an steal fegs an bubblies – smoke all day

Mojo i've to go out with ma da t'morrow

Mickybo out where with ye da

Mojo i can't tell ye it's a secret – he told me a can't tell

Mickybo ya can't have secrets if yer in a gang – ya have to tell

Mojo we always go to the park an he gives me a swing –
push higher da

Mojo's Da always higher – you've my back broke wee
lad – should be swingin yerself the age a ya

Mojo higher da higher

Mojo's Da we've to go for the icecream – we can't be late
for the icecream

Mojo after the swings we walk into town an ma da buys
me an icecream

Mojo's Da sit down an behave the girl'll bring the
icecream over now

Mojo you not gonna sit with me da

Mojo's Da i've to go an do a message – just sit there an
eat yer icecream an not a word out a ye

Mickybo what flavour do ya get – do ya get bubbly
flavour

Mojo nah – strawberry

Mickybo strawberry's alright but bubbly's better

Mojo see when i've finished my icecream i get another one

Icecream Woman (*Slow.*) there's another icecream – mind
ya don't get any on yer good shirt – yer da says yer
allowed thee – i think thee ice creams is too much for a
wee lad – my man ates anythin but he wouldn't ate thee
ice creams – yer da has ya spoilt rotten

Mojo after the three icecreams ma da's back from doin
his message – where'd ya go da

Mojo's Da didn't a say i had a message to do – well that
what a was doin

Mojo what message da

Mojo's Da never you mind – nothin that concerns you

Mojo he gives the woman the money for the icecream an then the two a them laugh

They laugh – ha ha ha.

next week da can we bring ma ma with us – she can sit with me while yer away doin yer message

Mojo's Da no she's not to know about this – ya understan this is our wee secret

Mojo why da

Mojo's Da do ya understan – i'm warnin ye now say nothin

Mojo why da

Mojo's Da cause i say so that's why

Mojo okay da

Mojo's Da look son if yer ma knew you were eatin icecream before yer dinner wouldn't she do her nut

Mojo she would do her nut da

Mojo's Da that's why it has to be a secret

Mojo right da – can we go to the swings on the way home da

Mojo's Da straight home for dinner i'm starvin

Mojo if ya ate the icecream like me ya wouldn't be starvin da

Mickybo does yer da not ate icecream

Mojo nah

Mickybo that's borin – yer da's borin mojo – mon we'll go over the timbers an burn wood

Mojo aye

They strike a match – whoof.

Mickybo wanna know what i heard

Mojo wha

Mickybo the whole a belfast is goin mad an we're all gonna get murdered in our beds

Mojo where'd ya hear that

Mickybo barney rip the balls

Mojo you see him

Mickybo nah – a was spittin through his letterbox an he shouted down the stairs – runnin about lookin for his big knife he was – he shouted fuck off an leave my letterbox alone – then he shouted belfast was mad an we're all gettin murdered in our beds

Mojo all of us

Mickybo everybody – ya couldn't get murdered in yer bed if ya weren't in it so we'll build a hut over the timbers an live in it

Mojo all of us

Mickybo think he's right

Mojo a don't know

Mickybo (*pushes open saloon door*) da are we all goin get murdered in our beds

Mickybo's Da (*drinking*) gooday gooday gooday digga – murdered in yer bed is it – that type a crack wouldn't happen to ye if ya were roamin the outback shootin kangaroos for a livin an drinkin soup from a billy can

Mickybo aye da billy can – ma i think we should all move out of the house an live in a hut me an mojo made over the timbers – there's plenty of room – there's nothin in it but a rubber bullet – the brits fired it down the street durin the riotin an i nabbed it – plenty a room ma – we'll all be safe in the hut ma

Mickybo's Ma would you like to hear my plan son – i was sittin on top of a mountain of dishes the other night listening to elvis on the radio and thinking of the time when the man that i love header and all that he is used to take me dancing – (*Sings.*) oh how we danced on the night we were wed we danced and we danced cause the room had no bed – there was this strange noise come out of the radio it sounded like the king had eaten something very large that didn't agree with him and was choking on his own boke – then a voice said we come in peace earth people – then the voice said don't lose your heads earth people if you lose your head you lose your money – things may be gettin a bit hairy but we're here to save you all especially wee mickybo mickybo's ma an the man that she loves header and all that he is – we're shippin you out to a planet where there's no dishes the stew makes itself the sky rains beer and the hills are made of bubblies – so we're alright wee honeybun – we don't need to live in the hut that you and mojo built over the timbers – cause the spacemen are coming to save us

Mickybo very funny ma

Mojo yer ma's a geg mickybo

Mickybo if we all get murdered in our beds it'll be yer fault ma cause we're not in the hut

Mickybo's Ma (*ruffles Mickybo's hair*) my wee honeybun

Mickybo ask yer ma an da

Mojo da

Mojo's Da get a good shine on them boy – ya can tell the cut of a man by the shine on his shoes

Mojo aye da

Mojo's Da yer a good kid

Mojo aye da – ma

No answer.

the sun's splittin the trees ma – will a open the curtains

Mojo's Ma no son

Mojo do ya think we should live in a hut ma

Mojo's Ma just me an you son

Mojo and my da an mickybo an his ma an da – they're a geg ma

Mojo's Ma no son i don't think we should live in a hut

Mojo right ma – i'm away out to play now – butch an sundance an the hut an the rubber bullet – mcmanus luigi riva ma

Narrator we played and sat in the hut waitin on the worst

They smoke a cigarette between them.

Mickybo don't be puttin a duck's arse on it

Mojo duck's arse me arse

Mickybo if everything was to burn down what would ya do

Mojo (*hosing*) be a fireman

Mickybo fireman be catmalogion

Mojo fireman be class

Mickybo my da says he read in a book that the fires in australia last for weeks and that postmen fly planes an earn a fuckin fortune

Mickybo's Da gooday gooday gooday digga – postman in australia uses planes – must be on a fuckin fortune – we're all goin to australia – remember that mickybo the whole fuckin lot of us

Mickybo aye da the whole fuckin lot of us

They blow smoke in the air.

if i can spit out the hole in that plank you owe me a marley

Mojo plank ma tubes

Mickybo i spit the best in our street

Mojo if ya miss you've to give me yer catty

Mickybo a marley for a catty – peel a grape an ate a bap – a catty's worth five marleys

Mojo yer big hole

Mickybo no bet – a bet ye a can do it though

Mojo welt on walter

Mickybo i got morons on my team goddamn morons on my team (*Mickybo spits.*) – mickybo is the spit master – bet ye i can spit an hit that nail

Mickybo i'm meltin mon we'll throw skimmers

They throw skimmers across the river.

ya think australia be like this

Mojo like wha

Mickybo throwin skimmers over the river

Mojo aye

Mickybo bet ye australia's weeker – bet ye the all go to school on horses

Mojo do ya really wanna go to australia

Mickybo aye – ya could get blown up here – that be cat

Mojo a wee lad in our school was in town with his ma an a bomb went off – an it blew one of his legs off

Mickybo right off in one go like

Mojo aye – but his trousers was still on him

Mickybo if ya foun his leg ya could sew it on to ye – three legs – keep the ball up forever

Mojo what would ya do if ya went to australia an there was bombs there too

Mickybo why would there be bombs there

Mojo don't know

Mickybo get my da to take us somewhere else

Mojo i'd like to go to america

Mickybo is australia near america

Mojo aye – they're connected by a bridge or somethin

Mickybo if ya went to america an i went to australia it would be like now – yer up the road an i'm over the bridge

Mojo if superman was here there'd be no bombs

Mickybo aye he'd hear them tickin with his x-ray ears

Mojo then he could just zoom down pick it up an throw it into space – everythin's safe there cause there's nothin to blow up in space

Mickybo batman couldn't do that

Mojo batman be useless in belfast

Mickybo he'd be too slow – he has to use the batmobile an ya have to fly if ya wanna save bombs

Mojo superman would've saved that wee lad in our school but batman wouldn't – what about spiderman he swings from buildins

Mickybo he couldn't throw a bomb into space

Mojo he could cover it in a web and then when it went off nothin would happen

Mickybo does superman go to australia

Mojo nah he only saves america

Mickybo maybe australia has their own

Mojo kangarooman

Mickybo he'd put the bomb in his hole then bounce off into the bushes

Mojo aye – think they'll blow the bridge up

Mickybo what would ya do if they did blow the bridge up

Mojo weeker – i could stay in yer house

Mickybo aye that be weeker – everyone have to swim to work wouldn't they

Mojo i hope they do blow the bridge up

Mickybo big bomb the size of a house blow it up

Mojo dynamite like butch an sundance used – quick we've only ten seconds before the bridge blows – take cover

Mickybo oh no the fuse has gone out

Mojo what will we do

Mickybo we have to save the city – stop everybody gettin murdered in their beds

Mojo we need a volunteer soldier

Mickybo i'm the major yer the soldier

Mojo i'm not doin it i'm too young to die – i have a wife an a shitload of kids

Mickybo it's an order soldier – if we're gonna save the city the bridge must go an yer gonna have to go with it

Mojo have i a last request

Mickybo yes

Mojo it has to happen – it's a last request so it must happen

Mickybo yes goddamn it man yes

Mojo i want you to die with me

Mickybo alright

Mojo we're dying to save the city

Mickybo light the fuse soldier

> *Mojo lights the fuse. Mickybo salutes. The bridge explodes and so do they.*

Narrator the bridge didn't blow – so after smokin their last fegs in the hut an watchin the river slip away mojo crossed the bridge and walked home – he didn't really want to go home but his stomach was empty so home it was – he walked slowly – the heat drew people out of their houses – they stood on street corners chewin the fat – those that didn't chew the fat hung flags an bunting an painted the kerbs – the heat – the people – the colour – it was a party – a party so big that no buildin could hold it so it spilled out onto the streets – the major was guardin the bonfire – a big heavy overcoat – the sweat lashin – the wine guzzlin – an wasps buzzin aroun his mouth

The Major (*swiping wasps away*) it's the wine – the wasps is after the wine

Mojo why ya wearin a coat when it's hot major

The Major always carry everything ya own wee man – never know when ya have to jump ship

Mojo you mindin the bonfire major

The Major that's the job give to me – big bottle a wine for the major

Mojo the gonna steal the bonfire major

The Major god bless the bonfire wee man – big bottle a wine

Mojo you gonna sleep in the bonfire major

The Major i am – never let it be said the major wouldn't sleep in a bonfire when he was bid

Mojo i'm away home now major

The Major god bless ulster wee man

Mojo except the wasps major – ya wouldn't want god to bless the wasps

The Major after the wine – bastards

Narrator just before he left mojo shot the major dead – bang bang bang bang – yer a dead man major – the street was alive – standin up straight – its face bright and shiny – an all the while the sun's beamin down

Mojo do wasps drink wine da – the major says wasps drink wine da

   Silence.

the major's funny da he eats wasps and lives inside the bonfire – you cut yer hand da

Mojo's Da a hit the wall a punch son

Mojo what ya do that for da

Mojo's Da i don't know

Mojo ya shouldn't do things like that da

Mojo's Da no a shouldn't

Mojo my ma's not standin at the front door da – where is she

Mojo's Da she's up the stairs – i wanna talk to you about somethin mojo

Mojo what da

   Silence.

Mojo's Da nothin – away up to yer ma see she's alright

Mojo are wasps bees da

Mojo's Da away up to yer ma mojo

Mojo are wasps bees ma

Mojo's Ma me an yous gonna stay with yer auntie rita for awhile mojo

Mojo why ma

Mojo's Ma a wee holiday – ya like yer auntie rita don't ya

Mojo no ma – she stinks a bleach and pinches my face – is ma da not goin

Mojo's Ma just me an you mojo

Mojo i don't wanna go ma

Mojo's Ma yer not stayin here with him – yer comin with me

Narrator mojo's ma packed a suitcase while his da stood and looked on in silence

Mojo (*trailed by the hand*) there's the women smokin in the street ma (*Shouts to women.*) we're goin on holidays – me an ma ma an a suitcase

First Woman away anywhere nice mojo

Mojo auntie rita's

Second Woman the weather'll be lovely there

First Woman send us a postcard

Second Woman bring us back a good lookin cowboy

The women laugh.

Mojo the smokin women want a good lookin cowboy ma

Mojo's Ma stop talkin mojo

Narrator mojo thought havin banter with the women was funny – his ma didn't – she had other things on her mind – things she thought but didn't speak – they walked the rest of the way in silence two suitcases draggin behind them – after a few days of his ma's fegs an auntie rita's bleach it was time for mickybo's – the major had shifted camp – guardin the bonfire at the top of auntie rita's street now

The Major the wee soldier laddie

Mojo i'm a cowboy today major

The Major (*swiping*) wasps – bastards

Narrator mojo shot the wasps – bang bang bang –
blatter blatter blatter

Mojo is mickybo in mickybo's ma

Mickybo's Ma he's not here

Mickybo yer a geg mickybo's ma – who has him – the
spacemen or the gypos – tell us a story mickybo's ma –
make us laugh

Mickybo's Ma tell ya a story – make ya laugh – i'm sittin
here without a slice a bread – not a pot to piss in an the
tv's shite – and mickybo's da the man that i love header
an all that he is has lost the spark of life than once made
him the man that he was – when's somebody gonna make
me laugh – mickybo's in the entry kickin a ball

Narrator nothing funny about that

Mojo where'd ya get the ball mickybo

Mickybo stole it – new one – go for the record – not
today though

Mojo me an ma ma's on holidays at ma auntie rita's – it's
wick – she bleaches the floorboards an keeps pinchin my
face – hate it

Mickybo wanna know what happened

Mojo aye

Mickybo it's bad like – it's not all bad like – it's like some
bad some good an some very big

Narrator the bad news

Mickybo gank the wank an fuckface burnt the hut an the
rubber bullet with a petrolbomb they found up the entry

Narrator the hut's gone – the good news

Mickybo i slit the tyres on fuckface's bike an built another hut – ya wanna see it it's weeker – no rubber bullet like but they'll be other riots – we'll get more

Narrator the hut's back and rubber bullets are on their way – the bad news

Mickybo it wasn't fuckface's bike it was his older brother's torture – torture's a header – he pokes the eyes out a mad dogs an tells his ma to fuck up

Narrator fuck up ma – the good news

Mickybo torture kicked the tubes out a fuckface cause i slit his tyres – an it had nothin to do with him

Narrator torture – the very big news

Mickybo fuckface wants a fair dig between me an you an him an gank

Mojo a fair dig with the both a them

Mickybo i said no problem that we'd gliss the bake of the two a them

Mojo they'll bury us

Mickybo yer from up the road – they wanna kick the tubes outta you anyway

Narrator there's fights to be fought an battles to be won but before all that there's some slabberin to be done

Mickybo we'll fight ya fuckface at two o'clock up the entry – no witnesses just the four of us

Fuckface no witnesses an no cryin to yer ma an da

Mickybo you'll be cryin fuckface – gonna kick the tubes outta ye

Fuckface i'm gonna rip yer eyes out an stick them up yer arse

Mickybo up yer arse – shout somethin mojo

Mojo up yer arse

Mickybo mojo's gonna kick gank up the balls an make them bleed – gank's balls are gonna bleed – big gank bloody balls

Gank i'm gonna kick mojo's balls into the lagan an him after them

Mickybo two o'clock fuckface

Fuckface smelly bastards

Mickybo you an yer ma's two smelly bastards

Fuckface up yer hole

Mickybo up yer hole

Mojo up yer hole

Narrator up the entry – ring ring ding ding

Mickybo mojo get wired in

Mojo you get wired in

Fuckface lappers gank the two a them's lappers

Gank lappers fuckface

Mickybo lapper that fuckface

Mickybo hits Fuckface and they tussle with each other. Mojo shadow boxes and watches the fight.

Mojo get wired in – kick gank up the balls

Fuckface bury im gank

Gank and Mojo aren't keen. They make half-hearted attempts to go for each other. Fuckface is on top of Mickybo holding him down.

torture – torture – i have im – ambush – ambush

Mojo barney rip the balls is in his yard – he's his big knife with him

Everything stops.

Mickybo fair dig over

Fuckface torture – torture – ambush

Mickybo punches Fuckface. Mojo makes a half-hearted attempt to hit Gank then spits at him.

Mickybo mcmanus luigi riva

Mojo riva riva

Mickybo run like fuck mojo

Mojo run like fuck mickybo

Narrator down the entry running like fuck over the timbers and into the hut

Mickybo ya think they saw us comin in

Mojo don't know

Mickybo did ya not look back

Mojo i just ran

Mickybo maybe the didn't chase us

Mojo aye

Mickybo do ya think the chased us

Mojo yeah

Mickybo so do i – that ugly bastard bloodied my nose (*Mickybo wipes his bloody nose with his sleeve.*) – did ya get gank

Mojo kicked im up the balls four times an spat in his bake

Mickybo we did them – didn't we do them

Mojo aye we did them

Mickybo do ya think barny rip the balls is with them

Mojo nah – what ya think

Mickybo nah

Mojo think they're out there waitin on us

Mickybo aye – torture an rip the balls with em

Mojo aye

Mickybo we'll get murdered

Mojo murdered – you hadn't slit the bike we wouldn't be gettin murdered

Mickybo they don't like you – we'd a got murdered anyway

Mojo they don't like you too

Mickybo aye but they don't like you more than they don't like me – they hate you – that's what they said – we hate mojo

Mojo i'm not fightin them again – the war's over – play in the park – better playin in the park

Mickybo after we get away we'll go to the park – if we were butch an sundance we could shoot our way out with real guns

Mojo shoot the faces off em

Mickybo member the two a them sittin all shot up talkin about australia

Mojo aye

Mickybo butch an sundance

Mojo aye

Mickybo where we goin when we get out a here sundance

Mojo the park

Mickybo no australia – butch an sundance are goin to australia

Mojo shoot our way out

Mickybo run out the hut shootin an head for the bridge at the end of the timbers

Mojo they get us they'll murder us

Mickybo they won't get us – they mightn't even be out there

Mojo real guns be weeker

Mickybo aye – ya ready then

Mojo right – one two three go

Mojo / Mickybo mcmanus luigi riva – don del a vista – flemanco – bingo – bang bang bang

They move from shooting to rolling down a hill.

Mojo race ya up to the top again

Mickybo nah it's borin – butch an sundance didn't roll down hills

Mojo the did when the bandits was after them

Mickybo it's borin – mon we'll get a bus an go to bolivia

Narrator a bus to bolivia

Mickybo hay mister this bus go to bolivia

Busman it does not – newcastle county down that's where this bus goes

Mickybo where's newcastle county down mister

Busman a long way from bolivia – i'd say it would be like bolivia though

Mickybo why haven't they burnt yer bus mister

Busman i've a big stick here that's why – bate them good lookin

Mickybo we've no money mister – take us to newcastle county down – we're the men for newcastle county down

Busman no money is it – newcastle county down – it's the twelfth – one bus there one bus back – no pishin on the seats

Mickybo one bus there one bus back – no pishin on the seats

   A bus to Bolivia.

Busman end of the road we're in bolivia

Mickybo right ya are mister

Busman and what would the lads be at in bolivia

Mickybo we'll be at robbin banks an drinkin beer out of a bucket

Busman wise men yous are

Mickybo wise men mister an no pishin on the seats

Busman all the way to bolivia an no pishin on the seats

Narrator bang bang bang bang – they shot the busman dead – then ran up a mountain – rolled down a hill –

smelt all the cow shite – threw stones in the sea an pished over the rocks – marched in front of the parade

Narrator hums the Sash. Mickybo twirls a stick.

then ran up the pier pretendin butch an sundance were bein chased by the posse

Mickybo (*both hiding*) who are those guys

Mojo who are those guys

Mickybo we can shoot or wait sundance

Mojo we can't wait butch i'm starvin

Mickybo we'll shoot it out then

Mojo they'll kill us

Mickybo mon we'll jump off the pier – they'll not follow us if we jump

As Butch and Sundance.

Mojo no i want to fight it out

Mickybo we'll die

Mojo we'll die if we jump

Mickybo we'll jump

Mojo no

Mickybo why not

Mojo i'm not doin it

Mickybo don't be silly

Mojo i just need one shot that's all

Mickybo why won't ya jump

Mojo i can't swim

Mickybo can't ya swim really like

Mojo course i can – grab the stick

Mickybo one two three go

Mojo / Mickybo bang bang bang bang (*Jump off the pier.*) – oh shit

Mickybo alright mister we're goin home

Busman how'd the lads go in bolivia then – did yas rob banks an drink beer out of a bucket

Mickybo we played with the band an jumped into the water when the posse was chasin us just like butch an sundance did

Busman fine men yous are

Mickybo we are mister – we're fine men just like our das

Busman butch and sundance there's yas go

Mickybo from belfast to bolivia an back again mister

Busman from bolivia to belfast an back again an not a bank robbed

Mickybo good luck mister

Busman fine lads yous are

Mickybo fine lads we are

Narrator butch an sundance makin a run for it to bolivia – two kids havin a geg – great lads – there was a crowd of people at the top of mickybo's street – blue flashin lights an screams you could hear forever – mickybo's ma held him tight – an all the while the sun shown down

Mickybo (*pushes open saloon doors*) we were in newcastle county down today da – we pretended it was bolivia and we jumped into the sea

Mickybo's Da newcastle is a fine place – me an yer ma used to go dancin there – newcastle is a fine place to go dancin

Mickybo we danced in front of the band da – it was a geg

Mickybo's Da good man mickybo havin a geg

Mickybo are you dead da

Mickybo's Da i am that son – every square inch of me

Mickybo why da

Mickybo's Da i was sittin havin a pint thinkin about the world and all its glory an someone shot me – blew the back of my head clean off

Mickybo was it sore da

Mickybo's Da nah son it wasn't sore

Mickybo bet ya there was a lot a blood da – when yer shot there's a lot a blood isn't there da

Mickybo's Da any god's amount of it son

Mickybo if superman was there he would've stopped the bullet da wouldn't he

Mickybo's Da aye son superman would've stopped the bullet

Mickybo does this mean we're not goin to australia da

Mickybo's Da i think it does son

Mickybo no gooday gooday gooday digger

Mickybo's Da no gooday gooday gooday digger

Mickybo see ye then da

Mickybo's Da good luck son

Narrator that evenin mojo sat on the banks of the lagan an threw skimmers across the water – he threw until his arms were sore an there was nothin left to throw – then he made his way home – over the bridge and up the road – the road was empty but for the major still guardin the bonfire – even though there was nothin left to guard – mojo's da came to visit that night – he had a bunch of flowers an shiny shoes – mojo's ma smiled at the flowers but it didn't last long – soon the bullets started to fly – mojo slipped up to his bed – he lay and thought about mickybo an his da – night night sleep tight an don't let the bed bugs bite – after a few days he called for mickybo – blatter blatter blatter

Mojo is mickybo in mickybo's ma

Mickybo's Ma there's nobody here

Mojo yer a geg mickybo's ma

Mickybo's Ma leave me alone an go away

Narrator mojo mickybo – great lads – mickybo's in the hut along with gank an fuckface – they're smokin fegs an talkin the talk of men – it's showtime

Fuckface wha do you want

   Silence.

Mojo ya wanna go to the park an we'll roll down the hill

Mickybo nah – that's for kids – rollin down the hill's just for kids

Fuckface where's mickybo's bike – where's his bike – me an gank saw ye ridin on his bike – didn't we see him ridin on mickybo's bike gank

Gank we saw ye on mickybo's bike – where is it

Fuckface say to him mickybo

Mickybo i want ma bike back mojo – ya stole ma bike an i want it back – my da bought me that bike an i want it back

Mojo i don't have yer bike mickybo – they stole it you said they stole it

Gank he's callin you a liar fuckface

Fuckface you calling me a liar – you an yer mates from up the road stole it

Gank steal the bikes

Mojo i don't have yer bike mickybo – i swear a don't have it – i'm yer mate

Fuckface he's mates with us now after what happened to his da – yer mates with us mickybo aren't ye

Mickybo aye – they saw ye on the bike – where's the bike mojo

Gank fight him mickybo

Fuckface aye mickybo hit him

Mojo i wanna go home

Fuckface yer goin nowhere until ya fight mickybo – ya said ya were gonna do it so do it mickybo

    Mojo and Mickybo face each other.

Mickybo get me ma bike or i'll dig ya

Mojo i don't have the bike mickybo you know i don't

Mickybo ya shouldn't have stole it – ya shouldn't have fuckin stole it

    Mickybo pulls Mojo to the ground and punches him.

Mickybo orange bastard – yas killed my da – ya dirty fuckin orange bastard

Narrator love many trust few and learn to paddle your own canoe – years later i was walking through the town – this town – belfast – a town with memories – i saw mickybo across the street – mojo mickybo

Mickybo mickybo mojo

Narrator we both pretended we didn't know each other and walked on – mojo mickybo

In the hut.

Mickybo mickybo mojo

Narrator what was the best day mickybo

Mickybo best day what way mojo

Narrator best day best day ya tube

Mickybo there were loads of best days ya geek

Narrator best day ever

Mickybo in the hut

Narrator aye in the hut – it was weeker in the hut

Mickybo after we had the fight with gank the wank an fuckface

Narrator aye

Mickybo they were all waitin outside the hut – the lot of them

Narrator all waiting to kick the tubes out of us mickybo

Mickybo butch an sundance against the world

Narrator as a child from now on.

Mojo where we going when we get outta here

Mickybo butch an sundance are going to australia

Mojo we'll shoot our way out

Mickybo run out the hut shootin an head for the bridge at the end of the timbers

Mojo what happens if they get us

Mickybo they won't get us – they mightn't even be out there – be weeker if we had real guns

Mojo aye – ya ready then

Mickybo right

Mojo one two three go

Mojo / Mickybo mcmanus luigi riva – bang bang bang bang bang bang

> *They freeze. As in the last scene of* Butch Cassidy and the Sundance Kid *we hear a call to 'Fire', followed by a volley of rifle shots. Another volley of shots. Louder. The sound of the rifle shots becomes deafening.*

CLOSING TIME

Closing Time was first performed in the Loft space of the Lyttelton stage at the National Theatre, London, on 9 September 2002. The cast, in order of speaking, was as follows:

Vera Pam Ferris
Iggy Patrick O'Kane
Robbie Jim Norton
Joe Lalor Roddy
Alec Kieran Ahern

Director James Kerr
Designer Rae Smith
Lighting Designer Steve Barnett
Sound Designer Rich Walsh
Costume Supervisor Sharon Robinson

Characters

Robbie
early sixties

Vera
late fifties

Joe
early sixties

Iggy
mid thirtiies

Alec
early fifties

A grubby pub/hotel. All the action takes place in the pub. There are two exits, one to the hotel the other to the street. At one end of the bar there is a large television screen. The television is always on but the sound is never turned up. At the other end of the bar is a public payphone. When people are not directly involved in conversation they watch the television, except Joe who sits with his back to the screen.

Morning. The bar is locked up. Joe is asleep at the counter, an empty bottle of vodka in front of him. Robbie is slumped over a table, surrounded by empty Babycham bottles. Robbie wakes and surveys his surroundings. He hears Vera and Iggy coming down the stairs and pretends to be asleep. Vera unlocks the hotel door then enters, followed by Iggy, who is badly hungover. Once in the bar Vera unlocks the door leading to the street.

Vera smell this dump – same bloody stink every day – fills the air it does – ya think other people live like this – bet ya the don't

Iggy (*sits at counter beside pay phone*) get us a pint vera will ye – am dyin – fuckin head's rippin open – bustin

Vera the shutter'll only wake 'im – a don't want that yet – if yer that bad am sure there's somethin on the table

Iggy that's not drink

Vera ya take enough a it it is – should eat somethin – want me t'make somethin t'eat – a've t'do breakfast for joe anyway

Iggy (*without waking Robbie he takes a bottle of Babycham*) kiddin me – food – no eats for three days – grub be bad news right now – eat in a coupla days time maybe – need a gargle – best thing

Vera the world be in a panic without it – aye

Iggy a've knocked it on the head a few times – at the moment that wouldn't be right though

Vera stands on a chair to open the window beside the front door.

Vera let some air in here – first thing in the mornin's bad – end up like mickey an donald there

Iggy will a fuck – know what am at – there's a cut off line or whatever – it's in yer head – it tells ye – that's the time t'pay attention t'what yer bein told – up t'that point ya wang away without – whatever – don't know – fucked

Vera many's a man's sat here an said that iggy

Iggy am the first t'mean it though – there's a difference – know what am at

Vera all know what we're at

Iggy vera what's the score with readies here – am skint – don't want t'be startin the day off with nothin – any chance ya could – y'know – give it back t'ye whenever am sorted out – it's just – y'know

Vera a've a few quid – keep ya goin

Iggy some women vera – not many like ye

Vera sits beside him and gives him some money from her bag.

Vera too good for this kip

Iggy darlin ya are – drinks – ya not openin up

Vera in a minute

Iggy cat rough – when my da was on the piss – first pop every mornin boke his ring – couldn't handle it – shouldn't a took it then – we should all do what he did – pack yer bags an sling yer hook

Vera do a look as if a haven't thought about it – there's mornin's a wake up an think a can't take any more a this –

somethin eatin away at me – a don't know what it is – but
it's in this place – come down the stairs he's lyin there –
must be another way – keep thinkin that

Iggy know what ya mean – i go for days not knowin
what the fuck's goin on aroun me sometimes – always
thinkin if a were somewhere else a'd know what the fuck
was goin on – always somewhere else like innit

Vera my case has been packed more than once – i've one
lyin in the back a the wardrobe from years back – packed
an all – nothin in it bloody fit me now – but sure what
would he do – he'd be in the gutter – left on his own –
couldn't leave 'im – couldn't bring 'im with ya

Iggy fuck 'im – let 'im paddle his own dixie – it's the
makin a people bein left on their jacks – only get one
crack at it vera – do what ya should be doin – none a that
regret chat – fuck that

Vera finish yer drink an we'll go back up stairs – the
day's work can wait – don't worry about him – his
head'll not raise until that shutter rattles

Iggy vera – ya must be jokin – look at the state a me – fit
for fuck all am – couldn't climb the stairs never mind
givin it that other trick – besides that – he might –
y'know – sortin out that situation – jesus

Vera you sure

Iggy better believe it am sure

Vera don't be comin lookin me t'night

Iggy yer the one does the lookin

Vera a wont be again

Iggy give me a break will ye – vera – just let me get
through the fuckin pint will ye – the state am in at the

moment – this is the crack a dawn y'know – lets get settled here – we'll see what happens later – let me – my head needs straightened out a bit that's all

Vera get yerself straightened out – that's the most important thing

Iggy watches television. Vera lights a cigarette.

Iggy good big box

Vera onc a pisspot's brainwaves – thought it would bring the punters back in

Iggy where's the chat t'turn the soun up

Vera he threw it out

Iggy threw it out why

Vera ask 'im – a don't know

Iggy politics or talks or somethin t'day

Vera gab all the want – not be buyin lunch here

Iggy suits – men in suits – wives must all be blind lettin 'em go out like that

Vera i look like a care

Iggy some fuckin talkin done – wha

Vera dummies meetin in the house

Iggy aye – my da used t'say there's too much fuckin talk in the world – take the spondolix off 'em – no fuckin about then

Vera (*puts cigarette out*) get somethin done here

Iggy aye vera open up

Vera takes keys from her handbag and opens the shutters. Robbie wakes. Iggy puts his empty bottle of

*Babycham in the bin beside him. Joe stirs but doesn't
fully wake. Vera wipes the counter down and puts a
glass of vodka in front of Joe. She pays for the drink
with coins on the counter. Vera pulls Iggy a pint. After
exchanging glances with Vera he pays for the pint.
Vera moves to Robbie and starts to clear the bottles
around him.*

Vera a think we're out a babycham

Robbie are we – hardly be missed – not that popular am
told

Vera popular enough with those who have t'break in
t'the yard t'get it

Robbie anythin be popular with those people

Vera what type a man drinks a crate a babycham

Robbie a thirsty one

Vera no man at all

Robbie very good – thank you vera – it wasn't the
babycham dampened that flame dear

Vera pisspot

Robbie aye

Iggy robbie why's there no chat for the soun on the box

Robbie still here are ye

Iggy why's there no chat

Robbie cause i own this place an a don't want there t'be
any chat that's why

Iggy grumpy head on

Robbie watch it an keep quiet

Vera sits facing Robbie.

Vera my love

Robbie yes dear

Vera all set for t'day – head clear is it darling – sharp?

Robbie razor blade – sweetness

Vera yer the man t'handle things

Robbie what is there t'handle – ask the guy for the readies – get the readies – sort it out

Vera am not goin with ya

Robbie that meant t'make a difference is it – i've organised it – i'll handle it – no problem t'me – better off on me own – man t'man – few gargles – that's the way t'do business – you don't go – be fine

Vera let you out on yer own

Robbie a know that

Vera be lost ya would – wee soul – wee lost soul – have ya the books sorted out yet – he'll want t'look at books

Robbie it'll be done – figures has t'be fresh in my head

Vera aye – fresh in yer head – do it right – am goin open up the kitchen an get joes breakfast sorted out – cause if i don't nobody will

Robbie a wee cupa tea

Vera it's what i live an die for robbie

Robbie thank you

Vera yer welcome – ya want some tea

Iggy stick with this – mixin them give ya the sickybad

Vera this place stinks – yous all need a bloody good hosin – a take it yer not eatin

Robbie maybe later

Vera aye – the books

Robbie aye

Vera exits to hotel. Robbie sits beside Iggy.

Iggy robbie

Robbie get yer head down alright last night – aye

Iggy with the gargle in me – out like a light – ya know the score yerself

Robbie room up at the top

Iggy at the top – aye – up at the top – oh aye

Robbie vera sort ya out did she

Iggy sort me out

Robbie aye – blankets – freeze the cleavers off ye up there – bad for business if guests get the cleavers froze off 'em

Iggy soun it was – blankets – everythin – soun

Robbie a good woman she is – likes t'look after people – it's in her nature

Iggy aye good woman – can't hear but a think united's sellin their keeper or somethin – face is up there must be sellin 'im – wanker anyway he is

Robbie i'm a funny fucker – know that – could be a stretcher case an still remember everythin said t'me – last night talkin t'you – a remember that

Iggy not worth rememberin – a lot a balls was it

Robbie about how fucked up ya felt – which yer entitled t'do – wantin advice ya were – a told ye t'take yerself off home – best place for ye – ya seemed t'reckon that – yer still here

Iggy rocket fuel an that robbie – all the plans go out the fuckin winda – ya know yerself

Robbie that right – ya hear what the lovely vera an me were talkin about there

Iggy a wouldn't do that – privacy an all that robbie – no way

Robbie did ya hear

Iggy a wee bit at the end – no more than that

Robbie we've t'see a guy t'day about readies or this place is fucked

Iggy that's a bad situation that robbie – a didn't realise . . .

Robbie doesn't matter what you realise – fuck all t'do with you – it's a business meetin – that's the point am makin – sometimes i might give the impression am not holdin it all t'gether – see me cowpted over that table ya might get the impression the war's over – i want you t'scrub the impression – is it scrubbed

Iggy scrubbed robbie

Robbie the impression you now stick with is robbie the businessman – robbie the man with his head well an truly fuckin screwed on

Iggy that's the way i see you robbie – yer a businessman – ya own this place – i respect that – i understan what yer sayin t'me

Robbie respect – aye – changes need t'be made y'see – big changes – what's the difference between you an joe over there

Iggy am conscious

Robbie very good – yer a very funny fella – that man has readies – that man pays his way – thirteen years he's been here – thirteen years he's paid his way – no longer a fuckin dosshouse – y'see – ya wanna stay here ya put yer hand in yer pocket – other than that come closin time ya fuck off home – understan what am sayin

Iggy it's all a bit haywire at the moment y'know – am hangin aroun tryin t'get my napper t'gether – that's what am doin

Robbie yer not listenin t'me – robbie the drinker's heart might bleed for ye – robbie the businessman doesn't give a fuck – a few gargles t'day then yer home

Iggy a want t'do that – y'know – a mean – intendin t'do that – a wanna go home – see her an the kids – that's important – ya know yerself – ya drink yer way through it – then ya go home – a know that – don't think a don't know that

Robbie drink yer drink

Iggy should a phone her – think a should phone first – look am nearly finished then am sailin home – type a crack – she'll understan that – understandable thing – that's why – should a phone her aye

Robbie robbie the businessman – doesn't give a fuck

Iggy right – thanks robbie – cheers

Vera enters from hotel with tea.

Vera that pipe under the sink's leakin again

Robbie have a look at it later

Vera a plumber be the wrong thing wouldn't it (*To Iggy.*) talkin about me was he – he does that – turn yer back an his mouth opens

Robbie don't flatter yerself dear – more important things – explainin the ways of the world a was

Iggy ways a the world – aye

Vera that be somethin you'd know about too robbie

Robbie it would vera that's correct – man a the world

Vera big plans robbie an still stuck here – must be hard for ya is it

Robbie the four corners a the earth dear – only a had you on my shirt tail

Vera globetrotter – listen t'that – what colour's the buses

Robbie waitin on one this years t'take you away

Vera the ones in t'town – what colour

Robbie bus colour

Vera colour a yer eyes – red – travellin man – only for me yer head be in the gutter

Robbie aye – no milk in this – forget that did ye – tell me this – what's the point in knowin the colour a buses if ya forget t'put milk in the fuckin tea

Vera like the babycham robbie there is none – alec hasn't arrived with the goods yet

Robbie not like 'im t'be late

Vera he's not late – got another phonecall about 'im last night – too drunk t'tell ye ya were

Robbie don't tell me now either – don't want t' know – whatever it is – leave me out

Vera i'll deal with it will a – like everythin else roun this kip

Robbie that's what that means – i say – a don't wanna know – that means – you deal with it

Vera he threw another wobbler he did – chased the wardens or whatever thay are roun the place with a stick – locked them in a room – stacked up all the furniture then tried t'set fire t'it

Robbie he's always at that crack – what

Vera a got the impression on the phone it was startin t'piss them off

Joe wakes.

Iggy alright joe – everythin alright

Joe still here

Iggy another day at the coalface joe – wha

Joe aye

Robbie alright kid

Joe aye

Vera breakfast not be long joe just waitin on alec with the bread an milk

Robbie alec went . . .

Joe a heard – talkin waken the dead it would

Vera rested yer head upstairs you'd hear nothin

Robbie would a not – alright vera aye

Vera the joys a spring joe

Iggy united's gonna sell their keeper joe – wanker he is

Joe keeper – keeper fuck

Robbie that's right joe – more important things

Vera listen t'me balloon head – what about alec

Robbie that's lovely innit – balloon head – lovely joe – wha

Joe lovely

Vera alec

Robbie alec's a balloon head – two balloon heads

Iggy three

Joe am in there

Robbie four balloon heads vera

Vera finished – this is his last chance – one more thing an he's out – that's what they said – an accordin t'them – it's our fault

Robbie our fuckin fault – what way our fault

Vera what way – he sits up here an you fill 'im fulla drink – that's what way

Joe the man's entitled t'a few gargles – what else – a mean – fuck he's entitled – has nothin

Robbie i'm t'blame – heap it all fuckin on there – backs not broke yet

Vera yer t'blame for everythin – ya know that robbie – don't be hidin from it

Robbie very good

Vera t'blame for everythin joe

Joe aye – the heap

Robbie down in that kip he's in he gets fuck all – all the do's feed 'im – don't give a fuck – the lock 'im out the rest a the time – he comes up here – he gets somethin t'do – a few odd jobs that half the time don't need t'be fuckin done – a few pints for doin them – they don't look after 'im we look after 'im – an i'm t'fuckin blame – a don't think so – an don't think a wont tell 'em that – burns a few sticks a furniture – fuck – the place is a kip anyway

Joe worse than alec there is

Robbie that's right

Vera he'll be through that door any second – sort it out globetrotter

Robbie the beautiful vera

Alec enters from street carrying a bag of groceries and a newspaper.

Alec sunny day out there robbie – go out an get the sun ya should

Robbie sunny enough in here alec

Alec puts groceries on counter and sets the newspaper in front of Joe.

Alec lizzy in the bakery was goin t'give me the bill vera – bill t'morrow a told her – think she'd know that vera – got a new watch – numbers – lights up in the dark – no batteries though – lizzy said she saw someone on the road – know who it was robbie – jimmy mac – walkin she said – no car – suit on 'im – new watch she said he had on 'im too – not as good as my watch – maybe the give 'im a watch in jail robbie

Robbie aye – fucker – must've let 'im out

Alec let 'im out aye robbie

Robbie bad fucker – alec – stay away from 'im

Alec he is robbie – jimmy mac's a bad fucker – good suit on 'im – no car – he's a bad fucker joe – isn't he

Joe aye alec – bad fucker

Vera robbie wants t'talk t'ya about somethin alec

Alec just talkin t'im there now vera – only jokin vera

Robbie sit down alec

Alec have t'tidy up robbie

Robbie leave that a minute

Alec can't leave it robbie – have t'do my work – get my lunch – go t'joes house – feed the cat – tidy up – have my tea – watch my programmes – cant leave it robbie

Robbie you've time alec don't panic – sit down there

Alec a like havin a pint when am sittin down robbie

Robbie pull 'im a pint

Alec pull us a pint vera

Vera it's nine o'clock in the day an we're givin 'im a pint

Robbie just pull 'im the fuckin thing

Iggy finishes what's in his glass and catches Vera's eye for another pint. Alec sits at a table. Robbie sits facing him. Joe puts some money on the counter and pushes his empty glass towards Vera.

Joe fire a tomato juice in that vera – take the edge of it

Robbie alec

Alec robbie

Robbie vera got a phonecall last night alec sayin that ya threw the head up again

Alec the don't like me down there robbie – talk about me when am asleep the do – the don't like me robbie

Vera sets the pint down.

Alec thank you vera – lizzy at the bakery vera – no sense

Vera no sense – alec – this'll not be long joe

Joe aye – give us a shout

Vera takes the groceries and exits to the hotel.

Robbie member what ya were at last night alec

Alec took t'my bed an the talked about me robbie – the don't like me robbie

Robbie ya tried t'burn the kip down again alec

Alec no robbie – no

Robbie listen t'what am sayin – ya did – understan – ya did

Alec a did

Robbie ya did

Alec no – went t'my bed an the talked about me robbie

Robbie ya come up here an ya do a bit a work – right

Alec after this pint robbie – do my work then

Robbie do yer work – have a few pints – that's it – no more nonsense alec ya understan – any more a that crack an ya can't come back here

Alec i'll stay here – the don't like me down there robbie

Robbie ya can't stay here – this is a hotel – not like the kip yer in

Alec me an joe – joe stays here – me an joe'll stay here

Joe ya wouldn't like it here alec – fuckin kip it is

Robbie good enough for you – no more nonsense alec or ya can't come back

Alec have t'do my work

Robbie jesus christ – behave yerself down there – an yer alright here – understan

Alec understood robbie

Robbie right – knock that in t'ya an away out an tidy the yard up – after that mop out the kitchen an finish off with takin a brush t'this place

  Alec finishes pint.

Alec money ready for the cat joe

Joe sort ya out before ya go

Alec sort me out before a go joe

  Alec exits to hotel.

Robbie put yer head away that

Joe he's hard goin

Iggy he always like that

Robbie what ya mean from birth or what

Iggy aye

Robbie no – postman was he – milkman

Joe somethin like that – delivery or somethin – don't know

Robbie doin his roun's – this is away at the start like –
twenty years an more

Joe would be that

Robbie jumped out a car they did – shot 'im in the head
an away – not right since – slowed 'im up y' know –
couldn't repair whatever damage was done – said
it wasn't him they were lookin for to – alec had taken
somebody elses shift or somethin – no good t'him that

Iggy nice place – wha

Robbie aye

Vera enters from hotel.

Vera that's ready joe

Joe right ready now (*Finishes his drink.*)

Vera (*to Robbie*) yer not sittin aroun – the pipe needs
sortin then the books

Robbie thank you for remindin me dear – fuckin order in
the chaos ya are – when ya die am getting a plaque
mounted out there let the world know what a martyr for
yer cause ya were

Vera assumin yer still aroun – crates of babycham take
their toll a hear

Joe (*starting to exit*) the fry's the thing

Iggy you'll be back in – not leave me on my todd

Joe later – cupla hours kip – get scrubbed up – fuck

Exits to hotel

Vera am goin up t'air the rooms – get rid a the stink

Robbie worked its way up there has it – maybe there's a
different type a stink up there

Vera the pipe an the books

Exits to hotel.

Robbie (*finishes his tea*) cold tea – own a hotel an ya end up drinkin cold fuckin tea (*Pours himself a drink and knocks it back.*) there are advantages – not many – a few – you sittin here – aye

Iggy nothin else for it

Robbie member what a said – t'days home time – i'll be in next door – ya need a drink give me a shout – ya understan

Iggy aye robbie

Robbie fixin pipes an cold tea – wha

Robbie exits to hotel. Iggy waits a moment then fills his glass from the pump. He watches the television.

Before lunch. Iggy, a few pints down the road, is still watching television. Joe is cleaned up and sitting in his usual seat, reading the paper. Robbie enters from hotel dressed in suit and tie etc. He carries a ledger.

Robbie what any man woman or child needs t'know about the world of accounting an how it can be shaped into an art form is in this book – ya could mistake this place for the hilton if ya read it with a clear head

He pours himself a drink.

Joe hilton alright

Iggy if it's not right whoever it is'll know

Robbie it is right – don't be talkin not right – right alright

Vera enters from hotel. Skirt suit – big blouse – make-up.

Vera that the first one a day aye

Robbie first one – oh sweetness

Vera credit where credit's due robbie – holdin out that long – what a man

Robbie not many of us left dear

Vera the book's done – he's goin t'what t'talk facts an figures y'know – this top man a yers

Robbie everythin spot on – personal friend a mine the man is – he knows the score – a few gargles isn't gonna make the difference one way or the other

Vera very professional – yer topman's gonna be impressed – no doubt

Robbie i'm professional – don't ever say i'm not professional – a know what am at – impressed – impressed all right – i'll show ya what he'll be impressed about (*Looks for something under the counter.*) where are they – you hide them

Vera oh jesus – where they always are – where they've been for ever

Robbie impressed – fuckin right (*Rolls out a set of plans on the counter.*) what's that – you see these before

Joe as often as a shave

Robbie aye – look at that

Iggy what – what is it

Vera ya mean ya can't tell by lookin at it

Robbie plans – that's what it is – impress people (*To Vera.*) haven't a clue what yer talkin about

Iggy bit rough lookin robbie

Robbie what would you know – rough lookin – plans they are

Joe rough plans

Robbie that's correct – ya can have rough plans ya know – they're allowed in the world

Vera why are the plans rough robbie – tell 'im why they're rough

Robbie ya know nothin – this is technical – right – technical

Vera technical – drew them when ya were pissed – another top man a yers – used t'get pissed in here – at some new pub in the town he was – both of ya's pissed – he's tellin ya what it was like – he couldn't speak – you couldn't write – jesus christ

Robbie it was an arthitect a was talkin to – that man knew what he was about

Vera architect – you were there – what was he joe

Joe was he not an architect

Vera he designed kitchens – an by the look a him he was fuckin useless at it

Robbie architect he was – top man architect

Vera robbie don't bring them – we'll look like fools

Iggy can't make head nor tail a them – what's that

Robbie what's that – i'll tell ya what that is – that's whats gonna help turn this place aroun

Iggy looks like a boat or ski run or somethin

Vera it's a big – window

Robbie two new gaffs down the road – what have they both got

Vera lots a people sittin in them havin a drink an enjoyin themselves

Robbie big windows at the front – people can see in – they like that – they see in – so they go in

Joe once they see in here they'll fuckin flood in

He puts money on the counter. Vera gets him a drink.

Robbie done up the would – wood an all that caper – pillars – booths – lovely big window – let the light in – belfast's changin isn't it – the keep sayin it's changin – so it must be fuckin changin – this place is changin – places down the road are fuckin kips – this place be like the way it was before

Alec enters from hotel.

Alec the kitchen's all mopped out robbie – will a brush up now robbie

Robbie aye alec you do that – the likes a that fucker jimmy mac gets a new start the same goes for us

Alec (*brushing up*) jimmy mac's a fucker robbie

Robbie aye alec

Vera how's it goin t'be different this time

Robbie different times that's why

Vera what happened with the compensation money –
you forget that

Robbie what happened – you tell me what happened

Vera i'll tell ya all right – it was alright up t'that point –
an sometimes alright can be good enough – ya drank
nearly every penny of it robbie – that there's somethin
here at all's only down t'me – change – join the
gravytrain – remortgage – get us back t'the good times –
drank that to robbie – ya know what – a probably
wouldn't've minded but there weren't even good times in
the drinkin of it

Robbie you had good times all right – and plenty of
them

Vera you stick t'yer top men an those fuckin plans there
– we'll see how that goes will we

Robbie we'll try an work somethin out with yer network
a friends will we – not too many on that list is there

Vera plenty on it before a met you – am goin out t'turn
the car

She gives Joe the keys to the hotel.

we're not expectin anybody

Joe aye

Vera there wont be but if anybody wanders in off the
street lookin lunch tell the chef had to leave to sign copies
of his latest book – what i cooked for the rich an famous
– but he left some sandwiches in the kitchen – i've a feelin
this isn't goin t'take long anyway joe

Robbie it'll take as long as any other business meetin

Vera don't be long

Vera exits to hotel.

Robbie she's some performer – wha (*Pours himself a drink – watches the television.*) charlton heston dead

Iggy the actor

Robbie no charlton heston the fuckin deep sea diver – yes the fuckin actor

Iggy don't know

Robbie on the news yesterday he was

Joe head a the gun lobby in america

Robbie didn't know that

Joe ben hur was a good movie

Robbie aye – better go out here – alright there

Joe aye

Robbie joe there might be a guy weigh in from the brewery – a don't think he will but he might – it's nothin – just tell 'im a had t'rush out – personal business – in fact keep 'im here – give 'im a drink i'll sort 'im out when a get back

Joe aye – should get paid for this y'know

Robbie aren't ya always in my thoughts – that's payment enough – alright alec

Alec alright robbie

Robbie member what a said now – take it easy t'day

Alec take it easy robbie

Robbie aye

Robbie exits to hotel with plans and ledger.

Joe think it was me owned this kip

Iggy could a won somethin

Joe who

Iggy charlton heston

Joe ben hur a good movie

Alec finishes brushing up.

Alec finished now joe – need the keys an the money for the cat joe – cold turkey for the cat – do that this afternoon after lunch joe

Joe gives Alec keys and money

Joe tidy over there is it

Alec tidy joe – all the rubbish in the wheelie bin

Joe best place for it alec

Alec best place for it joe

Joe wanna wee one – start ya off

Alec a wee one aye joe

Alec sits down. Joe gets him a drink.

Iggy what's the crack here when they're not about – we just wang away at the gargle buckshee

Joe no – you've a drink in front a ye – worry about the next one when ya have none

Alec downs his drink.

Alec am away for my lunch now joe – eat first work later – joe

Joe good luck alec

Alec exits to street.

Iggy you a house

Joe aye – big one across the way there

Iggy ya never said – three days talkin ya never said

Joe a lot a things a don't say

Iggy the house – is it empty like

Joe aye

Iggy don't get that – a mean – what – why don't ya live in it

Joe don't want to

Iggy what's yer man tidyin up if it's empty

Joe nothin – feeds the cat – sits there – a don't know what he does – don't care what he does

Iggy you check up now an again like or what

Joe a just told ye a don't go near it

Iggy furniture in it – aye

Joe everythin in it – same as the day a left it

Iggy a don't get this

Joe sit an drink yer pint

Iggy not like talkin about it

Joe that's right

Iggy we're sittin here y'know

Joe an wha

Iggy more to it than getting pissed or whatever – talkin – findin out about people an stuff – what they're about – fuck a don't know – just – talkin t'each other

Joe you do nothin but talk – every damn thing under the sun – talkin about it

Iggy it touches me – everythin touches me – the world – the whole lot – the big picture – it touches me

Joe aye – touched

Iggy if a've been doin all the talkin it's yer turn now

Joe a don't like talkin

Iggy tell us

Joe a just said

Iggy a know what ya just said – tell us

Joe my wife fucked off – right – that's it

Iggy cause a the drink like or what

Joe no – she just left

Iggy an what

Joe an nothin

Iggy the house – what's the crack with the house

Joe after she took off a didn't set foot in the house again – didn't feel right – just didn't feel right

Iggy what ya call her

Joe ruby – see where am sittin here – that's where she use t'sit – her seat (*Finishes his drink and pours himself another one.*) ya want one a these – it's paid for

Iggy not good with shorts – y'know

Joe up t'yerself

Iggy ah fuck it – give us one

Joe pours Iggy a drink.

184

Joe good luck

Iggy aye

Joe the two a us used t'come here – ruby an me – more
life about it then – house across the way – handy – she'd
come in on her own some a the time y'know – a wee
vodka – sit here an talk t'robbie – him an her got on well
y'know – talk t'anybody she would – good company –
she was known for that – known for bein good company
– most a the time she'd do my talkin for me – works like
that sometimes – yer one type they're another – fits –
makes sense – feels right or somethin – a don't know –
she would never light the fire – all the time we were
t'gether never once lit the fire or went out t'the yard t'get
coal – she said that was a mans job – used t'joke with her
that in another life she must a been in a coal minin
disaster – an that's why she wouldn't go near it – we were
meant t'go out t'gether this night – me an ruby an robbie
an vera – didn't go out that often or anythin – enough
goin on here – y'know – goin out to a brewery do we
were – they were presentin robbie with somethin – a
don't know – best run pub or somethin like that – he
invited me an ruby – one a those ones ya get dressed up
for it was – always gotta look yer best – a was the only
one not ready – come straight in here from work – did
that sometimes – all in good form the were – i just sat on
– wasn't thinkin about getting dressed up an that – come
the time t'go i had t'shoot over t'the house an fire the suit
on me an that – robbie says the couldn't be late in case he
missed his big moment – he wanted ruby t'go with them
an me meet them there – i was fine with that – big do's
aren't my – y'know – ruby said she'd sit here an wait on
me – that was that – the two a them took off in a taxi – i
went t'put my suit on an left her here – a was havin a
shave – we've all got used t'hearin blasts but this one
would've burst yer ears open – knew it was this place –

runnin over here thought a was goin t'throw up – place
was crazy – dust – bits a things everywhere – bits a people
– couldn't find her – screamin her name a was – couldn't
think where t'look – didn't want t'look for fear of findin
somethin – then she just walked out in t'the street – slow
motion – she just walked out an stood there – didn't
know what she was lookin at – blood all over her arms –
didn't speak – just held her – no injuries – blood must a
been somebody else's – said at the hospital that she was
in shock – felt like sayin tell me somethin a don't know –
the said that different people handle it differently an it
was just a matter a time – hang in there an it'll sort itself
out type a thing – she never spoke about it – hardly
talked at all – just waited – few weeks later a came in
from work this night an she was gone – packed her stuff
an just left – left a note sayin she was sorry but she had
t'go an wouldn't be back – haven't seen her since – funny
thing to – see that cat alec feeds – it arrived from
nowhere the day she left – tiny wee kitten – funny fuckin
thing that – waited – spendin most a my time here
anyway so a just moved in – haven't been back over the
road since

He takes a drink and pours himself another one.

Iggy fucked up place it is – what ya think she's doin or
what – or where or anythin

Joe i never tell that story – right – a don't want no more
talk about it – understan what am sayin

Iggy ya still love her like

Joe a just said no more – right

Iggy right – not right like is it – think a might phone my
wife – let her know what the crack is an that y'know

Joe go home

Iggy phone her first – always better t'phone first it is

Joe aye (*Finishes his drink.*) am goin t'go out an sit in reception in case this guy from the brewery weighs in – make the place a bit more respectable lookin

Iggy i'll sit out there with ye

Joe no i'll sit on my own – read the paper

Iggy aye – sure i'll be on the phone t'her anyway

Joe folds his newspaper and exits to hotel. Iggy finishes his vodka and pours himself another one. He leans over the counter and pulls himself a pint as well. He settles down to watch the television.

After lunch. Iggy is in the same position watching the television. He drinks the last of his pint.

Iggy news fuck – took ya three days t'ride somewhere t'say it – make sure then it wasn't a lot a shite – rich people in love an starvin babies lyin on the groun – aye – that's the message – now we're gettin there – the money message – two points up against the yak yak of outer fuckin do dah – we're in deep shit now

Joe enters from hotel with a tray of tea and sandwiches.

we're in deep shit now – we're up two points or down two points against the yo yo bin bin chats

Joe dow jones

Iggy aye him too

Joe there's tea in that – have a sandwich – brewery guy wasn't hungry

Iggy not now – too late now

Joe pours a cup of tea

Joe not goin t'believe this – know what the brewery guys name was

Iggy double vodka

Joe close – joe beer – that's who he is – he's joe beer the brewery man – hows about that – wha

Iggy aye names are all up the left – listen t'this – this is important – important this is – this come on the tv about two pints ago

Joe pay for them aye

Iggy aye a paid for them – listen t'this – some woman went t'some oliver hardy an wore this dress chat – shiny chats – wouldn't be my – y'know my trick – too glitzy – my wife not go for that type a thing – plain chats – this dress – must a cost a fuckin fortune too – this dress had no arse in it – an yer women wasn't wearin any trunks – ya could see her jamroll

Joe need t'watch what ya'd be sittin on

Iggy thought that – newspaper be bad – print

Joe plastic

Iggy that be cat too – don't get me wrong here she had a good jamroll – the point am makin is what the fuck y'know – it's up there – it's on the fuckin screen – there's punters in countries with fuck all runnin about in the nip all the fuckin time – dyin – have fuck all – an it's news like that some brass nail has a hole in her fuckin dress – know what a mean – somethin fuckin wrong about that like

Joe don't watch it then

Iggy it's there – have t'watch it

Joe don't talk about it then

Iggy what's the point in watchin it if ya don't fuckin talk about it

Joe a don't know – television – don't care

Iggy we should care

Joe aye

Iggy we should care but we don't that's the point am makin

Joe you've made it – right (*Checks his watch.*) alec be back soon for the afternoon shift

Iggy over in the house is he aye

Joe should be – bring the mail back with 'im

Iggy aye – there's somethin a want t'talk t'ya about – ask ya somethin

Joe what ya lookin – tenner – score

Iggy not that no – not that – maybe get that off ya later like – not now though

Joe what

Iggy am goin home

Joe now

Iggy no no not now – make a phonecall first – t'day sometime – t'night maybe – whatever – am goin home – that's that right – but say just in case a don't – say somethin happens maybe – don't know what the score is about ye y'know – might be home t'morrow instead a t'day – robbie's a gentleman – vera's a good woman – lovely woman – let me kip here anytime – that's soun –

am not sayin there will be but there might be a problem
there or somethin – a don't know – maybe vera or
somethin – talkin a wee bit fuckin funny she is – could all
go belly up y'know – if that's the situation – if that's the
way it goes – is there – is there any chance i could kip
down in that house a yers – empty house across the way

Joe no

Iggy no

Joe aye no

Iggy but a mean – it's lyin there

Joe that's our house – nobody stays there

Iggy our house

Joe yes our house

Iggy right – only askin y'know

Joe ya asked an ya got yer answer

Iggy you should sell it – get the readies for it – sell it –
price a houses roun here up through the fuckin roof

Joe are the

> *Robbie enters from the hotel. He doesn't look as
> smart as he did a few hours ago. He puts his plans
> and ledger on the counter.*

Iggy yer a gentleman robbie

Robbie still here – time you were off a think

Iggy still here robbie – still here – headin off soon

Joe well

Robbie no

Joe brewery man weighed in

Robbie fuck – what

Joe not a happy man robbie – waited as long as he could
– left his card – phone 'im immediately he says

Robbie fuck 'im he can join the queue – a need t'have a
word with ye about somethin

Joe wha

Robbie not now – she's in behind me – later – not now –
don't be mentionin the brewery guy t'her

Joe right

> *Vera enters from street. She slams the front door
> shut.She sits at the counter – nobody speaks. She gets
> up and walks behind the bar.*

Vera i'm gonna have a drink (*She pours herself a drink.*)
anybody else – robbie – don't let me down robbie

Robbie aye why not

Vera babycham

Robbie no

Vera nearly forgot – stupid bitch – all out a babycham –
iggy – joe – a drink – it's on the house – on our house

Joe am alright

Iggy aye – why not – it's all mapped out now anyway

Vera (*lifts plans and ledger*) put these away will a –
somewhere safe – wouldn't want anybody stealin them –
put them down here

Robbie you do that vera

Vera (*pouring*) is that enough in that – ya can have more
– it's alright t'have more

Robbie that's plenty

Vera ya sure joe – yer welcome to it

Joe i've tea here – take one later vera not now – keys

Joe hands Vera the hotel keys and she puts them in her handbag.

Vera anythin excitin happen joe when we were away

Joe not that a noticed vera no

Vera nothing exciting

Joe no

Vera sits beside Iggy, finishes her drink.

Vera another one a those please – know what i think

Robbie no what

Vera i think we should all just sit here an get pissed – bit of a change – you game for that iggy

Iggy i'm yer man

Vera (*handed drink*) thank you darling

Robbie yer welcome sweetness

Vera get pissed – so no news then boys

Iggy the world's up the fuckin left an there's a woman runnin roun the place with no arse in her dress – if ya were goin out of a night vera would ya wear somethin like that

Vera would depend on what mood a was in

Iggy wee lads in our street had no arse in their trousers – that's different though

Vera a have the body for it – what do ya think iggy –
would a have the body for it

Iggy certainly ya would

Vera joe – still have it enough t'flash a bit a flesh

Joe turn a few heads vera

Vera stomachs a think joe not heads – what do ya think
– will a get one a those dresses robbie – flash a bit a flesh
– you like that – a could wear it pullin pints – yer big
window – everyone see me – get all the punters in – what
ya think robbie – that be a bit of a turn on would it –
right it's decided – am gonna cut the arse out a all my
dresses – start now – get me the scissors

  Robbie hands her scissors.

here

Vera what way would ya go about this – do it yerself job

  She stands up, bends over and looks through her legs.

think this is the way the woman on the box did it – no
(*Stands up.*) have t'take it off (*Her back to Iggy.*) unzip
me – unzip me – come on – you've unzipped plenty a
them before am sure

Iggy only talkin a lot a nonsense vera – don't be cuttin
yer clothes up

Vera (*her back to Joe*) joe – do the business joe

Joe ya gonna get me that vodka now

Vera he'll get it – get joe a vodka – no takers then – no
point in askin you (*Sits down.*) useless – a hear united's
sellin their keeper – wanker he is from what a can gather

Robbie united who vera

Vera united with the wanker keeper – yous are no fun – need somewhere with a bit a fun – energy – light – we need light robbie (*Finishes her drink.*) – i'm goin down the road t'have a drink where there's light – no point in askin the old ones – ya want t'come with me iggy – stay here too long ya turn t'stone

Iggy am settled here vera y'know

Vera don't worry i've money on me – what are ya lookin at him for – am askin you t'have a drink with me – two adults havin a drink – no need t'look at him – robbie doesn't mind – wouldn't matter if he did – you don't mind do ya robbie – iggy an i go for a wee drink somewhere brighter

Robbie do whatever ya want vera

Vera do whatever ya want vera – see – let's go

They finish their drinks.

Iggy we'll not be long

Vera we'll be as long as we want – you can look after things robbie i'll doubt there'll be a rush

Iggy and Vera exit to street. Robbie pours himself a drink and sits beside Joe.

Robbie got off lightly there – wha

Joe more maybe

Robbie aye

Joe not work out no

Robbie fuck – not work out – what is it ya gotta do – a don't know – fuckin wearin me down it is joe – am sittin waitin on this fuckin head the ball arrivin – vera's givin it all that – understan'able – still doesn't make it easy

t'listen to – sittin lookin at all the punters in the place we
are – nice gaff – good shape of a counter – not like this
fuckin thing – went roun in a bend – ya could be standin
at it an there could still be plenty a room – know that
way – sittin thinkin fuck this am goin t'do a runner here
– go sit on a wall someplace an watch the world pass by
– wish t'fuck a had a – have t'pull yerself t'gether don't ye

Joe nothin else for it

Robbie ya reckon

Joe sometimes – other times no

Robbie a was lookin at the barman pullin a pint – kept
thinkin i used t'enjoy doin that – not brain surgery but – a
simple thing done well or somethin like that – thought
t'myself i could enjoy doin that again – then head the ball
danders in – haven't seen ye for a while – blah blah – old
times – all that – knew right away – this is my last roll a
the dice an this guy's turned in t'a fuckin balloon – didn't
say anythin t'her like – she knew anyway – seen enough a
them about this place – it was like ya knew it wasn't goin
t'work out but ya hoped it might so ya carry on with it –
it was like that – went along with it – talkin t'me like a
stranger he was – everythin was gonna be easy know that
way

Joe if everythin was easy we'd all be at it

Robbie correct – all telephone numbers – not interested
in plans or books or fuck all – just telephone numbers –
talkin about openin offices all over the show he is – am
tryin t'explain the situation t'im – he's all new start – new
this – everythin's possible – sayin how we all need t'tap in
t'this new foun energy – investigate the new opportunities
available – nothin – the guy's a fuckin joker – can't do
anythin for us – might be able t'do somethin if we have
collatoral – i explained we don't that's why we're here –

can't help – would love t'help but can't – another double
napper tandy – dead cert – then he starts in t'it –
lost everythin – wife – kids – house – business – gamblin
– tryin t'pull himself t'gether – tryin t'start up again – we
were gonna be his first clients – thought he could do it
but he can't – doesn't understan why – he just can't –
couldn't stop apologisin t'us – must've a big sign roun my
fuckin neck do a – he's leavin – what does he do – trys
t'tap me for a fuckin tenner – i'd a fuckin slapped 'im
only he looked too stupid

Alec enters from street.

Alec alright joe

Joe any letters for me over there alec

Alec no letters t'day joe

Joe nothin

Alec nothin joe

Joe all tidy are wa

Alec all tidy joe

Robbie have ya nothin t'be at alec – we're tryin t'have a
conversation here

Alec talk away robbie i'll just sit here

Robbie a don't want ye sittin there at the moment that's
what am sayin

Joe man's been graftin hard all day – allowed t'settle he is
– normally back before this alec – some grafter ya are

Alec i've done somethin

Joe done somethin what way

Alec must a done somethin – but a didn't do anythin

Robbie talk right alec

Alec did everythin the same – everythin the same as
always joe – tidy up – cold turkey in the catdish – pish
wish wish wish – no cat joe – all roun the place –
everywhere joe – it's not there – didn't do anythin
different joe – didn't lose it joe – just not there

Robbie calm down alec son

Alec joes cat robbie

Joe give 'im a pint – ya want a pint

Alec aye joe a pint

Robbie have a pint later alec not now

Joe he's upset for fuck sake – give 'im the pint

Alec never lost before – everyday there – never lost
before

Joe alec – alec – it's alright – it's nothin t'do with you
don't worry about it

Alec nothin t'do with me joe that's right – nobody better
touch it joe – i'll fuckin kill them – fuckin kill them a will

Joe it was an old cat alec

Alec it was an old cat joe

Robbie here

Alec (*pint*) cheers robbie – thanks robbie – cheers – it
was an old cat joe

Joe probably away t'die somewhere alec – that's what
they do – don't they do that robbie

Robbie oh aye away t'die – knock that in t'ya alec –
sunny day away out for a dander or somethin

Alec rather sit here robbie – give us somethin t'do

Robbie there is nothin for ya t'do

Alec tidy up the stairs

Robbie yer not allowed near the rooms ya know that

Alec just sit here then robbie

Robbie fuck (*Gives Alec money.*) buy a carryout an sit outside there with it

Alec never see me drinkin in the street robbie – never see me drinkin in the street joe

Joe nah alec

Alec buy batteries for my watch an radio – listen t'my radio at night robbie

Robbie aye do that

Alec don't look for the cat joe

Joe no point alec

Alec (*finishes pint*) back later robbie – listen t'my radio – have my tea – back later

    Alec exits to street.

Joe that cat arrived the day ruby left – know that

Robbie aye a know it – course a know it – an wha

Joe nothin – just sayin – strange like

Robbie everythin alright

Joe what ya mean alright – aye – alright aye

Robbie a need t'talk t'ya – just makin sure yer head's t'gether that's all – serious ya know – focused – know what am sayin

Joe stop talkin like that – say whatever ya got a say

Robbie ya know what am goin t'say – only got one thing to say – you know what it is

Joe do a

Robbie ya want another drink

Joe aye (*Drinks poured.*) you payin for that

Robbie aye am payin for it

Joe put the readies in the till then

Robbie fuck the till – sort that out later

Joe have t'look after business

Robbie this is what am doin now – right – am lookin after business – just think about this – it's about the house

Joe aye the house

Robbie other times we discussed this it's just been talk – this is more than talk – right – just listen – that's all am askin ya t'do at the moment – just listen – the house is lyin empty – understan why

Joe do ye

Robbie you've been here all this while – it's lyin there – i understan – fuckin right i understan

Joe right

Robbie for whatever reasons – an ya know them – it's down t'me a understan that – t'day was the last – fuckin – the last outside way a goin about this – a've nowhere else t'go – the house is lyin there – yer house is lyin there

Joe ruby an i's house

Robbie ruby an yer house – this could happen – it could be somethin made happen – a few ways a doin this – go t'the bank – no more fuckin head the balls involved in this – straight t'the right people – use the house as collatoral – get the readies fire it in t'place – have this place the way it should be – fuck those kips down the road – that's the one way – the other way would be t'sell it – get more readies i'd say – wouldn't need t'fire everythin in t'this place – keep some readies for yerself – you could buy in t'this place – i'd sell ya a whack of it – become a partner – ya live here anyway – so a mean – be handy – get a good feelin sittin here – when the place is buzzin an that – knowin you own some of it – or if ya didn't want that type a hassle – wouldn't be any hassle cause i'd be coverin that – ya didn't want the hassle ya could just lend me the money – pay ya back whatever a bank would pay ya back – all a this is solid – business – not just talk joe – another level – know what am sayin – understan there's punters say friends shouldn't get involved in this type a set up – that wouldn't be a problem with me an you – too long in the tooth – been down too many roads for anythin not right t'happen – it's a goldmine like – a real – y'know – fuckin goldmine it is – ya know that anyway – there's no point in me sayin the – ya know that

Joe aye

Robbie aye – i owe vera – whatever an all she does – i owe her – a can't fuck this up – this is about money an business – ya don't have t'say anythin now – a want ya t'think about it – you think about it

Joe aye – you've told me so a know what we're talkin about – i'll think about it – now's not the time for me t'be dealin with it – other things involved – not now

Robbie understan joe – but you'll think about it

Joe aye robbie a just said

Robbie we'll not talk about it any more – it's said – it's done – you'll think about it – don't be mentionin anythin t'her about it

Joe not mention anythin

Robbie no point in her knowin anythin at this stage

Joe right – no more

Robbie think about it – finished (*Looks at television.*) camilla parker bowles

Joe aye – some woman

Robbie aye – earn their readies easy the do – a may go an phone this brewery guy – money he's lookin – the quiz men be in soon – ya sittin there

Joe might dander down an get the late paper – maybe get somethin t'eat – ya want me t'sit here until they weigh in

Robbie aye – a want t'get this done now – don't want t'be phonin later with the gargle in me – give us a shout

Joe aye

Robbie fuckin tired am

Joe long oul day alright

Robbie exits to hotel with tea tray.

After the quiz. Robbie is clearing pint glasses from one of the tables. Joe is reading the evening paper.

Robbie did you know greenland was owned by denmark

Joe a did

Robbie waste a brains that isn't it like – know the answers t'everythin an not a fuckin job among them

Joe passes the time for them

Robbie (*behind the bar washing glasses*) ya need somethin t'fill it alright – if the bought more gargle it be better though – sittin over a pint half the day – in days gone by joe i'd a turfed them out on their arse

Joe aye

Robbie greenland an denmark a didn't know that – it's the type a thing that's hardly worth knowin though

Joe better off knowin it than not knowin it

Robbie that could be true – yer man asks the questions says he might try an get it off the groun at night – charge people in – he keeps the door i get the readies off the drink – that's if there is any drink – brewery man says they don't get paid soon they're goin t'stop deliverin – ya hear me

Joe a hear ye

Robbie yer man asks the questions says that kip down the road has it goin at night – big crowds at it – prize money an that (*Pours himself a drink.*) ya want one a these

Joe aye

> *Robbie pours Joe a drink, pays for it then sits beside him at the counter.*

Robbie made any decisions about what a said earlier

Joe no

Robbie still thinkin about it

Joe still thinkin about it

Robbie these things take time – not too much time but they take time

Joe aye

Robbie a was goin go in an make somethin t'eat – don't think i'll bother now – you had somethin – aye

Joe when a was down the road earlier – stew

Robbie any good

Joe alright – could a been hotter

Alec enters from street carrying a suitcase.

Robbie nice an slow – here we go – alright alec

Alec alright robbie aye – alright joe – do yer talkin robbie

Robbie aye alec

Alec sits down. Silence.

Alec jimmy mac's a fucker robbie

Robbie why's that alec

Alec you said he was – i knew he was anyway – i knew he was robbie

Robbie what's the suitcase for alec – better not be what a think it is

Alec the don't like me down there robbie – joe the don't like me down there

Robbie yer not stayin here – it's not a dosshouse alec – you can wicker about tidy up – fine – but yer not stayin here

Alec (*puts money on the counter*) give us a pint robbie – alright joe – didn't come back joe – cat didn't come back

Joe no

Alec beauty she was – not get another one like it – big fat cat full a cold turkey

Robbie drink that alec then maybe another then yer back down the road

Alec can't go back robbie – out ya go the said

Robbie i'll get vera t'phone them – she'll sort it out – it'll be alright

Alec no robbie no

Robbie what no robbie no

Alec jimmy macs watch – a belter – swap the watches – mines a beauty robbie look – look joe a beauty it is

Joe it is alec a beauty

Alec said i was a mad man – said my watch was shite he did – good watch – hit 'im a did robbie – jimmy mac's a fucker

Robbie a dig ya hit 'im

Alec hit 'im a few times robbie – bust his face – bust his face open a did robbie – played football we did when we were kids – house across the street – jimmy mac lived in the house across the street robbie – his big brother used t'let me have a go on his bike – up along the river – peddlin the bike up along the river – drivin the car – him drivin the car robbie – didn't say no – jimmy macs a fucker – bust his face open – the don't like me down there robbie

Robbie drink yer pint there alec – forget about all that alec – right

Alec forget about it robbie

Robbie somethin be sorted out – always sort somethin out alec

Alec somethin always sorted out robbie

Robbie (*to Joe*) what ya do about that – name a fuck – a mean – i can't – fuck y'know

Vera and Iggy enter from street. It's obvious they've been drinking. Alec watches the television.

Alec put on who wants t'be a millionaire robbie – like that show – put it on robbie

Robbie changes stations. Vera sits at the bar.

Vera sit down iggy – a know this isn't the type a kip we're accustomed to but sit down anyway

He sits beside her.

who wants t'be a millionaire – i do

Alec it's a good show vera – yer man's good

Vera good show alec – did you miss me robbie

Robbie my heart bled vera – countin every second a was

Vera (*looking in her handbag for money*) one last drink – gonna have one last drink with everybody (*Puts money on counter.*) – get the boy wonder a pint – alec – joe – everyone – get them all a drink – and you the light of my life a want you t'have a drink with me

Robbie gets drinks etc.

Alec c – it's c joe – isn't it c

Joe c – aye – fuck it – don't know – might be a

Iggy b it is

Vera loved it down there robbie ya would've – all laid out lovely – an the people – beautiful – not scumbags – all top men – yer type a people they are

Robbie glad you enjoyed yerself

Vera oh yes – top notch people

Alec a

Iggy should be b

Alec it's a

Vera packed t'the doors the place was – must be makin a fortune robbie – bringin the money t'the bank in wheelbarrows the must be – all in wee uniforms – professional place – professional – that would be the word

Robbie why don't ya get a job down there – woman a yer vast experience – all be out with open arms

Hands her a drink.

Vera an you know it too – one last drink – hey iggy – one last drink

Iggy aye aye – last drink aye

Vera cheers robbie

Robbie good luck vera

Alec d – it's d joe isn't it – d it is

Joe d

Iggy b again

Vera have t'go now

Robbie away t'yer bed aye

Vera bed – no no no no – somethin t'do – have somethin t'do robbie (*To Iggy.*) finish yer pint – i'll be back in a minute

Vera exits to hotel.

Alec d joe – a told ya it was d – a said d joe

Joe yer the man alec – millionaire

Iggy robbie we have t' – have t'talk here

Robbie drink yer pint an watch the t.v.

Iggy don't be getting the wrong – the wrong notion here – gonna say somethin t'help ya out – makin it clear it's nothin t'do with me – right – all i was doin was talkin an havin a gargle

Robbie what

Alec d again joe – it's d again

Joe an the man says d

Iggy am blitzed here right – head's startin t'go a wee bit – still tellin ya somethin though – i like you – know what am sayin – i like you that's why I'm sayin this

Robbie i don't like you

Iggy ya don't know me

Robbie i don't want t'know ya

Iggy ya don't – y'know – this is the fucked up side – an alright side too – there is – anyway – vera was talkin a wee bit strange down there – nothin t'do with me – her it was – kept wantin t'talk about leavin – leavin for good like – sayin she had enough an all that type a chat – don't know what she's up t'now like – just tellin ya this – don't agree with her leavin by the way – that's wrong – shouldn't fuckin leave – people should stick with it regardless a what the fuck's goin on – she kept talkin about me goin with her – don't know where she got that from now – not from me right – happily married i am –

phone her – have t'phone her – a just want t'wire ya off in case any – y'know – drunk she is – all be forgotten about whenever y'know

Alec b – has t'be b joe

Joe aye

Iggy maybe you should speak t'her or somethin – not right that she wants t'leave is it – flowers or somethin know what a mean – i do that type a crack – that's what i'm like – flowers an that sort it out – so that's what am sayin

Robbie that it

Iggy that's what am sayin – that's it

Robbie sure we'll see what happens – don't you panic about it – she gets a wee bit like that now an again

Iggy woman wha

Robbie aye

Alec b – am good joe – am good

Joe get you on it alec – win a fortune

Alec a fortune joe aye

   Vera enters from hotel with a suitcase.

Iggy robbie what am . . .

Robbie say nothin

Vera robbie

Robbie yes dear

Iggy vera don't be – a was just sayin t'robbie . . .

Vera iggy you don't have t'say anythin – it's not up t'you – i'll do the talkin – it's my resposibility

Iggy that's what am sayin – don't be . . .

Robbie let her say what she has t'say – right

Iggy right right right

Alec c – it's c this time joe

Joe in yer head alec – not out loud

Alec (*whispers*) c it is joe

Vera finish yer pint iggy – then we can phone a taxi – i'm leavin robbie – we're leavin – don't be blamin iggy – these things just happen – just leavin – don't want a scene – be decent that way robbie – i've had enough – enough is enough – can't grow old here – wasted too much bloody time here as it is – not that you care – i'm goin away robbie with another person t'start over again – a don't want a scene so we're just gonna leave – i've had enough – that's all there is to it robbie – i've had enough – we'll walk down an get a taxi iggy – i want t'go now – ya don't have t'say anythin robbie – a don't want ya t'say anythin – iggy

Robbie you do what ya have t'do vera

Vera hands Robbie the keys of the hotel

Vera you'll be needin these

Robbie aye

Vera iggy come on

Iggy this is all the drink talkin here – it's the drink talkin vera

Vera don't be worried about him – it's nothin t'do with him – he doesn't care – come on let's go

Iggy a don't know what – robbie

Vera what ya talkin t'him for – fuck him – we're goin so come on

Iggy sit down will ye – sit down

Vera a don't want t'sit down – finish the damn drink an we'll go

Iggy robbie a said – didn't a say – vera am not goin anywhere – jesus christ all a was doin was talkin t'ya y'know – fuck sake – i'm married for fuck sake – i love my wife – mightn't know that but a love her – a said this – robbie didn't a say this

Vera you make him say that – you made him say it didn't ya

Robbie he told me you were actin a bit strange vera that's all

Vera fucker – iggy listen – i know he's told you t'say all that

Iggy told me nothin

Vera he's a bad bastard – he wants t'torture me – that's what he's doin – torturin me – he doesn't love me – you fucker – he loves someone he can't have an he's fuckin torturin me because of it – i've t'watch him day after day drink every drop a manhood out a himself – nothin works – he drank himself so nothin works – does it on purpose – fucker – you said t'me ya wanted t'go so we'll go – don't listen t'him – i can't stay here – don't listen t'the fucker

Iggy i'm just havin a drink that's all am doin – i'm not goin anywhere – just havin a gargle

Vera (*to Robbie*) useless fuckin bastard – pisspot useless fucker – fucker – you fucker – phone my own taxi – my taxi to take me – take me

*She moves to the phone at the end of the bar and
rummages through her handbag for a phone number.
She can't find it but dials anyway*

nine – o – six – nine – o – six

*She smashes the phone with the receiver. She
composes herself, lifts her suitcase and exits to the
hotel. Robbie pours himself a drink*

Iggy robbie look – y'know – that was out a order that –
a mean – a said didn't a say – nothin a could do there –
didn't know she was gonna – sorry

Robbie sorry – an what ya goin t'do now

Iggy do now

Robbie yes – fuckin do now – what are ya goin t'do now

Iggy am not – nothin

Robbie want t'know what i think you should do – she's a
good woman y'see – vera's a good woman – i think you
should go up stairs to her – she'll be standin outside our
room – it's locked – you know the room a mean – go up
stairs give her those keys an tell her yer sorry – i think
that would be the thing t'do

Iggy maybe later robbie – not now – now's not right

Robbie get out t'fuck

Iggy that wasn't my fault

Robbie get out t'fuck

Iggy robbie – just let me sit here – a just want t'sit here –
alright alright look – this is it – this is it – her an the kids
have left me – everythin's fucked up at the moment – a
need a bit a time y'know – goin t'get her back like – get

her back all right – house is empty robbie – no one there – just let me sit here

Robbie yer either goin t'walk through that door or i'm goin t'throw you out it – what ya want

Iggy robbie please

Robbie don't have me say it again

Iggy finishes his drink and exits to street. Robbie sits down beside Joe. He sets the hotel keys on the counter.

Joe think it's d this time alec

Alec it's d – it is d joe

Robbie c it is

Vera enters from the hotel. Her and Robbie exchange looks. Vera lifts the keys from the counter and exits to hotel.

Alec a – it's a joe – a was goin t'say a

Robbie why didn't ya then

Alec don't know robbie – just didn't

End of the day. Slow, very slow. Robbie, Vera, Joe and Alec are all sitting apart from each other. They all have a drink in front of them. Varying degrees of drunkenness.

Joe what is that we're watchin alec – what is it

Alec that's the news joe

Joe news aye – alotta people shoutin there alec – looks like the lost somethin

Alec a lot a people shoutin joe aye

Joe lost money the have – do all the shoutin in the world – not goin t'get it back for them is it – what ya think alec not get it back

Alec not get it back joe

Joe what ya reckon robbie – all the shoutin you want not get somethin back ya lost

Robbie enough t'loose the have – no damage done

Joe there speaks a man who knows what he's talkin about – a businessman – you know what yer talkin about robbie

Robbie aye

Joe i'd say yer right – the wouldn't have a fuckin clue what it's like t'loose somethin – vera

Vera what

Joe they wouldn't have a fuckin clue

Vera no

Joe money – aye – different business all t'gether loosin yer cat alec – that be a different business

Alec a didn't lose the cat joe – don't be sayin a lost the cat – a didn't do that

Joe no alec no – lost as in gone for good – lost as in gone forever – never t'return – understan what am sayin there alec

Alec not comin back joe

Joe aye – not fuckin comin back – ya want another drink alec – this is the time a day t'rip in t'it – rip in t'it now robbie wha – get alec another drink there

Alec no more joe

Joe no more joe

Alec time for my bed – listen t'my radio – up early joe – always up early – get the work done

Robbie goin t'have t'go down an sort it out yerself alec

Alec the don't like me down there robbie

Robbie it'll be alright alec – just try an keep yer act t'gether

Alec am not goin down robbie

Robbie a don't give a fuck alec am tired – am fuckin tired – right

Joe ya can stay over in my place alec

Robbie what ya mean stay over there

Joe what a just said – he can stay over there – that suit ya alec does it

Alec suits me fine joe – finish my drink – a need the keys joe

Joe throws the keys to Alec

Joe there ya go

Robbie give 'im the keys back alec – yer not stayin there – he's not stayin there

Joe fuckin me who says comes an goes – keep the keys alec – away ya go

Robbie he's been drinkin all day – if he goes over there he'll fuckin . . .

Joe that's where he's goin – over there

Alec over there joe

Joe yer right alec

Alec (*finishes his drink*) listen t'the radio – up early in the mornin joe

Joe put all the lights on alec – see where yer at

Alec all the lights on joe (*Lifts his suitcase.*) right robbie – bill day t'morrow vera – get the bill a lizzy t'morrow – right joe

Joe right alec

Alec exits to street.

Robbie what the fuck you doin t'me

Joe do t'you – fuck all t'do with you

Robbie we talked t'day – i told ya what the fuckin score was – we talked t'day – think about it that's what you said – you were goin t'fuckin think about it

Joe thought about fuck all else

Robbie he's goin t'burn the place t'the groun

Joe that's right – burn the place t'the fuckin groun

Robbie that's right – that's fuckin right – what are ya talkin about – i need that place

Joe the cat's gone robbie – burn the place t'the fuckin groun

Robbie no – no no no – the cat's gone – look joe – joe – yer head's not right – all the gargle an that – yer sayin things there it's all fuckin nonsense – vera tell 'im that's all nonsense – joe ya can't burn a house down because a fuckin cat left – vera say t'im

Vera burn it t'the groun joe yer right

Joe big fire vera

Robbie don't listen t'that joe – she's fuckin – (*To Vera.*)
we're not doin that at the moment right – this is somethin
else

Vera burn the place t'the fuckin groun joe

Robbie go crawl after lover boy

Vera matches – whoof

Robbie it'll be alright joe everythin's soun – yer head's
not straight at the moment – we'll get alec back – it'll be
alright

Joe she's not comin back – ya not understan you stupid
fuck – she's not comin back

Robbie stop talkin like that – it's a fuckin cat that's all it
is a fuckin cat

Joe ruby – ruby's not comin back

Vera hear that robbie – hear what the man's sayin about
his wife

Robbie shut up – i'll go over an get alec – he can stay
here – no harm done if he's here

Vera not comin back robbie

Robbie what the fuck are you doin

Joe (*standing over Robbie*) doin – what am a fuckin doin
– burn the place t'the fuckin groun – that's what am doin

Robbie that it

Joe yes – that's it

Robbie been waitin all this time – sittin there waitin –
the right moment – just pick the right moment

Joe no – bigger than that – has t'be done – right thing t'do – can't go home – has t'be fuckin done – somethin has t'be done

Starts to exit.

Vera over t'watch the flames joe

Joe no

Vera where you goin then

Joe don't know

Robbie that door's getting shut – am closin up

Joe doesn't matter – not comin back

Joe exits to the street.

Vera i'm not stayin here robbie

Robbie no

Vera am tired – am goin t'bed – days are too long in this place

Robbie aye

Vera you goin t'lock up

Robbie i'll lock up – will a leave the front door open for 'im

Vera no (*Gives Robbie the hotel keys.*) come up t'bed

Vera exits to hotel. Robbie finishes his drink. He walks behind the bar and pours himself a drink. Before sitting at the counter he closes the shutters. He watches the television.

Robbie fuck

Robbie switches the television off. He lifts his drink then sets it down without taking any. He walks to the

front door and locks it. He walks back to the bar and downs his drink. He turns the lights off and exits to the hotel, locking the door behind him.

SCENES FROM THE BIG PICTURE

Scenes from the Big Picture was first performed in the
Cottesloe auditorium of the National Theatre, London, on
10 April 2003. The cast, in order of speaking, was as follows:

Bop Torbett Darren Healy
Maggie Lyttle Elaine Cassidy
Maeve Hynes Aoife McMahon
Joe Hynes Patrick O'Kane
Sammy Lennon John Normington
Connie Dean Kathy Kiera Clarke
Betty Lennon June Watson
Theresa Black Frances Tomelty
Dave Black Dermot Crowley
Frank Coin Harry Towb
Robbie Mullin Chris Corrigan
Shanks O'Neill Karl Johnson
Bobbie Torbett Ron Donachie
Sharon Lawther Eileen Pollock
Helen Woods Michelle Fairley
Paul Foggarty Ruairi Conaghan
Cooper Jones Gerard Jordan
Swiz Murdoch Packy Lee
Harry Foggarty Stuart McQuarrie
Spilo Johnston Breffni McKenna
Rat Joyce Andy Moore

Director Peter Gill
Designer Alison Chitty
Lighting Designer Hartley T.A. Kemp
Sound Score Terry Davies and Rich Walsh
Company Voice Work Patsy Rodenburg
Dialect Coach Majella Hurley

Characters

Bop Torbett
late teens

Maggie Lyttle
mid-teens

Maeve Hynes
late twenties

Joe Hynes
mid-thirties

Sammy Lennon
early seventies

Connie Dean
mid-twenties

Betty Lennon
late sixties

Theresa Black
mid-fifties

Dave Black
mid-fifties

Frank Coin
mid-seventies

Robbie Mullin
mid-thirties

Shanks O'Neill
early fifties

Bobbie Torbett
early fifties

Sharon Lawther
late forties

Helen Woods
late twenties

Paul Foggarty
early thirties

Cooper Jones
early twenties

Swiz Murdock
early twenties

Harry Foggarty
mid-thirties

Spilo Johnston
early thirties

Rat Joyce
mid-twenties

The play takes place over the course of a hot summer's day in an imagined area of present-day Belfast.

ACT ONE, SCENE ONE
The night before

ACT ONE, SCENES TWO TO TWELVE
The beginning of the day

ACT TWO
The middle of the day

ACT THREE
The end of the day

Whenever phone coversations are taking place
the person making the call walks into the scene of the
person receiving the call. The characters should speak
directly to each other even though they are on the phone.

There is a constant hum of the city in the air.

Act One

The beginning of day.
    The stage is filled with noise. A baby crying. A busy road. Loud music. Church bells ringing. Heavy machinery. Police sirens. Gun shots. People arguing. Screaming. The noise dies.

ONE

The street. The middle of the night. Cooper and Swiz are breaking into the shop. Maggie and Bop are keeping dick.

Bop Torbett this is dankers – mon we'll shift

Maggie Lyttle a told cooper i'd wait – he'll gurn if a don't

Bop Torbett they're just in there for the want of somethin to do it is

Maggie Lyttle stop brickin it

Bop Torbett everything's hassle – that fight at the club tonight – there'll be trouble about that – the druggie guy's a balloon

Maggie Lyttle a saw him an swiz's brother rantin in each other's faces

Bop Torbett swiz's brother's a bloodnut – think a might give it a miss from now on

Maggie Lyttle see the guy with his head lyin open –
blood all over the place

Bop Torbett nah i was in the thick of it with cooper an
swiz tryin to sort things out

Maggie Lyttle were ya

Bop Torbett yeah – a was

Maggie Lyttle too many headbins there – a don't want to
go back to school thinkin i've spent the whole summer
with them

Bop Torbett school – loose that lot a guff

Maggie Lyttle no bop that's right – i'll do what you do –
nothin

Bop Torbett not nothin – i don't do nothin

Maggie Lyttle nothin multiplied by itself ya do

Bop Torbett gonna get a job in the meat plant – bop the
meat man – that's not nothin

Maggie Lyttle shootin cows an cuttin the throats a pigs
all day long – what would ya want that for

Bop Torbett do alright – get some spondulix maggie
y'know

Maggie Lyttle couldn't picture myself doing somethin
forever

Bop Torbett forever what – end up like my da – worked
there an now has nothin – it's a starter that's all

Maggie Lyttle look – look – ya see that – look

Bop Torbett what – someone comin

Maggie Lyttle up in the sky ya tool – a shootin star or
somethin it was

Bop Torbett where

Maggie Lyttle it's away now – ya ever just look up at the stars

Bop Torbett nah

Maggie Lyttle i sit in the yard sometimes an look up at the sky – you should do that

Bop Torbett why

Maggie Lyttle why do ya need a reason – ya should do it that's all

Bop Torbett aye

Maggie Lyttle ya should

Bop Torbett must make a note of that – look up at the stars at night

Maggie Lyttle don't be an arse meat boy

Bop Torbett don't be sayin meat boy to them a don't want them slabberin

Maggie Lyttle you worry too much bop – mon me an you'll do somethin tomorrow

Bop Torbett like what

Maggie Lyttle like anythin – something different – get away out a here for a day

Bop Torbett away out a here where

Maggie Lyttle somewhere – we'll go swimmin up by the river other side of the park

Bop Torbett can't swim

Maggie Lyttle bop can't swim – who'd a thought

She kisses him.

Bop Torbett what ya do that for

Maggie Lyttle cause you can't swim – why ya not like it

Bop Torbett a did – just want to know why

Maggie Lyttle cause a like ya – you're a sweetie that can't swim

Bop Torbett what about cooper

Maggie Lyttle what about him – is he here – a told ya stop brickin yerself all the time – ya want to go swimmin with me or not

Bop Torbett do ya not have to be able to swim in order to go swimmin

Maggie Lyttle i'll teach ya – i'm a fish – i'll teach ya to be a fish – a fish an a meat boy

Bop Torbett swimmin in a river – aye dead on

Maggie Lyttle ya can watch me then

Bop Torbett what about cooper

Maggie Lyttle shut up

Bop Torbett he'll give me grief

Maggie Lyttle i think ya should go – ya might enjoy it

Bop Torbett aye alright but i'm not gettin in

Maggie Lyttle i'll teach ya to be a fish

Bop Torbett why do ya want me to go

Maggie Lyttle shut up – don't ask questions all the time

Bop Torbett i'll shut up then

Breaking glass in the shop.

what the fuck was that – am not stayin here – leave them two – i'll walk ya home – mon

Maggie Lyttle i'm waitin on cooper a told ya that

Bop Torbett am goin well

Maggie Lyttle away ya go then

TWO

*A house. The kitchen. Joe is sitting at a table having a
cup of tea. Maeve is at the counter making his lunch.*

Maeve Hynes cheese do ya – there is nothin else anyway
has to be cheese – too much meat bad for ya

Joe Hynes a thought we only had cheese

Maeve Hynes we do – need to keep you healthy – virile

Joe Hynes aye cheese – not get time to eat it anyway

Maeve Hynes why am a makin it then

Joe Hynes i'm only sayin a mightn't

Maeve Hynes shouldn't be workin without eatin

Joe Hynes a won't

Maeve Hynes not good for ya

Joe Hynes a just said a won't – be meetins all day instead
a graftin – listenin to the same shit an then havin to
report the whole bloody thing

Maeve Hynes a told ya not to take it on it's a thankless
bloody task

Joe Hynes none a the rest would do it

Maeve Hynes the have more sense that's why

Joe Hynes the asked me – that means somethin

Maeve Hynes the asked ya because the didn't want it – an you fell for it – shopsteward – somethin happens you'll be the first to go

Joe Hynes ya goin up to the hospital again today

Maeve Hynes ya know i am

Joe Hynes ya should go back to work – they'll not hold the job open forever

Maeve Hynes a know – i'll go back – just not right now that's all – julie needs me at the moment – that's important – she has no one – ya know that joe

Joe Hynes yes maeve i understand she has no one – it's just

Maeve Hynes it's just what

Joe Hynes you know what

Maeve Hynes a don't know what tell me – a cousin a mine's havin a baby – might even be today – she has no one – i'm there – so – tell me

Joe Hynes the timin of it – that's all – the timin of the whole situation doesn't seem spot on does it

Maeve Hynes what situation – if ya think i'm goin crazy joe just say it

Joe Hynes stop talkin like that maeve – that's not what a mean an ya know it

Maeve Hynes it feels like that to me

Joe Hynes alright – for whatever reasons and nobody's quite sure about that yet

Maeve Hynes no they're not

Joe Hynes for whatever reasons the doctor tells ya it's unlikely yer gonna be able to have kids

Maeve Hynes a know that – don't tell me things a know

Joe Hynes don't go into one here again

Maeve Hynes just tell me why i'm goin crazy joe

Joe Hynes stop sayin that – the tell ya that right – next thing some kid cousin a yers – who ya didn't give a monkey's about beforehand – had problems with her pregnancy an she's fired into hospital – now yer up there everyday

Maeve Hynes an what are ya sayin

Joe Hynes that's what i'm sayin – it mightn't be good for ya to be hangin around there all the time – that's all i'm sayin

Maeve Hynes she's a kid – she's havin a baby – i'm lookin out for her – that's all – why can't you see that as a good thing

Joe Hynes yer right – it's a good thing yer right – i'm wrong – forget i even fuckin spoke about it – do whatever ya have to do

Maeve Hynes a will – this about us – this is about us isn't it

Joe Hynes it's not about us maeve

Maeve Hynes it is isn't it

Joe Hynes no

Maeve Hynes whenever we were told that news i think you were glad

Joe Hynes how was a glad

Maeve Hynes glad we mightn't have kids

Joe Hynes what the fuck would a be glad about that for

Maeve Hynes why don't you talk to me about what the doctor says then – there's various treatments we could go for – you don't want to talk about that

Joe Hynes i don't have to – you never stop talking about it

Maeve Hynes you don't talk about it though

Joe Hynes maeve i've to go to work soon – i'm paid to hump meat but when a go in today i'm goin to get grief – so not now – none of this now

Maeve Hynes ya don't want it to happen – i know ya don't

Joe Hynes this has to do with money – that's what this is all about – money

Maeve Hynes forget about it – a don't want to talk about it now – go on to work – go hump meat

Joe Hynes nothing's secure – we can't make plans

Maeve Hynes that's what you say it is that's what it is

Joe Hynes that is what it is

Maeve Hynes leave it then

Joe Hynes right

Maeve Hynes ya want one round or two

Joe Hynes one'll do – no two – no fegs today i'll probably eat more

Maeve Hynes you stickin to it

Joe Hynes that's what we agreed isn't it

Maeve Hynes you'll be better off for it

Joe Hynes increase the sperm count

THREE

The shop. Sammy is sweeping up glass.

Sammy Lennon bastards – no good bloody reason – destruction that's all it is

Connie Dean enters. She is nervey.

watch yer feet on that glass there – see what they're doin to me – smash the bloody place up – no good reason y'know – full a drugs – wouldn't have happened years ago – destruction that's all it is – is there somethin yer lookin for dear

Connie Dean a don't know

Sammy Lennon ya don't know what it is yer lookin for

Connie Dean chocolate an nuts that's what a want ya do that

Sammy Lennon for cookin ya mean

Connie Dean no – sweets – a bar of chocolate an nuts – a big bar of chocolate with nuts in it – two big bars

Sammy Lennon you alright

Connie Dean three a them – three big bars – do ya have that do ya

Sammy Lennon it's there in front a ya

Connie Dean there's only two here

Sammy Lennon that's all there is – waitin on an order comin in

Connie Dean two'll do

Sammy Lennon five thirty eight dear

233

Connie Dean money yeah (*Hands him money.*) thank you

Sammy Lennon (*at till*) clear all the bloody glass up (*Connie exits.*) new windows an that – (*Turns.*) yer change – here – what the hell is up with people

Goes back to sweeping. Betty enters with two cups of tea.

what's wrong with this place – she just walked out without her change – people can hardly talk ya know that

Betty Lennon here drink yer tea

Sammy Lennon bet ya she was on bloody drugs too – this time a day – meant to be startin yer day's work not takin bloody drugs

Betty Lennon just drink yer tea sammy

Sammy Lennon aye drink my tea – look at the bloody glass everywhere

Betty Lennon we'll clear it up

Sammy Lennon aye – clear it up – sell the bloody place – we're gettin too old for this game betty dear

Betty Lennon who'd a thought i'd end up stuck with an old man

Sammy Lennon only three years of a difference

Betty Lennon five years – not three – five

Sammy Lennon i thought it was three

Betty Lennon no ya didn't – you know fine rightly

Sammy Lennon ya should've stayed in bed – get a bit more rest

Betty Lennon don't fuss sammy

Sammy Lennon i'm not fussin – a bit a rest that's all

Betty Lennon a slept well enough

Sammy Lennon there's nothin to worry about

Betty Lennon a know that

Sammy Lennon it's only a check up – the hospital said it's only a check up didn't the

Betty Lennon don't fuss

Sammy Lennon that's what the said though isn't it

Betty Lennon yes sammy that's what the said – it's fine

Sammy Lennon do you want me to go with ya

Betty Lennon no – no a don't – fussin round me – there's an order this afternoon you can't close the shop up

Sammy Lennon get a taxi

Betty Lennon i'll get a taxi

Sammy Lennon a don't like ya in taxis

Betty Lennon sammy stop it – it's fine – did ya phone the police yet

Sammy Lennon what bloody good did it do the last time – and the time before that – i've had enough – why don't we sell the damn place

Betty Lennon that doesn't stop us phonin the police

Sammy Lennon a don't want them involved – keep comin back here askin the same damn questions – makes me feel like a fool – a fool that can't look after his own business

Betty Lennon people don't think like that sammy

Betty Lennon protect ourselves that's what we're goin to be doin

Betty Lennon how are we goin to do that

Sammy Lennon beat the hell out a them that's what i'd like to do

Betty Lennon now you do sound like a fool

Sammy Lennon we'll get an alarm system – there's a bit of money put aside – get one that electrocutes them

> *Doorbell rings.*

(*To customer.*) watch the glass there – what can a do for ya

FOUR

A house. The living room. Theresa is putting make-up on to go out. She is dressed in black for a funeral. Dave has spent the night in the armchair.

Theresa Black sleepin in that armchair put yer back out

Dave Black a didn't sleep – tried a few a them tablets a yers – useless

Theresa Black you have to want to sleep for them to work – ya had any breakfast yet

Dave Black sort somethin out later

Theresa Black this look alright

Dave Black it's fine

Dave Black not too tight

Dave Black fine – over the top for the meat plant like

Theresa Black i've to go to a funeral

Dave Black a funeral

Theresa Black yeah a know

Dave Black anybody we know

Theresa Black some guy used to work there – before my time

Dave Black a funeral – today

Theresa Black masters is away i've to go on his behalf – better nip into the office before a go to the church see if he's left me any messages – leaves everything to the last minute then i've to sort it all out

Dave Black the amount of time ya spend there i'm sure it's under control

Theresa Black don't start

Dave Black i'm not – i'm just tired

Theresa Black you should've slept

Dave Black a couldn't – you did though

Theresa Black a thought ya weren't goin to start

Dave Black i'm not

Theresa Black i've had sleepless nights

Dave Black a know – i'm sorry – the abattoir closin for the day

Theresa Black more chance of me goin out with no make up on

Dave Black he doesn't like losin money that boy

Theresa Black he's down the south chasin business – if he doesn't get this contract i don't know what's goin to happen – i've to deal with it all too – not knowin what's goin to happen – it shouldn't be my job dealin with that

Dave Black tell him that

Theresa Black he'd only start up about how pushed he is tryin to keep the whole thing goin

Dave Black you don't owe him anythin – a day's work for a day's pay

Theresa Black i know that

Dave Black no control over anythin – that's what's wrong with us – no control – does the rest a them know what's happenin

Theresa Black he won't let me tell

Dave Black don't lie for him theresa

Theresa Black i'm not – a wouldn't

Dave Black none of it's worth it – none of it's worth a fuck

Theresa Black we have to work dave our situation doesn't change that

Dave Black our situation changes everything

Theresa Black why don't ya get ready for work

Dave Black i'm not goin to work

Theresa Black what about the job yer on

Dave Black fixin a few tiles on some woman's roof – what – i'm puttin things into perspective here – my boy's lyin in the cold earth somewhere – he's been lyin there for fifteen years – it's time we found him

Theresa Black our boy – not yers – ours

Dave Black yes – our boy

Theresa Black they're lookin dave – they've been lookin for months – they've ripped the countryside up – what more is there to do

Dave Black and today's the day they're goin to stop – i think we should be doin something – makin them not stop – not stop until the find him an we can be allowed to bury him – bury him so the fuckers that shot him don't have the last say

Theresa Black if the haven't found thomas by now dave the won't

Dave Black the will if the don't stop – i'm not lettin this be the last day

Theresa Black go to work

Dave Black no – somethin has to be done

Theresa Black what

Dave Black a don't know – it's funny yer dressed for someone's funeral and the one thing we want is a funeral of our own

Theresa Black it's not funny

Dave Black i think it is

Theresa Black i'll pick up somethin to eat on the way to work

Dave Black it's alright – it is – it's alright

Teresa Black (*kisses him*) a know that

Dave Black i'll phone ya

Theresa Black i'll be busy

Dave Black i'll phone ya any way

Theresa Black why don't you go an get dressed

Dave Black a will – i will

FIVE

A house. Frank Coin is tying his shoe laces. The radio is on.

Radio and the political talks continue although all parties involved have agreed they have reached an impasse – and finally – on the business front the euro has again dropped against the pound and the dollar

Frank turns the radio off.

Frank Coin another day ahead of us elsie – go out here and stretch my legs

SIX

A flat. Connie is looking out the window. Robbie is counting pills and putting them in plastic bags.

Robbie Mullin we need more bags – did i not ask you to check this

Connie Dean no – the sun's shinin – fills the street with colour it does

Robbie Mullin a did ask ya didn't a

Connie Dean no robbie ya didn't – you want me to go out an get some

Robbie Mullin i'll get them later

Connie Dean can we go somewhere today – a drive or somethin

Robbie Mullin no

Connie Dean why not

Robbie Mullin stop talkin i'm tryin to count these – just keep lookin out the window

Connie Dean there's no one there – a want to have a bath

Robbie Mullin stand there

Connie Dean there's no one there

Robbie Mullin shut up

Silence. Robbie counts.

you looked well last night – did a tell ya that

Connie Dean no

Robbie Mullin well ya did – a like it when ya look well

Connie Dean can a have my bath then

Robbie Mullin no just keep lookin

Connie Dean was last night bad robbie

Robbie Mullin the tried to wire me off an a told them to go fuck themselves – yeah it's bad – fuckin punks the are – more money they're lookin – squarin up to them's always bad – the don't like losin face – it's fucked – we're goin to have to split

Connis Dean leave the flat

Robbie Mullin yeah leave the flat

Connie Dean i like it here

Robbie Mullin the don't like bein fucked over – that means somethin's goin to happen

Connie Dean where we goin to go then

Robbie Mullin what's that matter to you – you've fuck all else place to go

Connie Dean i could live on my own – make my own way

Robbie Mullin some poxy fuckin bedsit whorin for a pill

Connie Dean i'm not a whore – and it wouldn't be a bedsit

Robbie Mullin what would it be – a fuckin palace

Connie Dean there's a man just parked his car across the street

Robbie Mullin (*at window*) where

Connie Dean there across the street

Robbie Mullin nah – never seen him before – too well dressed anyway that guy

He kisses her and feels her breasts then moves away.

this might work out alright

Connie Dean he's away down the street anyway

Robbie Mullin ya can be doin somethin an just get stuck in it – somethin needs to happen – dealin with scumbags – who are the – fuckin nobodies – wee bits here wee bits there – gettin nurses with fuck all to steal gear from the hospital – fuck that

Connie Dean ya know nothin else

Robbie Mullin a don't want to have to deal with lowlife scumbags any more – the fuckers would sell their children for a bag a pills – go up market – expand the business – start dealin with people that has a bit a money about them – and by the way there's plenty a fuckin things i could do – wouldn't suit you anyway if a was to run a fuckin bike shop or somethin would it

Connie Dean i could help out – there's things i could do

Robbie Mullin like what connie

Connie Dean can't think now don't ask me now

Robbie Mullin people who help out aren't fucked out a their heads half the time – make me a nice dinner after a come home from a hard day at the bike shop maybe – look after the kids – at the end a the day sort out the accounts – deal with the vat man

Connie Dean i'm not useless robbie

Robbie Mullin nobody said you were useless – yer just too used to this

Connie Dean why do you talk to me like that – a don't like it

Robbie Mullin i don't like havin to deal with lowlife fuckweeds all the time – ya want somethin to eat

Connie Dean a want a bath

Robbie Mullin what's in the kitchen

Connie Dean bread maybe – there's chocolate there

Robbie Mullin chocolate for breakfast

Connie Dean buy some food when yer gettin the bags

Robbie Mullin chocolate – where'd that come from anyway

Connie Dean i bought it the other day

Robbie Mullin the other day when – were you out

Connie Dean no – the other day it was – you were with me

Robbie Mullin i can't remember that

Connie Dean ya were there

Robbie Mullin don't lie to me

Connie Dean ya were there

Robbie Mullin right – bread – fuck – ya want a cup a tea

Connie Dean no

Robbie Mullin i'll make some anyway – keep lookin out the window

SEVEN

A house. The parlour. Bobbie and Shanks are dressed for a funeral. Shanks is drinking a tin of beer. Sharon and Bop are upstairs.

Shanks O'Neill ya spoken to her this mornin

Bobbie Torbett she hasn't surfaced yet

Shanks O'Neill she kip up there

Bobbie Torbett aye

Shanks O'Neill in yer scratcher

Bobbie Torbett aye – didn't get me eyes shut all night

Shanks O'Neill you an her givin it all that other message

Bobbie Torbett a was on the sofa – not gettin involved in all that caper

Shanks O'Neill a just thought ya might have slipped one in for old time's sake

Bobbie Torbett lyin on that has my back wrecked

Shanks O'Neill she still not bad lookin – she was always alright with the make up on

Bobbie Torbett doesn't matter how she looks i'm not getting involved

Shanks O'Neill an ole ride's an ole ride all the same

Bobbie Torbett she's a rocket

Shanks O'Neill she likes you though

Bobbie Torbett still a rocket

Shanks O'Neill blocked was she

Bobbie Torbett all over the show – cryin – huggin – all that fuckin gear

Shanks O'Neill turfed out

Bobbie Torbett that's what she said

Shanks O'Neill who's she with now

Bobbie Torbett don't know – couldn't make any sense of her

Shanks O'Neill she's weighed in blocked an he's turfed her out

Bobbie Torbett aye

Shanks O'Neill ya should've give her one

Bobbie Torbett a don't want to get involved again

Shanks O'Neill she wouldn't have remembered anything about it – a freebie

Bobbie Torbett what an the wee lad in the next room – fuck that – that's not the point anyway

Shanks O'Neill that her handbag

Bobbie Torbett no it's mine – don't be at that caper

Shanks O'Neill what (*Opens bag.*) a few quid gets ya a starter for the day

Bobbie Torbett yer a tosspot

Shanks O'Neill (*closes bag*) a tosspot with a tenner in his skyrocket – you'll not refuse a pint out of it

Bobbie Torbett you buy a pint – aye

Shanks O'Neill a buy plenty

Bobbie Torbett aye

Shanks O'Neill get a few pints at this funeral

Bobbie Torbett wee foggarty – one old fucker – couldn't bury him deep enough

Shanks O'Neill his sons be at it – they'd be good for a few pints

Bobbie Torbett the don't speak – the sons don't speak

Shanks O'Neill double dunter – pint from one – pint from the other – fuckin sweet

Bobbie Torbett what will a say to yer woman

Shanks O'Neill tell her to follow us round after the funeral

Bobbie Torbett what for

Shanks O'Neill bit of a laugh

Bobbie Torbett fuckin sure am not

Bop enters. He is just out of bed.

Bop Torbett who's up the stairs – couldn't sleep with the snores a them

Shanks O'Neill should be up at the crack a dawn yer age

Bop Torbett drink yer tin

Shanks O'Neill out all hours – chasin it – up some entry with a wee doll

Bobbie Torbett drink yer tin – there's a letter there for ya

Bop Torbett a know a got it – who's up the stairs

Bobbie Torbett member yer woman sharon – good while back it was

Bop Torbett the rocket

Bobbie Torbett aye – she had a bit of a bad night – had to put her head down somewhere that's all

Bop Torbett she's not stayin

Shanks O'Neill unless yer da takes a fancy to her again

Bobbie Torbett you want slapped – no she's not stayin

Bop Torbett she's not sayin

Bobbie Torbett a just said that

Bop Torbett i'm sayin no matter what she's not stayin

Bobbie Torbett never tell me what to do – i say who stays an goes – what was the letter about

Bop Torbett applied for a job down in the abattoir

Shanks O'Neill meat man like yer da

Bobbie Torbett a job down there

Bop Torbett the knocked me back

Bobbie Torbett there's other jobs

Bop Torbett it would've been handy

Shanks O'Neill toughens ya up that type a work – when we're at the funeral bobbie ya could say somethin to somebody

Bobbie Torbett say what

Shanks O'Neill put a good word in for him

Bop Torbett will ya do that

Bobbie Torbett the ones i know mightn't be there

Shanks O'Neill they'll all be there

Bop Torbett will ya ask for me

Bobbie Torbett i'll say somethin

Bop Torbett ya will

Bobbie Torbett aye

Bop Torbett am away back to my bed

Bobbie Torbett back to bed – get up there an get dressed

Shanks O'Neill if he's goin to be humpin meat he needs his rest – the poor child

Bobbie Torbett get yerself dressed

Sharon enters. Bop starts exiting.

Sharon Lawther good mornin – do ya remember me – sharon – it's a while back now – ya must remember me

Bop Torbett aye – ya alright (*He exits.*)

Sharon Lawther the grow up quick don't the – lovely wee lad ya have bobbie – makes me think a wouldn't have minded havin children myself

Bobbie Torbett he's alright – ya know shanks don't ya

Sharon Lawther certainly a do – it's not that long ago we were together bobbie ya know

Bobbie Torbett it's a right while

Sharon Lawther not that long

Shanks O'Neill bobbie was tellin me things weren't the best for ya last night – a bit a bother

Bobbie Torbett sharon we're just headin out to a funeral an that

Shanks O'Neill we've time yet

248

Sharon Lawther the bastard threw me out – havin a few drinks – next thing it's all nasty pills – nasty wee fucker he can be – never hit me like – looked like he might a done last night though – that's why a came round here

Bobbie Torbett it's not a situation a want to get involved with sharon

Sharon Lawther but ya wouldn't let him hit me bobbie

Bobbie Torbett no a wouldn't

Sharon Lawther that's why a came round here bobbie cause a knew you'd look after me

Bobbie Torbett he'll still be there will he

Sharon Lawther might be – don't know – nasty wee bastard – wouldn't get me behavin like that – few drinks alright – there's no harm in that – a bit of a laugh

Shanks O'Neill that's all we're at isn't it sharon – a few gargles an a wee bit of a laugh

Sharon Lawther that's right shanks – no harm in it

Bobbie Torbett ya goin round to see him then – get it sorted out

Sharon Lawther a don't want to be speakin with him

Shanks O'Neill just right – the dirty fucker

Bobbie Torbett aye a know dirty fucker – but ya have to sort it out ya understand that

Sharon Lawther wantin rid a me already

Bobbie Torbett we've to go to this funeral ya see – that's what am sayin

Sharon Lawther sure you go on – don't be worryin about me – i'll have a cup a tea – straighten myself out a bit then i'll go round to him – tell him if he ever pulls that stunt again me an him's finished – you go on i'll be alright

Bobbie Torbett you'll lock up

Sharon Lawther a know my way around bobbie – i'll have a cup of tea an i'll lock up – don't be worryin about me – where will yas be after the funeral – just in case somethin happens with him – where will yas be

Bobbie Torbett ya wouldn't know where we'll end up after this sharon

Sharon Lawther if needs be i'll maybe look for yas then

Bobbie Torbett i'm tellin ya anywhere it could be – we right – i'll get my jacket on (*He exits.*)

Shanks O'Neill you'll be alright

Sharon Lawther he loves me – he threw me out but he loves me

Shanks O'Neill wouldn't doubt it for a minute – i'd say after this funeral we'll end up in the tavern – if yer stuck that's where we'll be

Sharon Lawther it'll be alright – bobbie look after me

Shanks O'Neill course he will – we both will

Bobbie enters.

Bobbie Torbett ya right

Shanks O'Neill aye

Bobbie Torbett ya goin round to see him then

Sharon Lawther yes

Bobbie Torbett good

EIGHT

The shop. Helen enters.

Sammy Lennon the broke in again the did – wasters – didn't see anything on the way home did ya

Helen Woods no – wasn't much happenin a shut up early

Sammy Lennon aye – twenty regal is it

Helen Woods twenty regal – a should stop shouldn't a

Sammy Lennon i've these patches here – they're good – take the edge of it

Helen Woods need the willpower as well that's the problem

Sammy Lennon if a could sell willpower we'd be sailin

Helen Woods do you have any lighters

Sammy Lennon a do – no patches but a lighter – yer movin in the wrong direction

Helen Woods it's a present for someone

Sammy Lennon not one a them cheap ones then – man or woman is it for

Helen Woods a man

Sammy Lennon boyfriend is it

Helen Woods a friend – a boyfriend yeah

Sammy Lennon is he as good lookin as me

Helen Woods no chance

Maeve enters.

Sammy Lennon big smoker is he

Helen Woods it's the only hobby the two of us have

Sammy Lennon zippo – zippos are the best – the cost
a few quid more but the last ya a lifetime – if ya fall out
with him ya can ask for it back (*To Maeve.*) i'll get betty
down now

Maeve Hynes it's okay i'll wait (*To Helen.*) hello – lovely
day

Helen Woods it is

Sammy Lennon (*shouts*) – a customer – the zippos are
over here

   He and Helen move down the counter.

there's ones there with football teams on them – that
one's to do with bikes – is he into that type a thing – i'm
not myself but a know people are

Helen Woods more of a plain one

   Bettty enters. Helen and Sammy look at lighters.

Betty Lennon sorry – those stairs seem to be gettin
steeper every time a come down them – what can a do for
ya

Maeve Hynes nappies – my cousin's havin a baby –
today maybe – thought i'd bring her up some nappies

Betty Lennon a new baby – that's lovely – does she know
what it is

Maeve Hynes no – she wanted the surprise – the hospital
told her to bring nappies up – you'd think that would be
the one thing there'd be plenty of wouldn't ya

Betty Lennon you'd wonder where the money goes – just
over here

   Joe is in the abattoir. He makes a call on his mobile.

Helen's phone rings. Joe walks into the scene. Helen answers her phone.

Sammy Lennon you work away there i'm not goin anywhere – maybe it's him – the lighter man

Helen Woods hello

Joe Hynes well how's it goin

Helen Woods it's you

Joe Hynes you expectin someone else

Helen Woods no

Joe Hynes where are ya

Helen Woods on my way to work – just called into the shop – where are you

Joe Hynes work – fuckin pain – rest a them's cleanin up – just thought i'd give ya a bell

Betty Lennon these are the best a think

Maeve Hynes they'll do then – a was thinkin of some cream as well – you know the way sometimes the get a rash

Betty Lennon suda cream

Joe Hynes you alright

Helen Woods yeah

Joe Hynes what's wrong

Maeve Hynes there was this baby in the ward yesterday – the size of it – tiny wee hands

Sammy Lennon all grow up into hoods no matter what size the start off

Joe Hynes can ya not speak

Helen Woods not really no

Joe Hynes someone there

Helen Woods that would be right

Maeve Hynes the have dolls the mothers practise on you'd swear the were real – cry an everything the do

Joe Hynes who – who's there

Helen Woods you'd know them alright

Betty Lennon a big tub or a small one

Maeve Hynes a big one – no point in savin pennies for things like that

Joe Hynes maeve

Helen Woods yes

Joe Hynes fuck yer jokin – were ya talkin to her

Helen Woods said hello

Joe Hynes fuck – give me grief this mornin she did – crazy bitch – babies again

Helen Woods that's very interesting

Sammy Lennon (*to Betty*) is the baby place up near where yer goin – (*To Maeve.*) goin for an appointment today she is

Betty Lennon it's the other side a the buildin

Joe Hynes what's she at

Maeve Hynes what's the name of the buildin

Betty Lennon a can't remember – it's just a check up – the older ya get the more the want to check up

Helen Woods can't really say

Joe Hynes ya want to talk later – i've to go to the office anyway – find out what's happenin here

Helen Woods yes

Joe Hynes right

Joe exits. Helen moves back to counter.

Sammy Lennon take yer time lookin dear there's no hurry – (*To Maeve.*) if yer leavin it until the afternoon you an betty could go up together – a don't like her goin up on her own an she won't let me close the shop

Maeve Hynes a said i'd be up there early just in case – in case she goes

Betty Lennon don't be listenin to him – i'll go up on my own – i've told him not to fuss

Maeve Hynes any other day

Betty Lennon of course

Sammy Lennon anythin needed for babies we have it here – no need to be lookin elsewhere

Frank Coin enters and waits to be served.

Helen Woods this one here a think

Sammy Lennon yer boyfriend will like that one – good plain solid lighter – you and him hardly be at the baby stage yet

Betty Lennon sammy

Sammy Lennon i'm only talkin – (*To Helen.*) i'm only talkin dear

Helen Woods that's alright – no we're not at that stage yet

Maeve Hynes until the baby actually arrives a don't think men have much interest in all a that

Helen Woods no probably not

Maeve Hynes when the have them in their arms it's a different matter

Helen Woods how much is that

Sammy Lennon sixteen an the cigarettes – four sixty-twenty sixty please – he'll not need to be buyin another lighter for the rest of his days

Betty Lennon (*to Maeve*) that'll be six forty an two thirty – eight seventy altogether

Helen Woods better be off to my work

Sammy Lennon there's nothin else for it dear

Helen Woods (*exiting – to Frank*) ya weren't about last night – we all thought the world had stopped

Frank Coin didn't a fall asleep in front of the fire – lookin forward to a pint a was too

Helen Woods i'll keep ya one this evenin

Frank Coin my name's on it

Helen exits.

Sammy Lennon (*to Maeve*) nice girl that – runs the pub down the way – whatever man she ends up with be lucky to get her (*To Frank.*) the usual – a pint a milk and a few slices of chicken

Frank Coin that be right

Maeve Hynes i'll go on – hopefully haven't missed the big event

Betty Lennon i'm sure she'll wait

Maeve Hynes she's waited this long

Betty Lennon that's right

Maeve exits.

Sammy Lennon two or three slices is it

Frank Coin two

Betty Lennon (*to Sammy*) don't be sayin to people about takin me anywhere

Sammy Lennon a don't like ya goin up there on yer own that's all

Betty Lennon stop bloody fussin (*To Frank.*) how's things today

Frank Coin good enough – sure one day much the same as the rest

Betty Lennon that's right and the truer it gets the older you are

NINE

The abattoir. Theresa's office. She is on the phone.

Theresa Black i understand mr masters is at a meeting and can't be disturbed – what i'm tellin you is he has to be disturbed – yes a know only too well that you're just doin what you've been told – but a need to – right – right – if he comes out for any reason at all – tell him to phone theresa – it's very important – he has to phone me – right thank you (*Phone down.*) dosey bitch

Joe enters.

yes joe

Joe Hynes what's the score here

Theresa Black i'm tryin to get in contact with him – he's at a meetin

Joe Hynes ya haven't spoken to him

Theresa Black he left a message on the machine for me this mornin an all it said was – i'm waitin on the euro

Joe Hynes the train

Theresa Black the currency

Joe Hynes what does that mean waitin on the euro – i'm not goin back down to tell them we're waitin on the fuckin euro

Theresa Black that's all a know

Joe Hynes phone him

Theresa Black i've left three messages for him

Joe Hynes waitin on the euro

Theresa Black the rate of it

Joe Hynes i know

Theresa Black good rate get the best price

Joe Hynes what happens if the rate's not good

Theresa Black i know as much as you do

Joe Hynes a have to say somethin to them

> *Dave on a busy street. Makes a call on his mobile. Theresa's phone rings. Dave walks into the scene.*

Theresa Black sorry joe – yes – what – i'm busy

Dave Black i'm on my way to the bbc

Theresa Black what bbc – did ya not go to work

Dave Black i'm on my way to the bbc

Theresa Black what for

Dave Black i'm goin on the radio

Theresa Black the radio

Dave Black aye

Theresa Black the get in contact with ya

Dave Black no

Theresa Black i don't understand – i'm in the middle a somethin here dave

Dave Black so am i – i'm in the middle a somethin to – i'm goin round to get on the radio

Theresa Black arrive an demand to go on

Dave Black that's right – there's people on the radio all the time – no reason why i shouldn't be – bring it out in the open – put pressure on them – that's the right way to do it isn't it – isn't it

Theresa Black the just don't let people do that

Dave Black won't know until a try – i'm phonin to say that's what i'm doin – just in case ya hear me

Theresa Black i'll hardly have time

Dave Black aye whatever – i'll phone ya later

Theresa Black right

Dave exits.

Joe Hynes what am a goin to say down here

Theresa Black what are ya goin to tell them

Joe Hynes aye what am a goin to tell them – the know there's a container at the dock – the want to know why they're standin around then

Theresa Black you know as much as i do

Joe Hynes there's no problem with gettin paid is there

Theresa Black there'll be wages at the end a the day

Joe Hynes what am a goin to tell them

Theresa Black tell them – tell them – tell them the meat's to be inspected at the dock – that's why we can't unload it yet

Joe Hynes an what about somethin to do

Theresa Black get them to clean the yard

Joe Hynes we've done that

Theresa Black tell them there's an inspection of the yard as well – get them to do it again

Joe Hynes inspection – they're not fuckin stupid ya know

Theresa Black it's the only thing i can think of

Joe Hynes this isn't on

Theresa Black no

Joe Hynes it's not – somethin has to be sorted out

Theresa Black a know – it's not up to me but i'm tryin – you can see that can't ya – go an tell them about the inspection

Joe Hynes when will ya know the full story

Theresa Black you'll know when i know

TEN

The pub. Bobbie and Shanks are at the bar. Helen is serving them.

Shanks O'Neill first of the day

Bobbie Torbett weren't ya garglin in the house

Shanks O'Neill first a the day in here

Bobbie Torbett square the woman up there

Shanks O'Neill oh aye – alright now – a pint in front a ya – tosspot was it

Bobbie Torbett square her up

Shanks pays for the drinks.

Helen Woods was there many at it

Shanks O'Neill not as big a crowd as you'd like if ya were dead yerself

Bobbie Torbett there's been bigger alright – not surprisin miserable fucker he was

Helen Woods did the mention about comin back here

Bobbie Torbett you'll not be rushed off yer feet

Shanks O'Neill see the sons weren't talkin still

Bobbie Torbett no

Shanks O'Neill you'd think with a funeral an that

Helen Woods maybe sort out some sandwiches for them

Shanks O'Neill aye helen make a few sandwiches – forgot to eat yesterday

Bobbie Torbett forgot fuck all – told ya to go home an eat – wouldn't hear of it – food's only for wankers apparently

Shanks O'Neill when i've a drink in me a go a bit deaf in both my ears

Bobbie Torbett not too deaf when yer asked what ya want to gargle

Shanks O'Neill it's only certain words a can't hear

Helen Woods home

Shanks O'Neill what

Helen Woods i'll go in here an see if there's anythin for sandwiches just in case

Shanks O'Neill smoked salmon be nice

Helen Woods aye – any punters come in give us a shout

Bobbie Torbett will do

Helen exits.

nice wee girl that

Shanks O'Neill too young for you – do me though

Bobbie Torbett i'm just sayin

Shanks O'Neill she does a line with yer man

Bobbie Torbett who

Shanks O'Neill guy works at the plant – married like – don't know his name – in here now an again – always on the phone

Bobbie Torbett him

Shanks O'Neill aye him

Bobbie Torbett fuck yer woman callin round last night – she starts thinkin like that she'll end up callin round everytime the two a them give each other a dirty look

Shanks O'Neill she'll not

Bop Torbett not be back today anyway

Shanks O'Neill no

Bobbie Torbett not know where we are – don't want her spoilin a good drink

Shanks O'Neill no – what do ya call masters' secretary

Bobbie Torbett theresa – she's a right woman now

Shanks O'Neill she was there

Bobbie Torbett saw her – always liked her – losin the son didn't do her any favours

Shanks O'Neill ya should've been over at her sayin about the wee lad an the job – she'd be the one to talk to

Bobbie Torbett say nothin about the meat plant when he's about

Shanks O'Neill ya not want him workin

Bobbie Torbett a don't want him workin in that fuckin kip

Shanks O'Neill carryin the meat never did me any harm

Bobbie Torbett carryin what meat – not a day's work in ya

Shanks O'Neill i worked there with the best a them a did

Bobbie Torbett aye

Shanks O'Neill no aye about it

Bobbie Torbett aye – you just keep thinkin that – he's not endin up like i did – back wrecked an not even a fuckin thank you for it – so say fuck all

Shanks O'Neill aye

Bobbie Torbett i'm tellin ya

Shanks O'Neill a heard – i'm not fuckin deaf

Bobbie Torbett right

Silence. Helen enters.

Helen Woods no smoked salmon – a bit a ham an chicken – it'll have to do

Bobbie Torbett do them rightly

Helen Woods ya like to have somethin at these things – doesn't look good if there's nothin

Paul enters.

Shanks O'Neill here we go

Bobbie Torbett what do ya call him

Shanks O'Neill harry

Bobbie Torbett sure

Shanks O'Neill aye

Bobbie Torbett harry sorry for yer troubles

Paul Fogarty paul – my name's paul – i've a brother harry

Bobbie Torbett paul – of course – sorry for yer troubles anyway

Shanks O'Neill aye paul sorry for yer troubles an that

Paul Fogarty aye bad day – you want a pint or are you alright

Shanks O'Neill go another pint

Bobbie Torbett we'll have a drink for yer da – great man he was – knew him well

Paul Fogarty (*to Helen*) three pints there

Helen Woods a wasn't sure whether to put some sandwiches out

Paul Fogarty ya want a few sandwiches

Shanks O'Neill a couple a sandwiches do rightly paul

Bobbie Torbett aye

Paul Fogarty do enough for the three a us – more if ya want some yerself

Helen Woods i'll get ya the pints then i'll sort the sandwiches out

   After getting the drinks Helen exits.

Paul Fogarty (*to Bobbie*) ya worked with my da then

Bobbie Torbett a did – worked with him for a right few years

Shanks O'Neill a worked with him myself

Bobbie Torbett good worker he was yer da – always said that about him – good worker

Paul Fogarty ya think there'd a been more at the funeral

Bobbie Torbett people's funny fuckers about funerals – makes them think about dyin – the don't like that

Paul Fogarty a thought the abattoir might a closed though

Shanks O'Neill money hungry whores the are paul

Paul Fogarty there was a few there a didn't know – but then a man has a life of his own whether he's yer da or not

Bobbie Torbett that's right – only a knew them in my own right there was ones at my da's funeral a wouldn't've known he knew

Shanks O'Neill aye that's right

Paul Fogarty we'll have a drink to him anyway

   All lift pints.

to big dan god rest him

Shanks O'Neill big dan

Bobbie Torbett big dan

Paul Fogarty i'll nip out here an see – in case any others are about ya know

   Paul exits.

Bobbie Torbett big dan – who the fuck is big dan

Shanks O'Neill what ya mean who the fuck is he – his da – the guy the just fired into the ground

Bobbie Torbett big dan's not his fuckin name

Shanks O'Neill yer tellin me he got his own da's name wrong

Bobbie Torbett i don't know what the fuck he did

Shanks O'Neill he'd know his own da's name bobbie for fuck's sake

Bobbie Torbett no big dan – man a worked with was called john – ya not know him

Shanks O'Neill not really no – maybe the guy ya worked with wasn't him

Bobbie Torbett the man a worked with wasn't him – how the fuck can it not be him – john foggarty ya called the man – that's his son harry

Shanks O'Neill paul

Bobbie Torbett aye whatever – paul – harry – that's his son anyway – an i'll tell ya another thing – he was the size of a fuckin sixpence – nothing big about him

266

Shanks O'Neill maybe it was his brother or somethin

Bobbie Torbett how can the guy a worked with be the brother of the guy a worked with – you lost yer fuckin mind

Shanks O'Neill ya know what a mean – ask him

Bobbie Torbett ask him – i've just been to the guy's da's funeral an a told him a worked with his da for years – an then i'm goin to say by the way what's yer da's name – fuckin wise up

Paul enters.

Shanks O'Neill i'll ask him

Paul Fogarty nah – doesn't look like anyone else comin

Shanks O'Neill paul – yer da

Paul Fogarty aye

Shanks O'Neill john ya called him

Paul Fogarty aye

Shanks O'Neill you said god rest big dan

Paul Fogarty aye right – in the house that's what he liked us callin him – sure he wasn't big either

Bobbie Torbett a knew that – he wasn't a big man at all – the meat he was carryin was bigger

Paul Fogarty big dan god rest him

Shanks O'Neill aye – saw yer brother at the funeral

Paul Fogarty fucker

Shanks O'Neill you an him not get on no

Paul Fogarty haven't spoken this – must be fifteen years – fuckin useless bastard he is

Shanks O'Neill he'll hardly be weighing in then

Paul Fogarty a wouldn't want him near me – sure the three of us is enough

Bobbie Torbett three's plenty

Paul Fogarty knock that into ya we'll have another

Shanks O'Neill that's the game

ELEVEN

The street. Bop and Maggie. She has swimming gear with her.

Maggie Lyttle yer just goin to stand here all day

Bop Torbett don't know

Maggie Lyttle a thought ya wanted to go with me

Bop Torbett a don't feel like it

Maggie Lyttle i'm not goin on my own

Bop Torbett get cooper to go

Maggie Lyttle i didn't ask cooper

Bop Torbett we'll go some other day

Maggie Lyttle are ya goin or not

Bop Torbett no

Maggie Lyttle right

They stand in silence. Cooper and Swiz enter. Cooper has a large plastic bag of sweets.

Cooper Jones the bop fella – and the maggie girl – who wants some sweeties – sweeties for the children – all types a sweeties

Bop Torbett they from last night

Cooper Jones last night was last night today is today

Swiz Murdoch cooper an swiz – the criminals

Maggie Lyttle nothin more than tea leaves

Swiz Murdoch masterminds of the criminal world

Cooper Jones look – born with no fingerprints – maggie baby want some sweets

Maggie Lyttle give us a bar a chocolate

Cooper Jones the bop fella sweeties

Bop Torbett nah a just put one out

Cooper Jones no other takers – fuck that then (*Throws bag away.*)

Bop Torbett (*to Swiz*) ya not at work today

Swiz Murdoch fuck work

Cooper Jones the swizman says fuck work

Swiz Murdoch not for us – too good lookin for that place – aren't a too good lookin for that place maggie

Maggie Lyttle better lookin cattle there

Cooper Jones moo – moo

Swiz Murdoch moo – moo

Cooper Jones the moo people

Swiz Murdoch where'd ya go last night bop

Bop Torbett nowhere

Cooper Jones moo – moo maggie – go moo

Maggie Lyttle take off ya header

Cooper Jones go on

Maggie Lyttle moo – fucking – moo

Swiz Murdoch lapped the show

Maggie Lyttle more sense he has

Cooper Jones the bop fella has more sense – have i no sense dearest

Maggie Lyttle yer just a big lig

Cooper Jones i'm deeply hurt – the woman of my dreams thinks i'm a big lig – an me who just give her chocolate

Swiz Murdoch a don't like it when he runs off

Bop Torbett a didn't run off

Cooper Jones the swiz fella – the man who says fuck work

Swiz Murdoch fuck work

Cooper Jones bop isn't into the hurdy gurdy – stop gettin on his case

Swiz Murdoch lapped the show

Cooper Jones leave him

Swiz Murdoch moo

Cooper Jones (*to Maggie*) what's in the bag – ya goin somewhere

Maggie Lyttle i'm not standin here all day

Cooper Jones waste yer talents standin here all day – a don't think so

Maggie Lyttle a was goin to go swimmin

Cooper Jones the swimmers – the piss in the water there

Maggie Lyttle the river up by the park

Cooper Jones ya want me to go – i'll go

Maggie Lyttle ya want to go swimmin

Cooper Jones in school i used to swim the shit out a the rest a them

Swiz Murdoch moo

Maggie Lyttle you've no gear with ya

Cooper Jones that meant to matter – we'll go now – the water's callin me and when the river calls the trunks get wet

Swiz Murdoch ya be about later sort some gear out

Cooper Jones oh aye – we'll be back later

Maggie Lyttle unless ya plan livin there

Cooper Jones moo

Swiz Murdoch moo

Cooper and Maggie exit. Bop and Swiz stand in silence.

just me an you bop – ya goin anywhere

Bop Torbett nah – you

Swiz Murdoch aye – last night the druggie – my brother wants me to stand outside his flat – nothin major just wants to know the fucker's movements – ya wanna go – be better than standin here

Bop Torbett the guy's a screwball

Swiz Murdoch just standin lookin – don't be lappin the show again bop

Bop Torbett i'm not

Swiz Murdoch get a few fabulets out of it do us for tonight – mon

Bop Torbett aye alright

TWELVE

The flat. Robbie is dressed in a suit. He is getting ready to go out. Connie is restless. She is still at the window.

Connie Dean why can't a go with ya

Robbie Mullin yer not goin you'll get in the way

Connie Dean i'm sick a stayin here on my own

Robbie Mullin i'm not takin all the gear and there's readies in the bedroom as well – that's why yer stayin – stop fuckin hasslin me – not like yer asked to do much is it

Connie Dean what happens if someone comes

Robbie Mullin the won't

Connie Dean i'll be on my own – ya shouldn't leave me on my own robbie

Robbie Mullin a don't want the place empty – that money is all we've got – place is like a fuckin fortress anyway what ya worried about

Connie Dean i'm just worried

Robbie Mullin don't be treatin me like one of those fuckin half wits works down in that meat place – the think it's all right that they get a pile of grief from whatever scrubber they've shacked up with before the leave for work – that's not me an don't ever fuckin think that it's gonna be me – ya got that

Connie Dean i'm only sayin

Robbie Mullin you goin out with me changes the situation – if the situation changes that might make it difficult to get rid a things – what would happen then – tell me

Connie Dean a don't know

Robbie Mullin no ya don't fuckin know – the money in there not goin to do us long – have to fuckin slum it – i'm not doin that – we need more money – that's the only thing these people's interested in – the colour of yer readies – do all the talkin ya want but unless ya have the money to back it up you'll be treated like a joke – doesn't matter what deals or whatever you've pulled off before – means nothing – an that's the right way to do it too

Connie Dean ya goin now

Robbie Mullin soon

Connie Dean i need somethin before ya go

Robbie Mullin there's odds an ends in that drawer – don't be gettin all fucked up

Connie Dean a don't get all fucked up

Robbie Mullin a mean it – ya need yer head about ya

Connie Dean in the drawer over there

Robbie Mullin didn't a just say

Connie Dean ya goin to bring back some food

Robbie Mullin like what

Connie Dean somethin nice

Robbie Mullin somethin nice – aye – pack a few suitcases while i'm out

Connie Dean a don't know what to take

Robbie Mullin whatever the fuck we need

Connie Dean there's two wee lads across the street – just standin there the are

Robbie Mullin (*looks*) don't know them – you know them

Connie Dean a don't go anywhere – if you don't know them i don't know them

Robbie Mullin just kids – have fuck all to do but hang around – wouldn't worry about it – just kids – i'll phone later right

Connie Dean right

Robbie Mullin take it easy – member what a said

Connie Dean you'll phone me

Robbie Mullin get the cases packed – yer the only person i can trust – remember that

> *He kisses her, then lifts his bag and exits. Connie goes straight to the drawer.*

THIRTEEN

The pub. Helen is behind the bar. There are two plates of half eaten sandwiches on the counter. Bobbie, Shanks and Paul are standing at the bar. Bobbie is in the middle of telling a joke.

Bobbie Torbett i've never seen a horse that fast in my life – but tell me this – why'd it run into the oaktree – yer man says – a don't know – it just doesn't give a fuck

> *Laughter except Shanks.*

Shanks O'Neill i don't get that

Bobbie Torbett it just doesn't give a fuck

Shanks O'Neill an what

Bobbie Torbett doesn't matter

Shanks O'Neill it's not funny

Bobbie Torbett aye

> *Harry Fogarty enters. He stands at the other end of the bar.*

Harry Fogarty (*to Helen*) a pint please (*Silence.*) yous boys at the funeral

Bobbie Torbett aye – knew yer da well

Harry Fogarty you want a pint

Shanks O'Neill do rightly

Harry Fogarty (*to Helen*) another three pints

Paul Fogarty (*to Helen*) i don't want one

Harry Fogarty take one

Paul Fogarty (*to Helen*) a don't want one

Harry Fogarty not such a big crowd there

Bobbie Torbett there's ones that has nobody at them

Harry Fogarty except the poor bugger that's dead

Bobbie Torbett funerals wouldn't be the same without them

Harry Fogarty ya knew my da then

Bobbie Torbett aye – a worked with him – carryin the meat

Harry Fogarty hard ole number that

Bobbie Torbett it can be

Paul Fogarty yer not wanted here

Harry Fogarty i'm havin a pint

Paul Fogarty have it some place else

Helen sets drinks up.

Helen Woods there's sandwiches there – a wasn't sure how many – ya want me to make more

Paul Fogarty he's not stayin

Harry Fogarty it's alright luv a drink'll do me (*Raises glass.*) my da

Bobbie Torbett big dan god rest him

Shanks O'Neill to big dan god rest him

Harry Fogarty big dan – a forgot about that (*To Paul.*) not raisin your glass

Paul Fogarty not with you ya fuckin ponce

Harry Fogarty that it – you goin to sort me out are ya – big lad – don't be makin a fool a yerself in front a these people

Paul lunges. Bobbie holds him back.

Paul Fogarty get out to fuck – frightened a you – fuck off

Harry Fogarty let him go

Paul Fogarty fuckin ponce

Bobbie Torbett it's yer da's funeral lads

Paul Fogarty he doesn't give a fuck whose funeral it is

Harry Fogarty a give as much of a fuck as you do

Paul Fogarty ponce

Harry Fogarty i'm warnin ya

Paul Fogarty don't fuckin warn anybody

Bobbie Torbett give it a break here

Helen Woods i don't care whose funeral it was any trouble an ya have to go

Bobbie Torbett there'll be no trouble

Helen Woods take yer drink an eat yer sandwiches

Bobbie Torbett that's right eat the sandwiches

Everything is settled.

Harry Fogarty we need to talk

Bobbie Torbett that's a start

Harry Fogarty i've a letter here

Paul Fogarty want me to read it to ya

Harry Fogarty some man at the funeral give it to me – a didn't know him – it's from my da

Paul Fogarty what he give it to you for

Harry Fogarty don't know – my da wanted us to read it together he said

Paul Fogarty that's not goin to happen

Harry Fogarty it's what my da wanted – i'm goin to sit down over there at that table – you want to sit down with me fine if ya don't it's up to you.

Harry sits at the table.

Bobbie Torbett yer better goin over

Shanks O'Neill that's right

Bobbie Torbett big dan – the man's dead an that's what he wanted – yer always better of doin what dead people want – bad vibes from the grave isn't good

Paul sits at the table.

Harry Fogarty i'm not happy about this either

Paul Fogarty just open the letter harry an read it

Harry Fogarty (*opening letter*) a bigger crowd would've been better

Paul Fogarty people's other things to do

Harry Fogarty aye

Paul Fogarty what's it say

Harry Fogarty read it yerself

Paul Fogarty settle yer differences – that's it – a note that says settle yer differences

Harry Fogarty there's another sheet a paper here

Paul Fogarty what is it

Harry Fogarty his own writing it's in – a list

Paul Fogarty a list a what

Harry Fogarty jesus – a list of everything he owned – look at that – man sat down and wrote everything out that he owned – doesn't look like much does it

Paul Fogarty no – fuck this – we to divide this up then aye

Harry Fogarty ya want to go somewhere else an do this

Paul Fogarty where

Sharon arrives with her suitcase and sets it down beside Bobbie and Shanks.

Act Two

ONE

The middle of the day. The shop. Robbie and Sammy are in mid-conversation. Betty is checking a list of goods that have been delivered.

Sammy Lennon like freezer bags ya mean

Robbie Mullin they'd be too big

Sammy Lennon too big – next down from that would be sandwich bags – (*To Betty.*) did the deliver any sandwich bags

Betty Lennon no – but he has to come back this afternoon

Robbie Mullin i'd really need them now

Sammy Lennon might be some over in the corner there

Betty Lennon that's that checked off – whatever comes in this afternoon sammy you've to check off – you forgot the last time

Sammy Lennon i didn't forget – tryin to pull a flanker on me he was

Betty Lennon just check it off sammy

Sammy Lennon ya see sandwich bags about here

Betty Lennon can't remember seein them – i've done my list so i'm away to organise my taxi

Sammy Lennon aye you do that

Bettty exits.

things are still in a bit of a mess here – i'd a break in last night – everythin messed up – not sure where everythin is

279

Robbie Mullin kids was it

Sammy Lennon aye bloody kids – oven bags – what would they be – no – same size as the freezer bags

Robbie Mullin peelers are never about when ya need them

Sammy Lennon damn the fear of it – didn't phone them – the only thing a have here are kids' party bags – that hardly be of any use to ya

Robbie Mullin let's have a look at them

Sammy Lennon there's twenty in that

Robbie Mullin twenty's plenty – right size – kids' party bags – aye they'll do – security ya need

Sammy Lennon a was thinkin that – an awful price a hear

Robbie Mullin i've a card here – always worth yer while keepin these things – ring them

Sammy Lennon a will – although you'd wonder whether it stops them or not – drugged up to the eyeballs nothin stop them

Robbie Mullin baseball bat is the job

Sammy Lennon now yer talkin – i've an ole club up there a was thinkin of goin up to get it

Robbie Mullin split a few nappers open

Sammy Lennon ya wonder what the hell's goin on – wee girl in here this mornin – first thing – drugged up she was – what way is that to be before the world's awake – she looked ill to me – eatin the amount of chocolate she bought make anybody ill – not that i'm complainin about sellin it

Robbie Mullin chocolate

Sammy Lennon aye – must've been for her breakfast

Robbie Mullin right – what a owe ya for the bags

Sammy Lennon give us a pound

Bettty enters

Betty Lennon every taxi firm booked – nothin for at least half an hour

Sammy Lennon ya gonna be late

Betty Lennon a don't like rushin

Robbie Mullin where is it yer goin

Sammy Lennon she's headin up to the hospital

Robbie Mullin i've business up there – i'll give ya a lift

Betty Lennon you don't mind

Robbie Mullin not at all

Sammy Lennon i hate her in taxis – read somewhere that it's them that delivers the drugs all over the city – never know what would happen

Betty Lennon the can't all be doin that sammy

Robbie Mullin better safe than sorry – i'll wait for ya outside – parked out the front

Robbie exits.

Sammy Lennon that's a right fella that

Betty Lennon you remember about the new order

Sammy Lennon yes – don't you be worryin about anythin it's only a check up

Betty Lennon stop fussin over me

Sammy Lennon ya got everything

Betty Lennon i've my bag that's all a need

Sammy Lennon not be long anyway

Betty Lennon aye

TWO

The abattoir. Theresa's office. She is about to make a phone call. Dave enters.

Dave Black (*to workers below*) aye – ya wouldn't know a day's graft if it spat in yer eye

Teresa Black (*puts phone down*) what are you doin here

Dave Black that's lovely

Theresa Black ya know what a mean

Dave Black the wouldn't let me on the radio – said the might later but a wasn't goin to hang around for that

Theresa Black i said the wouldn't

Dave Black a know ya did – how's things goin here – they're givin out down there about hangin around

Theresa Black still waitin to hear word

Dave Black gettin close to the wire is it

Theresa Black there's been easier days

Dave Black aye right – a want ya to phone yer brian an get me a lend of his car – i'm goin to drive down to the dig

Theresa Black what for

Dave Black see if a can get somethin done

Theresa Black yer suspended from drivin

Dave Black he doesn't know that

Theresa Black still

Dave Black still nothin – phone him – i'd do it only he'd give me a lot a shit over the phone – ya know what he's like – think he was the only one ever to own a car

Theresa Black i'm not phonin him

Dave Black the only other way's the bus – phone him

Theresa Black i'm not phonin him

Dave Black why you doin this to me

Theresa Black i'm not doin anythin

Dave Black correct – yer not helpin me are ya – a don't understand yer attitude

Theresa Black i'm in the middle a work

Dave Black since they've started diggin there's been a change

Theresa Black there's no change – i've work to do – i'm under pressure here can you not see that

Dave Black it's like ya don't want them to dig

Theresa Black don't be bloody stupid

Dave Black a don't understan that – the have to look theresa – if the don't look the won't find him

Theresa Black go get yer bus

Dave Black why don't ya come with me – if both of us are there together the case for keepin it all goin would be better – stronger

Theresa Black i'm needed here

Dave Black what if the ask where ya are

283

Theresa Black nobody's goin to ask anythin dave

Dave Black what if the do – say i start shoutin the odds – this is important to us – you have to keep diggin because it's important to us – what if someone says – where's yer wife – where's the mother of this child – sorry but she couldn't make it today – busy at work she tells me – what type of person are they goin to think you are

Theresa Black the type that's kept us goin all these years – the type that gets on with what the have to do in order to keep our lives together – do you know what it's like to have to look an listen to you this last fifteen years – all the time wimperin in my face – like ya were the only person ever felt any pain – yer like an open wound

Dave Black i'd rather be like that than the way you are

Theresa Black what way would that be – lookin after you ya mean – go to work dave – eat yer food dave – go to the doctor dave – go to sleep dave – they're goin to stop diggin an now yer goin to do something – it's too late

Dave Black least a haven't given up – if our child was to walk through that door right now a be ashamed for ya – you couldn't look him straight in the eye

Theresa Black get out

Dave Black oh i'm goin all right – i'm goin to where you should be only ya haven't the balls to go – you couldn't look him in the eye because you've stopped carin

Theresa Black get out

Dave Black another thing – tell yer brother to stick his car up his fuckin hole

Dave exits. Theresa composes herself then lifts the phone.

THREE

The river. Maggie and Cooper are drying off after a Swim. Frank Coin is some distance away sitting on a park bench.

Maggie Lyttle what was it – oh aye – i used to swim the shit out a them when a was at school – spoof

Cooper Jones a did – haven't been in the water for a while that's all (*Poses.*) what do ya think a that – there's wankers pays a fortune to be like that – with me it's just natural

Maggie Lyttle big girlie spoof

Cooper Jones didn't a save you from drownin there

Maggie Lyttle gropin me under the water isn't savin me from drownin

Cooper Jones it keeps yer head up above the water

They lie on the grass.

Maggie Lyttle i think a could live here

Cooper Jones fuck all but fields

Maggie Lyttle the city's fuck all but streets

Cooper Jones streets are good fields are fucked – country people are a bit iffy

Maggie Lyttle iffy what way

Cooper Jones always on about sheep – sheep an cows – like those balloons down at the plant – ask swiz about them

Maggie Lyttle swiz is a dick

Cooper Jones ya not like swiz no

285

Maggie Lyttle he's a dick

Cooper Jones he's alright

Maggie Lyttle he's too nasty – see it in his face sometimes

Cooper Jones he is nasty – but then all his ones are nasty bastards – got a job

Maggie Lyttle thought you were a fuck work type a guy

Cooper Jones a do think like that but this job's sound

Maggie Lyttle head commando of the head commandoes

Cooper Jones i'd make a fucking fine commando let me tell ya

Maggie Lyttle on dry land

Cooper Jones doin the door at the club

Maggie Lyttle did ya not say a job

Cooper Jones a get money – an none a that other sandwiches for lunch shit

Maggie Lyttle a job job

Cooper Jones a job job is a no no – be alright – the guy's that doin it is movin on soon to something else

Maggie Lyttle rocket science

Cooper Jones the very thing – he deals with rockets already doesn't he – i'll let ya in for nothin

Maggie Lyttle that meant to be a bonus is it

Cooper Jones see the guy on the door that's my fella – jesus you're one lucky duck

Maggie Lyttle yer so full a shit

Cooper Jones darling

Maggie Lyttle yer so full a shit darling

Cooper Jones tell me this

Maggie Lyttle this is goin to be somethin deep isn't it – yer not normally into the deep but yer goin to surprise me

Cooper Jones what might be deep for me mightn't be for you

Maggie Lyttle a bet ya a know what yer goin to say

Cooper Jones what

Maggie Lyttle any chance of a blowjob

Cooper Jones a wasn't goin to say that but we're both thinkin along the right lines (*He rolls over on top of her.*) the heat makes me horny does it not you

Maggie Lyttle it does

Cooper Jones (*hand between her legs*) ya want to hear what my plan is

Maggie Lyttle in front a that ole lad over there

Cooper Jones fuck him – (*Shouts.*) go away home ya lonely ole fucker

  They kiss.

FOUR

The flat and the street outside. Connie has the music on. She is packing, dancing, drinking and trying on tops. Bop and Swiz are in the street watching the flat.

Swiz Murdoch the inside a that flat be the business

Bop Torbett ya reckon

Swiz Murdoch that's where the spondi is – that's the work ya want to be at – fuck that chasin cattle business

Bop Torbett the not bothered about ya not weighin in today

Swiz Murdoch don't care

Bop Torbett not sack ya

Swiz Murdoch sack away all the like – get a few quid for doin this – some fabulets on top a that – better off

Bop Torbett i'm gettin my da to put a word in for me

Swiz Murdoch the sack me ya can have my lunchbox – ya think he has a jacuzzi – bet ya the fucker has a jacuzzi – bet ya he gives her one in it – yer woman – his girl – i wouldn't be too long wangin one into her – all that water an bubbles up round yer jamroll – maybe get cramps – cooper maybe has a touch of the cramps now – what do ya reckon bop – cooper wangin away

Bop Torbett nothin to do with me

Swiz Murdoch think the rest of us has no eyes – the lovely maggie – i'd give her one – although cooper catch ya yer fucked – it's all about not gettin caught – a gave my brother's girl one – he's not with her now – don't be sayin just in case it gets back to him – a don't think he liked her – just right the dirty bitch

Connie appears at the window. She has no top on.

fuck look at that – look at yer woman – (*Shouts up.*) show us yer diddies big girl

Connie laughs and flashes her breasts.

that's it ya girl ye – get the lot off dear – look at the diddies on her

Connie moves away from the window.

she's in there on her own – bored off her napper – fuckin meat plant aye

Connie is back at the window. She has a top on.

there she's back again – get them out for the boys dear

Connie throws a bunch of keys out on to the street. Swiz picks them up. Connie moves away from the window.

we're in young man we're in

FIVE

The hospital. Betty is sitting on her own. Maeve enters.

Maeve Hynes ya made it then – the taxi driver didn't steal ya for the slave trade

Betty Lennon sammy worries too much – i got lost walkin about this place – sittin here havin a rest

Maeve Hynes it's a wonder anyone can find their way around here

Betty Lennon it is a bit confusin

Maeve Hynes the whole place is badly designed – look where we are sittin outside the cancer an two steps away is the labour – it's a bit insensitive

Betty Lennon a suppose it is

Maeve Hynes women goin in there to have babies beside a ward where they're all dyin – coughin an splutterin everywhere

Betty Lennon not everyone in there is dyin i'm sure

Maeve Hynes once yer in there there's not much hope –
a don't blame those poor souls a blame the hospital –
could've planned it better

Betty Lennon yer cousin isn't it – has she had the baby yet

Maeve Hynes not yet – should be soon though

Betty Lennon just nipped out for a breather

Maeve Hynes the midwife asked me to leave – she said a
was too nervous an a was makin the mother nervous –
i've to calm down

Betty Lennon i'm sure they'll let ya back in

Maeve Hynes she needs a face she knows to hold her
hand

Betty Lennon people need support at times like this

Maeve Hynes it isn't easy in there holdin yer nerve

Betty Lennon no i'd say not

Maeve Hynes the poor girl's hooked up to everything – it
makes ya think what can go wrong

Betty Lennon she's in the best place

Maeve Hynes that's true – it's just ya worry don't ya

Betty Lennon some worry an some don't – sammy
worries about everythin under the sun – ends up ya can't
tell him anythin he makes a fuss – things you should be
tellin him

Maeve Hynes some a the women in there – you'd worry
more about the wee babies then ya would anythin else –
what type a life's out there for them

Betty Lennon most seem to get through it

Maeve Hynes but to see them – wee girls – fegs in their mouths – the baby in the cot an they're up at the smokin room puffin away – not interested in holdin the children – there's one in there – face covered in tattoos an the hair dyed off herself – wouldn't hold the baby – gets the nurse to look after him – the shouts of her – what type a life is that wee child gonna have – his mother won't even hold him – i'd half a mind to lift the child up an give it a nurse myself

Betty Lennon you'd need to be careful about that – the mother wouldn't thank ya for it

Maeve Hynes i've half a mind to do it none the less – they should be taken off them an given to people that's goin to care for them – that's the worry isn't it – that bad things are goin to happen to those wee children – bloody disgrace

Betty Lennon don't be getting all upset

Maeve Hynes i can't help it – it just makes me feel crazy

Betty Lennon you're to go back in there remember

Maeve Hynes the shouldn't have children – here's me rantin on an a haven't asked ya about yer check up

Betty Lennon it's nothing – everything's alright

Maeve Hynes were ya havin tests taken or were the given ya the results of ones the had taken – i was in here a few months back – needle after needle – x rays – more needles – a sample of this a sample of that – treated like a bloody piece of meat ya are – the nurse was lovely though – the doctor a had no time for but the nurse was lovely – the job the have to do too – can ya picture what it's like in that ward for them – dyin or not dyin lookin after those poor souls must be a messy business

Betty stands to leave.

Betty Lennon i'd better go

Maeve Hynes once i've got the better of my nerves i'll head back in – she needs me to look after her doesn't she

SIX

The abattoir. Theresa sits behind her desk in her office.

Teresa Black (*speaking on the intercom*) would joe hynes come to the office please – joe hynes to the office

Joe enters.

Joe Hynes get some exercise up and down those stairs today – by the way one a the wee lads down in the bonin yard – stupid wee bastard he is – messin about with the knives – he's opened his hand up – first aid box was no good so he's on his way to the hospital – he hardly be back so i'll collect his wages for him

Theresa Black did ya write it all down in the accident book

Joe Hynes aye – a told him all about the claim forms an that

Theresa Black thought it was his fault

Joe Hynes his fault or not he'll be off work won't he – he'll need a few quid

Theresa Black a was talkin to masters – it's not as straightforward as he thought it was

Joe Hynes it couldn't be straightforward – that would only get the job done

Theresa Black the deal he's workin on isn't completed –
the guy who owns the processin factory is still waitin on
a better price so he won't sign

Joe Hynes we're all fucked then

Theresa Black listen a minute – i want to get one thing
clear first – i'm not meant to be tellin ya this

Joe Hynes why ya tellin me then

Theresa Black because a think it's the right thing to do –
it has to be up to you

Joe Hynes i don't want things left up to me

Theresa Black he's managed to organise something with
the bank – they've agreed to give him money before the
end of the day but the won't give him all he needs – either
he pays for the container at the dock or covers the wages

Joe Hynes he has to cover the wages – there's no
question about that

Theresa Black right – if the container isn't unloaded
today it has to go back – he'd still get charged under a
time penalty though – if he pays for the container with
money he hasn't got he'll have to incorporate that cost
into the deal he's workin on at the moment – that along
with the euro will put him over his margins – he could
lose the whole lot – with nothin comin in that means
there's goin to have to be lay offs

Joe Hynes what are ya tellin me then

Theresa Black i just said joe

Joe Hynes the deal – what's the deal

Theresa Black unload the container which at least means
he has something to sell

Joe Hynes he hasn't bought it yet

Theresa Black he can sell it before he buys it

Joe Hynes fuck

Theresa Black the wages would be covered but probably not today

Joe Hynes yer askin me to tell them to work – then tell them they're not gettin paid

Theresa Black better that than lay offs

Joe Hynes the container doesn't matter does it – it's not long term

Theresa Black no it's only a way of keepin things tickin over for a few days while something else can be sorted out – it's the other deal that's important

Joe Hynes if he doesn't get that

Theresa Black he thinks he is goin to get it – there's just a bit of a waitin game goin on

Joe Hynes i'm meant to be tellin the union all this ya know

Theresa Black what good's that to any one

Joe Hynes the bottom line is i've to go down an tell them to unload a container an then wait an hope the get paid – who's goin to do that

Theresa Black don't tell them

Joe Hynes don't tell them what

Theresa Black don't tell them the mightn't be gettin their money at the end of the day

Joe Hynes you've put me in a position here

Theresa Black unload the container – in the long term it's the best thing to do – but it's yer decision

Helen is behind the bar in the pub. She makes a phone call on her mobile. Joe's mobile rings. Helen walks into the scene.

Joe Hynes sorry about this

Helen Woods i'm bored joe – surrounded by monkeys here – come over an see me

Joe Hynes i'm talkin to somebody here

Helen Woods are ya talkin about meat joe – tell me what yer goin to do with yer meat joe

Joe Hynes i'm sure something can be sorted out

Helen Woods i'm hungry joe – i'm goin to eat all yer meat – juicy pink meat

Joe Hynes that sounds interestin

Helen Woods big joe the meat man – (*Laughs.*) i'm bored joe – come on over – i've a present for ya

Joe Hynes as well as the meat thing

Helen Woods if yer not here ya won't know

Joe Hynes sometime later

Helen Woods i'll be waitin meatman

Helen exits.

Joe Hynes mobile phones – they're a curse – the union give me that one – jesus that's a joke

Theresa Black what are ya goin to do

Joe Hynes take a meat cleaver to masters that's what

Theresa Black joe – what

Joe Hynes i'll get them to unload the container – drag it out a bit – not mention anythin about the wages – if nothin comes through by the end a the day there'll be a fuckin riot

Theresa Black i'll chase him all afternoon

Joe Hynes this container comin from the dock now

Theresa Black not just yet

Joe Hynes ah come on theresa

Theresa Black he's to find a bank to sign a form – he's drivin round lookin for one right now

Joe Hynes god bless him

SEVEN

The pub. Helen is behind the bar. Paul and Harry are standing. Bobbie, Shanks and Sharon are at their table. Harry addresses everyone.

Harry Fogarty listen to this a minute

Shanks O'Neill speech speech

Bobbie Torbett listen to the man

Harry Fogarty there's a couple of items on the list we can't agree on – both of us want this sorted out – so – we'll tell you what the are and why each of us wants them – then ya vote on it

Shanks O'Neill welt away – what's first up

Bobbie Torbett houl yer whist there – goin to a funeral is one thing – big dan god rest him – gettin involved between families an that is another

Harry Fogarty you'd be doin us a favour

Sharon Lawther do what dead warriors do – burn the lot

Shanks O'Neill whoof – except the stuff ya can sell

Bobbie Torbett we're bein asked to do somethin here – whatever way it goes that's the law a the land

Harry Fogarty aye (*To Helen.*) this includes you by the way dear – that alright

Helen Woods i'm not doin anythin else at the moment

Harry Fogarty the first thing is my da's suit

Paul Fogarty only suit he had

Sharon Lawther is it a good suit – a good suit is the makings of half a man

Harry Fogarty yer only suit is yer good suit – i want to keep it to wear it – right – you go

Paul Fogarty i think it should go to charity – let somebody who needs it get the use of it

Shanks O'Neill i'll take it

Harry Fogarty wearin yer dead da's suit is passin something on

Sharon Lawther that's a nice suit you've on ya

Paul Fogarty yer right he doesn't need another one

Shanks O'Neill give it to me

Bobbie Torbett i've a question here – is the suit not too small for ya – big dan wasn't that size

Harry Fogarty the can be altered can't the

Bobbie Torbett fuck – it would need to be altered a right bit

Harry Fogarty it's my da's an i want it instead of a complete stranger gettin it

Shanks O'Neill i'm hardly a complete stranger

Bobbie Torbett yer getting nothin

Paul Fogarty somebody could get the use of it

Harry Fogarty vote then – whoever thinks i should get the suit put their hands up

Shanks O'Neill it should be a secret ballot

Bobbie Torbett things should always be kept in the family i think

Sharon Lawther whatever bobbie says is right

Bobbie Torbett this is serious

Sharon Lawther i'm agreein with ya

Bobbie Torbett give a reason

Sharon Lawther right – if it doesn't go to him you've no way a knowin who might get it – could be a murderer or anythin

Shanks O'Neill ya would know if i got it

Bobbie Torbett it wouldn't fit you

Shanks O'Neill it doesn't fit him

Bobbie Torbett it makes sense it not fittin him it makes no sense it not fittin you

Shanks O'Neill i vote for charity

Attention turns to Helen.

Helen Woods my mother died an i still have all her shoes in the house – it wouldn't feel right anyone else havin them

Harry Fogarty i get the suit – right

298

Shanks O'Neill what's next up seein a just missed out on a suit

Harry Fogarty my da had a lot a gardenin equipment

Bobbie Torbett up at them allotments a know that

Shanks O'Neill i've no garden that's me out

Harry Fogarty i think we should split it – he thinks we should just leave it – do nothin with it

Bobbie Torbett what's the point in that

Harry Fogarty tell them why ya want that

Sharon Lawther i vote . . .

Bobbie Torbett we're not votin yet

Sharon Lawther hurry up well

Paul Fogarty the allotment was his pride an joy – any free time he had he spent it up there – the two a us used to go up there with him – that's the only place the three of us spend time together (*To Harry.*) he told me not to mention this – i'm only sayin it now because of what we're at

Harry Fogarty he told me not to mention somethin as well

Paul Fogarty what

Harry Fogarty you say

Paul Fogarty alright then fuck it a will – because of this waster my da had to sell the allotment – he came to me an says you had lost money gamblin an ya needed it back so he had to sell the allotment to get it for ya

Harry Fogarty that's what he told ya

Paul Fogarty cause that's what happened

Harry Fogarty he told me you lost money in a game a cards – ya couldn't afford it and he had to sell the allotment to pay it off – that's what he said

Paul Fogarty what would he do that for

Harry Fogarty i don't know

Bobbie Torbett the allotment yer talkin about is up round the embankment isn't it

Paul Fogarty aye

Bobbie Torbett over in the corner beside like a hedge fuckin thing

Paul Fogarty aye

Bobbie Torbett durin the day i walk up there – yer da sold nothing – every day a was up there i'd see him workin away

Paul Fogarty big dan

Harry Fogarty john

Bobbie Torbett yes

Harry Fogarty up at the allotment

Sharon Lawther bully for big dan – we need another drink here

Bobbie Torbett up there yes (*To Sharon.*) easy on the gargle

Sharon Lawther go buy a drink

Shanks O'Neill (*to Sharon*) we'll get that sorted in a minute

Paul Fogarty (*to Bobbie*) ya sure

Bobbie Torbett i'm not sayin again

Paul Fogarty a was only sayin

300

Bobbie Torbett don't fuckin say

Harry Fogarty don't be gettin all heavy here

Bobbie Torbett what way

Harry Fogarty don't be slabberin at anyone

Bobbie Torbett that right

Shanks O'Neill bobbie

Bobbie Torbett shut up – a was tellin ya information that was of use to ya – and he's talkin to me like a fuckin child and now yer tellin me i'm slabberin – a don't like that

Harry Fogarty do ya not

Bobbie Torbett no a don't

Shanks O'Neill i'd leave it lads – different ball game with this man

Paul Fogarty nobody was sayin that to ya

Bobbie Torbett that's alright then – my mistake

Harry Fogarty right – i'll get another drink in here

    Paul and Harry move to the bar.

Sharon Lawther only gentleman in the place ya are

Bobbie Torbett a thought ya were goin round to yer sister's

Sharon Lawther not want me here bobbie

Shanks O'Neill yer alright sit there

Sharon Lawther aye i'm alright – goin to the ladies do my face up a bit – mightn't want rid a me then (*Passing Paul and Harry before she exits.*) i vote you to split it up – a spade each

EIGHT

The flat. Music is playing. Connie is trying on tops to see which ones she will pack. Swiz and Bop are on the sofa smoking a joint.

Connie Dean i like this one – wear it if we're goin somewhere special

Bop Torbett aye that one that's a good one

Swiz Murdoch the chill out gear

Connie Dean never get wearin it – no point in takin it

Swiz Murdoch all look the same to me – goin on holiday are ye – topless beach is it – not need any a them

Connie Dean movin out – on our way – movin out and movin up

Swiz Murdoch today like

Connie Dean today – the man that looks after me had a bit a trouble at work – you nice boys wouldn't know about that

Swiz Murdoch us nice boys wouldn't – bop sure we wouldn't

Connie Dean i like it round here

Swiz Murdoch aye round here's the business – me an ya have a boogie – a goin away party

Swiz and Connie dance.

Connie Dean (*to Bop*) mon dance

Bop Torbett my legs are too heavy

Swiz Murdoch that child already has a girl – me on the other hand i've no one

302

Bop Torbett my hands are the big – must have the biggest hands in the world

Swiz Murdoch fuckin massive the are

Bop Torbett (*laughing*) biggest hands ever made – gloves the size of a ship i'd need for these big fuckers

Swiz Murdoch he's gone

Swiz kisses Connie and starts to pull her skirt up.

Connie Dean (*stops him*) no no no no no – chill out there a bit

Swiz Murdoch what ya mean – it's party time – no audience – we'll go in there (*Takes her hand.*) mon

Connie Dean a just want a bit of a laugh

Swiz Murdoch we'll have a laugh in there – mon

Connie Dean no

Swiz Murdoch what the fuck does that mean no

Bop Torbett she says no

Swiz Murdoch fuck up you

Bop Torbett what about the hands

Swiz Murdoch (*to Connie*) i didn't come up here for no

Connie Dean a don't want everything like that all the time

Swiz Murdoch the window – what the fuck was all that about

Connie Dean it was funny – a thought that was funny

Swiz Murdoch i like funny – i'm all for funny – a don't like being fuckin messed about though

She kisses him.

Connie Dean i'm sorry

Swiz Murdoch don't fuckin tease

Connie Dean never get to talk – just chill out – see what happens

Swiz Murdoch see what happens what

Connie Dean don't rush in (*She kisses him on the cheek.*) nice girls don't like rushin in

Swiz Murdoch later

Connie Dean two nice boys

Swiz Murdoch nice boys alright

Bop Torbett nice boys with massive fuckin hands

Robbie at the hospital. He makes a call on his mobile. The phone rings in the flat. Robbie walks into the scene.

Connie Dean oh shit that'll be him

Swiz Murdoch fuck him leave it

Connie Dean can't leave it – fuck – don't say anything

Swiz Murdoch aye

Connie Dean don't fuckin say anything

Swiz Murdoch stay cool dear

Connie answers the phone.

Robbie Mullin what kept ya

Connie Dean nothing – nothing – packin

Robbie Mullin everythin alright

Connie Dean just sortin some clothes out robbie – just sortin some clothes out

Robbie Mullin those wee lads still hangin about outside

Connie Dean they're away – no one about out there now – away

Robbie Mullin if the come back let me know

Connie Dean of course robbie a will

Robbie Mullin of course ya will – ya let me know everything don't ya

Connie Dean yes robbie

Robbie Mullin can't have people lying to me sure a can't

Connie Dean no robbie

Robbie Mullin can't have lies

Connie Dean no

Robbie Mullin called into that shop nearby earlier – got some bags – nice man owns that place – tellin me about some spaced out junkie type in his shop this mornin – bought a lot of chocolate

Connie Dean robbie a just needed a walk – there was nothin to eat

Robbie Mullin don't speak

Connie Dean a didn't

Robbie Mullin now listen to me – take no more gear – not a tablet not a joint not a fuckin drink – nothing – just stand beside that window and look out on to the street – i'll be back soon

Robbie exits.

Swiz Murdoch what about another spliff

Connie Dean both of ya have to go now

Swiz Murdoch given ya grief over the phone – fuck him

Connie Dean he'll be back soon – just go

Swiz Murdoch sort him out – bop beat him with his big hands

Connie gets money from her purse.

Connie Dean (*to Swiz*) here look take that

Swiz Murdoch what's that for

Connie Dean just take it and leave – just take the money and leave

Swiz Murdoch what about later

Connie Dean (*screaming*) get out – get fuckin out

NINE

Theresa's office is empty. Dave is sitting on a grass bank. He is surrounded by the noise of heavy machinery, diggers etc. Theresa enters the office and sits at her desk. There is a message on her answering machine.

Dave Black theresa it's me – listen love i'm sorry about earlier on – a didn't mean what a said – a know ya care – today's a bad day that's all – you're doin yer best at work a know that – none of that's easy – it's just – a don't know – i can't do anything here – a spoke with the police and that – there's nothing can be done the say – they've been told to finish at midnight tonight – he was nice about it this guy – that's not an easy job either – they've been told what to do and that's that – not bein able to do

anything is the part a can't take – havin no control when
ya feel ya should be doin something – i'm goin to stay
here a while longer – have this feeling that a should – the
workmen gave me a few sandwiches so i'm alright that
way – police told me if the got more information the
would act on it – not that that's likely – but ya never
know – it's a nice day here – the sun's shining – a had this
thought that no matter where he was buried i hoped the
sun was shining – that would keep the earth warm – he
wouldn't be lying in the cold ground – everybody's doin
their best – right – anyway – you don't have to phone me
back – i'll let ya know when i'm comin home – somebody
here can give me a lift – talk to ya later – and don't worry
theresa it's alright

TEN

Bop and Swiz in the street outside the flat.

Swiz Murdoch fuckin header – hear the screams of her

Bop Torbett i liked her

Swiz Murdoch look at that – she gave me a score – give
ya a tenner of it later on

Bop Torbett a score

Swiz Murdoch aye – a know – fuckin eejit (*Jangles keys.*)

Bop Torbett you lift those

Swiz Murdoch on the way out

Bop Torbett what ya goin do with them

Swiz Murdoch give them to my brother – wire him off
they're doin a runner tonight

ELEVEN

The shop. Sammy is behind the counter. Maggie and Cooper are at the other end of the shop.

Cooper Jones ya want a bottle a this

Maggie Lyttle no

Cooper Jones stick one in yer bag

Maggie Lyttle no

Cooper Jones lapper

Sammy Lennon what's goin on down there

Maggie Lyttle go an pay for it

Cooper Jones watch this (*At counter.*) what's yer panic – do you not want me to buy somethin

Sammy Lennon were you in here earlier on – you an another one

Cooper Jones me – in here – no – i've been helpin my old granny to do her shoppin all day – she has to walk all the way to supermarket cause she says you're too dear – a robber without a mask she says you are

Sammy Lennon you were in here an ya lifted sweets an run out

Cooper Jones a was with my granny i told you that

Sammy Lennon yer barred – put that back an get out

Cooper opens the bottle and drinks.

you'll have to pay for that

Maggie Lyttle cooper – let's go

Cooper Jones pours the rest of the bottle on the floor.

Cooper Jones no wonder my granny doesn't come in here

He pretends to throw the bottle at Sammy, Sammy is startled, Cooper laughs.

Sammy Lennon i'm warnin ya don't come back

Cooper Jones don't fuckin warn me

Cooper lifts a bottle of water while him and Maggie exit. They stand outside the shop.

Maggie Lyttle grow up for christ sake

Cooper Jones i'm only messing – i'll go back in an pay him for the water

Maggie Lyttle stop pesterin him

Cooper Jones ya want a drink a this (*She takes a drink.*) ya goin go to the club tonight

Maggie Lyttle don't know

Cooper Jones go on go – i want ya to go

Maggie Lyttle do we have to go – can we not do somethin else

Cooper Jones like what

Maggie Lyttle i don't know there must be something else to do – go to the pictures

Cooper Jones what for

Maggie Lyttle to see a movie

Cooper Jones what ya wanna see a movie for – goin out an just sittin there watchin somethin – i don't get that

Maggie Lyttle it's just somethin to do

Cooper Jones go to the club – have a laugh – that's doin somethin – that other thing it's just borin – watchin other people do things – somebody makes up a story about people in america and you sit an watch it – what's the point in that

Maggie Lyttle no point yer're right

Cooper Jones a need to be hangin about the place anyway – might need me on the door or somethin

Maggie Lyttle i'll go myself

Cooper Jones to the pictures

Maggie Lyttle yes

Cooper Jones on yer own

Maggie Lyttle by myself – on my own

Cooper Jones tonight

Maggie Lyttle aye

Cooper Jones who goes to the pictures on their own – no one

Maggie Lyttle i'll start a new craze

Cooper Jones do what ever ya want then

Maggie Lyttle a will do whatever a want

Cooper Jones a know ya will – that's cool

Maggie Lyttle a don't need you to tell me what to do

Cooper Jones a didn't tell ya to do anythin

Maggie Lyttle do what ya want – go to the pictures – like you were givin me permission

Cooper Jones i'm goin to the club that's what i'm doin

Maggie Lyttle a know that

Cooper Jones a don't understan – what

Maggie Lyttle nothin

Cooper Jones what

Maggie Lyttle nothin

Cooper Jones i'll go to the pictures next week

Maggie Lyttle a don't want ya to go now

Cooper Jones didn't ya just say

Maggie Lyttle a want to go on my own

Cooper Jones have i done somethin here

Maggie Lyttle no

Cooper Jones somethin a don't know about

Maggie Lyttle nothin ya don't know about

Cooper Jones only a bit of a laugh ya know

   Sammy enters brandishing a club.

Sammy Lennon get away from here – go on move on

Cooper Jones i'll pay for the water

Sammy Lennon i don't want yer money – just get away from my shop – i'll hit ya with this – i'm warnin ya

Cooper Jones (*laughs.*) you hit me with that (*To Maggie.*) mon we'll go

Maggie Lyttle i'm goin home

Cooper Jones you'll be about later – on the corner – i'll see ya later

Maggie Lyttle maybe

TWELVE

The backyard of the pub. The inside of the pub is also visible but it is just background. Helen is kneeling in front of Joe. She stands up. Joefixes his trousers.

Joe Hynes i need to get back to work

Helen Woods jesus joe you can wait a few minutes surely

Joe Hynes a few minutes – it's just over there everything's – dodgy

Helen Woods i bought you somethin

Joe Hynes a haven't forgotten somethin have a

Helen Woods ya haven't forgotten anythin – a just wanted to buy ya somethin that's all – last ya a lifetime apparently – here

Joe Hynes (*smiles*) right

Helen Woods ya not like it

Joe Hynes no it's lovely

Helen Woods have ya already got one – i'll get it changed – i only got it round the corner

Joe Hynes i've stopped smokin – maeve's idea – well we've both been talkin about it

Helen Woods you and her decided

Joe Hynes aye – it's her really

Helen Woods (*lights a cigarette*) ya never mentioned anythin about it

Joe Hynes the lighter's lovely – she read somewhere that smokin might damage yer sperm

Helen Woods (*offers him a cigarette*) ya haven't stopped then – you've just told her you've stopped

Joe Hynes no a have

Helen Woods take it

Joe Hynes i've stopped

Helen Woods i like you smokin

Joe Hynes there must be other things about me helen

Helen Woods i like lookin at ya smoke – the way ya smoke – i like it

Joe Hynes well i'm sorry but what can a do

Helen Woods tell her ya don't want to stop

Joe Hynes but a do

Helen Woods a thought ya said it was her makin ya

Joe Hynes it's the right thing to do

Helen Woods so it's you – you want to do it

Joe Hynes humpin meat all day – haven't a fuckin breath left in me

Helen Woods ya should've said

Joe Hynes a didn't know about the lighter

Helen Woods that's not it

Joe Hynes what then

Helen Woods we should've talked about it – not you an her you an me

Joe Hynes i'll keep the lighter in case a start up again – which the way things are goin could be soon

Helen Woods i'll bring it back

Joe Hynes no a want to keep it – was she in the shop when ya were buyin it

Helen Woods yeah

Joe Hynes fuck

Helen Woods what

Joe Hynes nothin – i'm just thinkin the two a you together – a bit close like isn't it

Helen Woods i didn't like bein there in her company – it didn't feel right

Joe Hynes yer bound to bump into her now an again

Helen Woods i don't like it

Joe Hynes what do ya want me to do

Helen Woods a don't know

Joe Hynes ya don't want me to leave her

Helen Woods would ya leave her

Joe Hynes a don't know

Helen Woods that's why i don't want you to do it

Joe Hynes it's not the right time

Helen Woods jesus christ – when is the right time

Joe Hynes me leavin might put her over the edge

Sharon Lawther (*shouts from pub*) can we get some service here please – there's people's eyes hangin out with thirst

Helen Woods a better go back in here

Joe Hynes i'll call back over later

Helen Woods aye

Joe Hynes do ya want the lighter back – it's just maybe with me not smokin and her bein in the shop when ya bought it – if she saw it – ya know – she might – ya know

Helen Woods no that's fine – i'll bring it back – better go out the back way – don't want ya walkin through the pub

Joe Hynes nah

Joe exits. Helen lights another cigarette.

THIRTEEN

The flat. Robbie is punching Connie. Throughout the beating Connie is silent. It is something she has gotten used to.

FOURTEEN

A busy street. Betty is trying to cross the street. She is confused. She drops her handbag and the contents spill out. She kneels down to pick them up.

Act Three

The end of the day. The pub. Helen is behind the bar serving Frank Coin. Harry and Paul are standing at the counter. Bobbie, Shanks and Sharon are at a table. She is drunk, she is resting her head on the table.

Helen Woods (*giving Frank his pint*) there ya go – didn't a tell ya there was one waiting on ya

Frank Coin an a few more on top a that

Helen Woods out walkin today

Frank Coin usual

Helen Woods beautiful day for it

Frank Coin it was

Frank sits at a table away from the rest.

Harry Fogarty (*to Helen*) tins dear

Helen Woods how many you want

Harry Fogarty (*to Paul*) how many we want

Paul Fogarty ten

Harry Fogarty (*to Helen*) give us a dozen

Paul Fogarty couldn't be ten

Harry Fogarty i'll square up for this

Paul Fogarty ya will not

Harry Fogarty let me do this

Paul Fogarty i'll get for the sandwiches then

Harry Fogarty right

They pay for the tins and sandwiches.

(*To Helen.*) good job (*To Bobbie etc.*) we're away on here

Bobbie Torbett right – it was a good day – yer da was well looked after – (*To Harry.*) that other thing earlier – sorry – a few drinks ya know

Harry Fogarty forgotten about

Paul Fogarty thanks for makin the effort – not to be forgetten

Bobbie Torbett had to be done

Shanks O'Neill good day – good send off

Harry Fogarty been better if there was more at it

Paul Fogarty aye

Shanks O'Neill (*to Paul*) a wee word in yer ear there

Paul Fogarty (*to Harry*) you go on out i'll see ya out there

Harry exits.

Shanks O'Neill god rest yer da an that y'know

Paul Fogarty aye

Shanks O'Neill i'm stuck for a few quid – any chance ya could – y'know – drop us somethin – bad timin but – y'know

Paul Fogarty death put things in perspective

Shanks O'Neill perspective aye

Paul Fogarty a tenner do ya

Shanks O'Neill plenty

Paul Fogarty can't bring it with ye

Shanks O'Neill yer a gentleman

Paul exits. Shanks returns to table.

Bobbie Torbett man's just buried his father

Shanks O'Neill no better time

Sharon Lawther get me somethin to eat bobbie

Shanks O'Neill hang on in there darlin

Bobbie Torbett (*about Sharon*) see what a mean

Shanks O'Neill she's alright

Sharon Lawther we'll go back to the house bobbie an i'll cook something – i can cook ya know – don't think a can't a can

Bobbie Torbett we're havin a drink

Sharon Lawther cook with the best a them

Bop enters. He stands at the bar. Bobbie walks over to Bop.

Bobbie Torbett ya been round to the house – get somethin to eat

Bop Torbett i'm alright

Bobbie Torbett want a pint – sit down with us have a pint

Bop Torbett sit with them two

Bobbie Torbett wise move – shouldn't be here myself

Bop Torbett go on home then

Bobbie Torbett aye – i'll be headin round soon

Bop Torbett a left somethin on the pan for ya

Bobbie Torbett right

Bop Torbett did ya ask for me

Bobbie Torbett a did

Bop Torbett well what the say

Bobbie Torbett there's nothin on at the moment – an the way things are lookin that's goin to be the case for a good while – sorry but that's what the said son

Bop Torbett they're not takin anybody on

Bobbie Torbett there's other types a work son – it doesn't have to be that

Bop Torbett who were ya talkin to

Bobbie Torbett who was a talkin to – fuck it – i'm not doin this – i'm not doin it – a wasn't talkin to anybody – the abattoir's a kip

Bop Torbett go sit down with yer mates an get drunk

Bobbie grabs Bop then lets him go. Bop exits.

Bobbie Torbett jesus – just tryin to explain somethin – should've sat down an had a drink – a could a explained something

He sits down at the table.

(*To Shanks.*) go up an get a drink

Shanks goes to the bar.

Sharon Lawther i'd have made a good mother ya know bobbie – plenty of love in me – people don't see that but it's there – you see it bobbie don't ya

Bobbie Torbett aye

TWO

The abattoir. Theresa is in her office. The fire alarm is ringing. Theresa is putting her coat on. Joe enters carrying a football.

Joe Hynes it's not the real thing – one a the lads smashed the glass with the ball

Theresa Black i was goin to call ya up anyway – he signed the contract   everything's clear for a month

   The alarm stops.

Joe Hynes a month

Theresa Black that's as long term as he could get – i'll get these cheques signed (*Signing cheques.*) get everyone away home – he said he wants a meetin with ya first thing monday mornin

Joe Hynes a meetin about what

Theresa Black there was no details joe – all he said was there's goin to have to be changes – a don't care – today's been sorted out that's all i'm interested in

Joe Hynes short term contracts

Theresa Black he didn't say that's what it was

Joe Hynes changes he said

Theresa Black changes

Joe Hynes that's what it is

Theresa Black once i've all these signed will ya give them out – a don't want them all comin up here

Joe Hynes aye sure – ya alright

Theresa Black bit of a headache just

Joe Hynes changes – that could mean fuckin anythin – turn the whole lot into a packin plant – that's half a them laid off – either that or the short term contracts – either way it's walkin time – no big bucks for him then

Theresa Black there is no big bucks joe

Joe Hynes he doesn't keep this place goin for the love of it

Theresa Black he's not makin a fortune – i have a feelin given half a chance he'd close the place – he's never happy

Joe Hynes who is – there's not many in here wake up in the mornin kissin the sunshine

Theresa Black i'm just sayin joe – from talkin to him i think he's had enough

Joe Hynes fuck him i've had enough

Theresa Black we've all had enough – we don't own the place though do we – us havin enough means a shoutin match in the house or an extra pint on the way home – him havin enough means the place closes – wait until monday

Joe Hynes fuck it – yer right – monday mornin's a long time away – know what a think

Theresa Black no joe tell me what ya think

Joe Hynes you don't care what a think do ya

Theresa Black not really no – but tell me anyway

Joe Hynes i think we have as much control over what happens as the lumps a dead meat we carry about the place

Theresa Black i think yer right

Joe Hynes i know i'm right – see when a started here know the only thing a had on my mind – say no a don't joe – cause a bet ya ya don't know what it is

Theresa Black no a don't joe

Joe Hynes the only thing a had on my mind was losin weight

Theresa Black an look at you now it's worked

Joe Hynes it has – ya know my wife don't ya – maeve

Theresa Black i've met her – lovely girl

Joe Hynes lovely girl – i always fancied maeve – but she never seemed too keen – and i got it into my head it was because a was too fat – so in order to get her round to my way of thinkin a thought i'll have to drop the weight – a mate a mine says get a job in the abattoir the weight'll fall of ye – that's why i'm here – over ten years ago that was – an it worked because a got the girl – funny as fuck how things work out isn't it

Theresa Black i'm bustin my sides

Joe Hynes you could put a sofa in here an charge people – yer a good listener

Theresa Black go down an give the cheques out

Joe Hynes know what i'm thinkin – know what would happen if i didn't weigh in on monday mornin

Theresa Black what

Joe Hynes fuck all – that's what would happen – i'm takin the wee lad's cheque

Theresa Black aye

> *Joe exits. Theresa signs a cheque then folds it and puts it in her handbag. She takes a hand mirror from her bag and studies her face in it.*

THREE

The shop. Sammy is behind the counter. He is about to make a phone call. Betty enters. Sammy puts the phone down.

Sammy Lennon where have ya been – i was just about to phone the police betty – what happened

Betty Lennon nothing happened

Sammy Lennon a thought something had happened to ya

Betty Lennon i bought some clothes that's all – a dress – a bought a new dress

Sammy Lennon why didn't ya phone me – ya could've phoned me betty

Betty Lennon (*takes dress from bag*) do ya like the dress

Sammy Lennon it's lovely

Betty Lennon do ya like the dress – it took me a long time to pick this dress – do ya like it – look at it

Sammy Lennon yes a like the dress

Betty Lennon it'll suit me won't it – it's the type a thing i look well in

Sammy Lennon you should've phoned

Betty Lennon stop being an old fool

Sammy Lennon i was worried – what happened at the hospital – i thought maybe ya got bad news or somethin and ya went off somewhere

Betty Lennon where would a go sammy

Sammy Lennon i don't know – what happened

Betty Lennon it's fine – everything's fine

Sammy Lennon what did the doctor say

Betty Lennon she said everything's fine

Sammy Lennon and have ya to go back or anything

Betty Lennon did the rest of the order arrive

Sammy Lennon he was here – tried to pull another fast one – a box of crisps he said we already had

Betty Lennon ya checked everythin then

Sammy Lennon double checked it – you'll not be pullin any fast ones here i said to him

Betty Lennon what he say

Sammy Lennon what could he say

Betty Lennon maybe we should sell up

Sammy Lennon need to get one of those alarm systems in first – anybody buyin the place would expect it – a phoned up about them – there's a fella comin out tomorrow

Betty Lennon that type of thing might be costly sammy

Sammy Lennon if it's too costly (*Takes out the club from under the counter.*) this is plan b

Betty Lennon don't be stupid

Sammy Lennon it worked today – one of those hoods was in the place – they're barred – it's the only type a behaviour the understand betty – he was goin to throw a bottle at me – i let him know though – told them not to come back – their business wasn't wanted here – chased him off with this – the have to know ya mean business

Betty Lennon put it back upstairs

Sammy Lennon a will not – it's stayin behind the counter

Betty Lennon i'm goin to phone up an get somebody round to value the place

Sammy Lennon the shop and the house – we sell the house we'll have to buy another

Betty Lennon unless we want to live in the street we would

Sammy Lennon where would we go

Betty Lennon move up the road a bit

Sammy Lennon those houses are too big for us – wouldn't have the money for one of those even if the weren't too big

Betty Lennon they're buildin smaller ones round the corner from the bigger ones

Sammy Lennon new houses betty – what would we want with a new house

Betty Lennon we'll see – talk about it later

Sammy Lennon aye – see the type a money involved – this place mightn't be worth as much as we think

Betty Lennon maybe – i'm goin up to lie down – you be alright here on yer own

Sammy Lennon me and my friend here will keep things tickin over

Betty Lennon sammy a don't want ya

Sammy Lennon i'm only jokin – go have yer lie down – know what a was thinkin

Betty Lennon what

Sammy Lennon i'll cook us both a nice meal tonight – we haven't done that in a while

Betty Lennon no we haven't

Sammy Lennon i'll cook us both a nice meal later on –
after you've had yer sleep – maybe close the place a bit
early tonight

Betty Lennon that would be nice

Sammy Lennon aye it would

FOUR

The allotment. Paul and Harry are drinking tins of beer.

Harry Fogarty cheers

Paul Fogarty good luck

Harry Fogarty god rest ya da

Paul Fogarty god rest him – still can't work out why he
did that – let the two of us think he got rid a this place

Harry Fogarty there's plenty a things ya don't know
about people isn't there

Paul Fogarty think he was tellin us something

Harry Fogarty what way – he wasn'e one a the world's
thinkers was he

Paul Fogarty just tryin to work this out

Harry Fogarty there is no workin out to it – he just
wanted the place to himself – see inside the shed's still the
same

Paul Fogarty is it

Harry Fogarty everything fuckin perfect – spotless

Paul Fogarty i hated the way he made us scrub
everything clean

Harry Fogarty in order to do a job right what have ya got to look after

Paul Fogarty you've got to look after yer tools

Harry Fogarty a fuckin surgeon's tools wouldn't be as clean as those

Paul Fogarty he loved this place

Harry Fogarty a savin grace for people that don't say much

Paul Fogarty my ma god rest her was never up here

Harry Fogarty never

Paul Fogarty he wouldn't let her come up

Harry Fogarty she wouldn't have come up anyway – the house was hers the allotment was his

Paul Fogarty don't think she was too keen on us comin up here y'know

Harry Fogarty she didn't give a fuck

Paul Fogarty don't know

Harry Fogarty my da's shed – member yer wee woman – daly ya called her – buck teeth dirty fingernails – her da had to go on the run at some stage or somethin

Paul Fogarty aye – him an my da were mates were the not

Harry Fogarty aye – member her

Paul Fogarty a do

Harry Fogarty me an her used to go at it some steam in that shed – some girl she was

Paul Fogarty i know that

Harry Fogarty how'd ya know that

Paul Fogarty she told me

Harry Fogarty told ya when

Paul Fogarty told me when me an her were goin at it some steam in the shed

Harry Fogarty ya never said

Paul Fogarty what would a say for

Harry Fogarty dirty bastard – i liked her – don't like her now cause she did the dirty on me – liked her then though – you did that on me

Paul Fogarty what about you and the home brew

Harry Fogarty the home brew was good – better than this shite – that was a different matter

Paul Fogarty how was it a different matter

Harry Fogarty my da assumed it was yers – i didn't do the dirty on ya – stealin someone's girl is doin the dirty

Paul Fogarty she wasn't yer girl – wasn't she goin out with yer man brennan – brother only had one hand – the only reason my da assumed it was me was because ya told him it was me

Harry Fogarty he must've thought you looked like a drinker or somethin

Paul Fogarty he beat the shite out a me for that

Harry Fogarty beat the shite out a the two of us for plenty a things

Paul Fogarty whenever he went for the belt ya knew it was serious

Harry Fogarty there was a few times he was very nearly gettin fuckin choked with it

Paul Fogarty felt like that myself – member i poured the weedkiller over the roses – fuck

Harry Fogarty never seen him like that – thought the tears were goin burst out a him

Paul Fogarty standin there lookin at the rose bush – ya thought somebody had just fuckin died – not a word out a him – he didn't speak to me for weeks – see just where yer sittin – right where those weeds are – what we goin to do with this place then

Harry Fogarty it's not like we can divide it up or anythin is it

Paul Fogarty not like him to let weeds grow

Harry Fogarty aye – sell it

Paul Fogarty ya want to do that

Harry Fogarty don't think so

Paul Fogarty either we look after it or we let it go

Harry Fogarty ya look after the gardenin part of it right – and i'll use the shed for women

Paul Fogarty what women

Harry Fogarty some women

Paul Fogarty no women

Harry Fogarty right scrub the shed idea then

Paul Fogarty listen – when somebody dies ya bury them

Harry Fogarty easiest way i'm told

Paul Fogarty that's like death – buryin is death – something's dead there's no growth – what about burial with growth – in memory of my da know what i'm sayin

Harry Fogarty no

Paul Fogarty dig those weeds up and plant some flowers
– my da's flowers

Harry Fogarty now

Paul Fogarty yes certainly now – on the day he was
buried ya see it has to be done today like – before
midnight – the day he was buried

Harry Fogarty the day he was buried – yer not usin my
shovel by the way

Paul Fogarty what one's that

Harry Fogarty the one with the black handle

Paul Fogarty that one's mine

Harry Fogarty fuckin sure it's not

Paul Fogarty fuckin sure it is

FIVE

*The flat. Connie is putting make-up on her bruised face.
Robbie is finishing the packing. He sets a shoulder bag
beside Connie.*

Robbie Mullin the gear is in that bag – you look after it
– don't let it out a yer sight – an don't be dippin into it
either (*Takes a bag of pills from the shoulder bag.*) here
take that

She doesn't move.

take it – have them on the way down if ya want

*Robbie exits to the bedroom. Connie takes a pill and
puts the rest in her handbag. She continues to put*

make-up on. It is painful. Robbie enters with a wad of money.

ten grand roughly – that's our lot – put it in yer handbag

Connie Dean we need to stop at a chemist – i need more make up

He touches her face she pulls away.

you'll have to go in and get it – i'll tell ya what to get

Robbie Mullin right – there'll be somewhere on the way out – get it in a garage would ya

Connie Dean no

Robbie Mullin we'll find somewhere – are ya nearly ready – we need to get goin a don't want to be drivin all night

Connie Dean ya want me to look my best don't ya – this takes time

Robbie Mullin ya want a drink

Connie Dean no

Robbie Mullin (*getting a drink*) give the ole doll that runs the shop a lift to the hospital today – her husband talkin away to me about hoods breakin into his shop – he says they're all high on drugs – then he says he's worried about his wife getting a taxi because he thinks they're all drug dealers – so a give her a lift in a car full a gear – people haven't a fuckin clue have the

Spilo Johnston and Rat Joyce walk into the room. They are gunmen.

Spilo Johnston neither one a you say a word

Robbie Mullin i've money ya can take it – i'm movin out anyway there's no need

Spilo Johnston a just told ya not to speak – don't say a fuckin word – kneel down in the middle a the floor

Robbie Mullin jesus don't

Spilo Johnston ya speak again an i'm goin to put one in yer napper right now

Robbie kneels.

we need a tie an a hankie (*To Connie.*) hey you turn round – what happened to yer face

Connie Dean nothin

Spilo Johnston he do that to ya – yer some fella aren't ya (*To Connie.*) get me a hankie an a tie

Connie exits to the bedroom followed by Rat Joyce. Spilo looks about the room, checks the CDs etc. Connie and Rat enter. Spilo stuffs the hankie in Robbie's mouth and ties his hands behind his back.

Spilo Johnston that's better – (*To Connie.*) nobody mentioned you – sit down – don't panic just listen – (*He talks to her with his gun.*) ya listenin

Connie Dean yes

Spilo Johnston good – yer gonna take whatever bag belongs to ya and go – yer not to come back here ya understan

Connie Dean yes

Spilo Johnston yer seen round here again yer goin to end up the same way as him – when ya leave ya speak to no one ya got that

Connie Dean yes

Spilo Johnston a don't know what ya think of this scumbag here – personally speakin if he did that to my face a

wouldn't be too happy with him – the point is – phonin
the peelers isn't goin to do him any good but it'll do you
a lot a harm – and don't think we won't be able to find
ya we will – ya understan all that

Connie Dean yes

Spilo Johnston well take yer stuff and away ya go

*Connie lifts her handbag and the shoulder bag. She
stands beside Robbie.*

Connie Dean can a hit him

Spilo Johnston only i've to do what i've been told i'd let
you shoot him – welt away

Connie Dean bastard

Connie punches Robbie and spits on him. She exits.

Spilo Johnston she certainly doesn't like you – couldn't
blame her – i've been told to tell ya this is a warnin – you
want to be the man in the big picture shoutin yer head off
– sayin things ya shouldn't say – i'd advise ya to do it
somewhere else – but ya know that – bags packed an
everything – too late – what a bummer

*He pushes Robbie to the ground and rolls him over
face down.*

hold his legs down

*Rat does this. Spilo shoots Robbie in the back of both
knees. He is going to shoot him in the ankles but the
gun jams.*

give me yers

Gives him the gun.

you ever do this before

Rat Joyce no

Spilo Johnston away ya go then

Rat shoots Robbie in both ankles. They exit.

SIX

The pub. Helen is behind the counter. She is flicking the lid of the lighter open and closed while looking at her mobile phone which she has in her hand. Frank, Bobbie, Shanks and Sharon are at their usual tables. Joeis in the abattoir, he is changing out of his work clothes. Maeve is at home. There is a cot in the room. A baby is crying. Maeve lifts the baby from the cot to stop it crying. Frank walks from his table to the counter.

Frank Coin (*to Helen*) waitin on a call

Helen Woods thinkin a makin one

Frank Coin always better off makin them than not

Helen Woods time for a half un is it

Frank Coin that time alright

Helen gets Frank his drink and he sits down at his table. Helen makes a call. Joeis in the abattoir. His phone rings. Helen walks into the scene.

Helen Woods hello

Joe Hynes how's it goin (*Silence.*) hello are ya there

Helen Woods yeah i'm here

Joe Hynes i'll be over soon

Helen Woods i'm goin home joe

Joe Hynes that's alright i'll meet ya round at yer place then

Helen Woods a was thinkin of havin an early night – on my feet all day

Joe Hynes ya not want me to come round

Helen Woods a don't think so

Maeve is nursing the baby. She makes a phone call.
She walks into the scene.

Joe Hynes hold on a minute there's somebody beepin me – hold on – hello

Maeve Hynes where are ya

Joe Hynes where do ya think a am i'm at work

Maeve Hynes a wee baby boy – she had a wee baby boy – nine poun something – looks just like her

Joe Hynes maeve i've a union guy holdin on here

Maeve Hynes how'd it go today

Joe Hynes hold on a minute – ya still there

Helen Woods yes

Joe Hynes maeve's on the other line

Helen Woods i'll just go on then joe

Joe Hynes no no wait – i'll get rid of her just wait – hello – a can't stay on here

Maeve Hynes tell me how it went

Joe Hynes it's sorted out

Maeve Hynes that's good – ya want to see the baby joe it's beautiful

Joe Hynes a have to go

Maeve Hynes when are ya comin home

Joe Hynes don't know

Maeve Hynes you'll not be long i've a surprise for ya

Joe Hynes what

Maeve Hynes you'll see when ya get here

Joe Hynes it didn't cost money did it

Maeve Hynes not a penny joe

Joe Hynes right

Maeve Hynes don't be long

   Maeve exits.

Joe Hynes she's away (*Silence.*) a can't hear ya

Helen Woods a didn't say anythin

Joe Hynes i'll call over to the pub before ya go

Helen Woods no don't

Joe Hynes what's the matter

Helen Woods nothin – just tired – i'm goin to go on here

Joe Hynes phone me later

   Helen moves back into the pub and starts collecting glasses from the tables. Sharon returns to her seat from the toilet.

Shanks O'Neill don't ya feel better for that

Sharon Lawther aye – give us a feg

Shanks O'Neill (*he does*) a told ya a good boke get it all out a yer system – isn't that right bobbie a good boke is the makins of ya on days like this

Bobbie Torbett aye (*To Sharon.*) you alright

Sharon Lawther do a look alright

Bobbie Torbett (*to Shanks*) what ya call the barmaid

Shanks O'Neill in here nearly everyday ya don't remember what ya call her

Bobbie Torbett just tell me her fuckin name

Shanks O'Neill helen her name's helen

Bobbie Torbett have to have a word with her

Shanks O'Neill buy another gargle when yer up there

Bobbie Torbett i've had enough (*He moves to counter.*) helen

Helen Woods same again

Bobbie Torbett no – no more – is it alright if a have a word with you a minute

Helen Woods i've no money on me

Bobbie Torbett no not that – this mornin – when the world was a clearer place – i remember you sayin that ya were short staffed here or somethin

Helen Woods why ya lookin a job

Bobbie Torbett a don't think so – i have a wee lad – about eighteen he is – ya see him in earlier

Helen Woods good lookin fella

Bobbie Torbett takes after his ma – he's a good kid – he needs work – he's lookin a job in that fuckin kip across the way – can i tell you this – no good sayin to him he won't listen – i don't want him over there – you see – it does somethin to ya – i worked there all my days – start out as a kid – then workin there – talkin with men all the time – shoutin and slabberin – it hardens ya – i was the

337

hardest man in that place – what use has it done me – none – only i'm minus a wife now – i don't want that for him – ya understand that – so is there any chance ya could fit him in here – least be a starter for him – not get him involved in that – would you do that

Helen Woods can he start tomorrow

Bobbie Torbett yer a darlin – here first thing he'll be – a darlin ya are

Sharon stands beside Bobbie at the bar.

Sharon Lawther ya want a drink

Bobbie Torbett cheers helen luv – no – don't you be takin anymore

Sharon Lawther i'm just havin this one (*To Helen.*) a gin an a pint

Helen gets the drinks and Sharon pays for them.

Bobbie Torbett i'm drinkin whatever's there then i'm headin home

Sharon Lawther ya not goin to ask me to go with ya

Bobbie Torbett no – go round to yer sister's

Sharon Lawther a wouldn't be welcome there

Bobbie Torbett stayin with me sharon isn't goin to work out ya know that

Sharon Lawther a don't know that

Bobbie Torbett well i do – go back round to the flat an sort it out

Sharon Lawther there is nothing to sort out

Bobbie Torbett if he's gone all the better

Sharon Lawther he was never there to go

Bobbie Torbett never there what

Sharon Lawther i live on my own bobbie – a have done this years

Bobbie Torbett what was all that last night then

Sharon Lawther didn't want to be on my own anymore that's all

Bobbie Torbett what's in the suitcase

Sharon Lawther nothing

Bobbie Torbett jesus sharon luv – what the fuck

Sharon Lawther there's times when i think about you bobbie an last night was one a them – thought we could spend a few days together see what might happen

Bobbie Torbett nothing's goin to happen

Sharon Lawther no

Bobbie Torbett what ya goin to do

Sharon Lawther sit an have a drink with shanks – he's an obnoxious little bollocks but better that then nothin

Bobbie Torbett i'm not a fuckin expert on these matters but why don't ya try an straighten yerself out

Sharon Lawther bobbie for fuck sake

Bobbie Torbett a know

Shanks O'Neill my mouth's dryin up here

Sharon Lawther ya sittin down

Bobbie Torbett just to finish what's in front a me – look after yerself

Sharon Lawther yeah

They move to the table. Sharon sits. Bobbie stands.

Shanks O'Neill sit down there

Bobbie Torbett i'm goin on here

Shanks O'Neill goin on where

Bobbie Torbett goin on home

Shanks O'Neill we'll all go then

Sharon Lawther no i'm not

Bobbie Torbett i've to go home to my bed – you sit here with sharon keep her company

Shanks O'Neill an what about after

Bobbie Torbett go round to yer own house – i'm sure yer ma would like the company

Sharon Lawther you live with yer ma

Bobbie Torbett him an his ma have great fun together

Sharon Lawther (*laughing*) ya live with yer ma

SEVEN

The street. Swiz, Cooper and Bop are lively.

Cooper Jones moo

Swiz Murdoch moo

Cooper Jones mon bop give it a moo

Bop Torbett moo – moo – moo – moo

Cooper Jones get some a these wee dolls round the club show them the business

Swiz Murdoch wee dolls is it – you on yer own tonight –
no lovely maggie bop

Cooper Jones says she's away to the pictures – fuck it

Swiz Murdoch what were the tales from the riverbank

Cooper Jones moo

Swiz Murdoch what

Cooper Jones don't be sayin fuck all

Swiz Murdoch rather eat my own eyes out

Cooper Jones first time – fuckin beezer

Swiz Murdoch first one in – hear that bop – cooper an
maggie the pokey people

Cooper Jones pokey man

Swiz Murdoch any good

Cooper Jones aye it was good

Swiz Murdoch that's you in love now

Bop Torbett moo – moo – moo

Cooper Jones yer right bop – bop's right

   Maggie enters.

Swiz Murdoch the maggie – no swim suit

Maggie Lyttle dick

Swiz Murdoch moo dick

Cooper Jones thought ya were headin off to the pictures –
couldn't stay away

Maggie Lyttle a went smart arse

Cooper Jones the makin movies shorter these days

Maggie Lyttle the queue was too long

Swiz Murdoch how'd the swimmin go maggie did ya have a good time

Maggie Lyttle ya weren't there – work it out

Swiz Murdoch cooper said he had a good time – we had a good time bop didn't we

Maggie Lyttle standin here all day aye

Swiz Murdoch oh no – where were we bop

Bop Torbett round at the druggies' flat

Swiz Murdoch in the druggies' flat

Cooper Jones doin what

Swiz Murdoch doin who – that right bop doin who – isn't that right bop

Bop Torbett aye

Maggie Lyttle you two – a don't think so

Swiz Murdoch two of us standin outside the flat she comes to the window – what happens next – gets the jugs out – next thing in the jacuzzi

Maggie Lyttle aye dead on

Swiz Murdoch bop am a right or wrong – tell them – go on

Bop Torbett we were round there

Maggie Lyttle in the jacuzzi with the druggie girl

Swiz Murdoch bubbles up to our arses

Cooper Jones the bop fella

Swiz Murdoch everybody was in the water today – an what did yer uncle swiz get us (*Produces dope.*) a big chunk a blow – sky high for the water babies

342

Cooper Jones chill out gear

Swiz Murdoch chill out gear

Cooper Jones the chill out gear maggie

Maggie Lyttle roll one up then

Cooper Jones roll one up is right

Swiz Murdoch i've no skins

Cooper Jones you any

Maggie Lyttle i don't smoke what would a have them for

Cooper Jones bop

Bop Torbett no

Cooper Jones fuck that i'm not eatin it – a hate that it takes hours

Maggie Lyttle buy some

Cooper Jones the shop – bop's the man for the shop – skins an water – this is the plan

Swiz Murdoch plans are good

Cooper Jones the old fucker barred me today so no money is to exchange hands here

Maggie Lyttle can we not just buy them

Cooper Jones no

Swiz Murdoch no is right

Cooper Jones bop's on the team

Swiz Murdoch no lappin the show like ya did last night

Bop Torbett a didn't

Cooper Jones ya gonna do it

Bop Torbett aye what

Cooper Jones give us all the money ya have

Bop Torbett what for

Cooper Jones so we know ya didn't pay for them

Bop Torbett i'm not givin you two my money

Cooper Jones i'm heart broken ya don't trust us –
maggie'll look after it

Swiz Murdoch he trusts the lovely maggie

   Bop gives Maggie the money.

seven quid – not goin to do much damage with that

Bop Torbett you owe me a tenner

Cooper Jones go forth an come back with water an skins

Bop Torbett the skins are behind the counter

Cooper Jones there in lies the challenge

Bop Torbett i'll buy the skins an steal the water

Cooper Jones no

Maggie Lyttle they're behind the counter – what is he
invisible

Swiz Murdoch he pretends he has a gun

Bop Torbett i'm not doin that

Swiz Murdoch lappin the show

Cooper Jones it's a joke that's all – stick yer finger in yer
coat pocket – give it some verbals – then on yer way out
the door take yer hand out a yer pocket an wave at him –
what's the problem there – he'll even find that funny
himself

Bop Torbett wave bye bye to him

Cooper Jones wave bye bye to him

Swiz Murdoch piece a piss – moo

Bop Torbett right i'll do it

Swiz Murdoch moo chill out moo

Maggie Lyttle i'll go with him

Cooper Jones he'll be alright on his own – you'll be alright on yer own

Bop Torbett aye

EIGHT

The abattoir. Theresa's office. She is sitting in the dark. Dave is standing in a field. The diggers have stopped. He takes a few deep breathes then makes a phone call. The phone rings in the office. Theresa turns the light on. Dave walks into the scene. Theresa answers the phone.

Theresa Black yes

Dave Black what are ya still doin there

Theresa Black nothin – i'm leavin now – where are ya at home

Dave Black no

Theresa Black come on home dave – i need you to come home

Dave Black they've found the body (*Silence.*) theresa did you hear what a said they've found the body

Theresa Black i heard – how can the be sure it's him

Dave Black it's him

Theresa Black how can the be sure

Dave Black i recognise the shoes – it's his shoes (*Silence.*)
you alright

Theresa Black i'm alright – how did the find him – where
was he – did the use a digger – it didn't hit him or
anything did it

Dave Black he was near a hedge that had grown there –
the dug him out with shovels – the can't move him just
yet – they're waitin on someone comin with a coffin

Theresa Black put a blanket over him

Dave Black there is a blanket over him – when the coffin
comes the have to take him away for official
identification

Theresa Black his shoes

Dave Black i know – i'm goin to stay with him

Theresa Black yes

Dave Black i got them to leave me alone with him – i –
i said a few prayers over him and told him that we loved
him – oh my god theresa (*Silence.*)

Theresa Black it's alright dave

Dave Black it's not alright (*Pause.*) look there's no point
in ya doin anythin now – a know ya want to be here but
there's no point in comin down now – come down
tomorrow yeah

Theresa Black yeah

Dave Black bring some of my clothes down would ya

Theresa Black like what

Dave Black anything – somethin dark – look i'm goin to have to go here – something's happenin a don't know – maybe the coffins arrived or somethin – so i'm goin to go alright

Theresa Black yeah

Dave Black you alright

Theresa Black yeah – i'll be down first thing in the mornin

Dave Black the found him theresa – the found our boy

Theresa Black go you on and get things sorted out dave – i'll be down in the mornin

Dave Black right – don't be sittin there all night go home

Theresa Black a will

Dave Black i'm away on

Theresa Black right

Dave exits. Theresa is motionless.

my baby

Her scream is silent then she howls with grief.

NINE

The allotment. Paul and Harry have stopped digging. They have found guns.

Paul Fogarty guns – fuckin guns

Harry Fogarty want are ya lookin at me for i didn't put them there

Paul Fogarty what are the doin there

347

Harry Fogarty the mightn't be his

Paul Fogarty no that's right the mightn't be his – who put them there then the fuckin gun fairy

Harry Fogarty somebody else might a planked them

Paul Fogarty guns for what

Harry Fogarty shootin deer – that's why ya don't see any a them up round here – we live in belfast what do ya think the were for – they're in good nick

Paul Fogarty how ya know that

Harry Fogarty what do ya mean how do a know it

Paul Fogarty you seem to know a lot about them

Harry Fogarty a know nothing about them

Paul Fogarty are the yers

Harry Fogarty aye a brought ya up here to shoot ye – fuckin eejit – they're clean that's what a meant – spotless – well looked after

Paul Fogarty they're my da's then

Harry Fogarty he could a just been lookin after them for somebody – the knew he had an allotment – say the said look would ya bury them for a while – that happens

Paul Fogarty not that that's good – it's not – but if it's not that

Harry shrugs.

what does shruggin yer shoulders mean

Harry Fogarty it means ya know as much as i do

Paul Fogarty if he wasn't keeping them for someone it means the were his

Harry Fogarty i know that

Paul Fogarty and if the were his what – he might a used them – in fact no might about it – if the were his he used them

Harry Fogarty he didn't use them

Paul Fogarty then what the fuck was he doin with them – and why were the buried

Harry Fogarty well it's not the wild west is it – ya hardly go around wearin them on yer fuckin holster

Paul Fogarty where's the joke here

Harry Fogarty the gun fairy – was that not a joke – an stop talking to me like that – buried guns or no fuckin buried you'll get a slap

Paul Fogarty what's wrong with you – get a slap – fuckin wise up – so my da's a murderer

Harry Fogarty don't be sayin that

Paul Fogarty it could be true

Harry Fogarty it's not true

Paul Fogarty how do ya know

Harry Fogarty he was my da for christ sake – a think i'd know if he was a murderer or not

Paul Fogarty ya didn't know he buried guns did ya

Harry Fogarty that's different

Paul Fogarty how's it different

Harry Fogarty anybody can bury guns only some can use them though

Paul Fogarty this is why he lied about the allotment

Harry Fogarty looks like it – solves the problem too of what we're goin to do with it

Paul Fogarty fuckin creates a problem

Harry Fogarty not for me it doesn't

Paul Fogarty it does for me

Harry Fogarty all we got a do is put them back where the were – let this place grow over an forget about it

Paul Fogarty forget about it

Harry Fogarty he's dead now there's not much we can do about that – not like we can ask him is it – even if we could it's hardly likely he'd tell ya – which must be part of the reason he stopped us from comin here

Paul Fogarty what

Harry Fogarty to protect us

Paul Fogarty to protect us – fuck that was big of him

Harry Fogarty yeah it was – whatever he was involved in he didn't want us to get involved in it in any way

Paul Fogarty does it not bother you that my da might a shot someone and in all likelihood the poor fucker that he shot is dead

Harry Fogarty a told ya stop talkin like that

Paul Fogarty not sayin it isn't goin to make it any less true is it

Harry Fogarty there's nothing we can do

Paul Fogarty yes there is

Harry Fogarty what

Paul Fogarty phone the peelers an tell them what we've found

Harry Fogarty are you out a yer fuckin mind – that's never goin to happen right – but tell me anyway what good would it do

Paul Fogarty we could find out what the story is

Harry Fogarty tell me this did ya love my da

Paul Fogarty don't be askin stupid fuckin questions

Harry Fogarty did ya or didn't ya

Paul Fogarty of course a did he was my da

Harry Fogarty right – i loved him too – and now he's dead

Paul Fogarty and what

Harry Fogarty say it's the worst which it's not – say my da did shoot somebody and they're dead – and now he's dead – what – it goin to bring whoever he shot back to life – no – all that's goin to happen is that the world's goin to know that my da shot someone and he's not around to tell anybody why

Paul Fogarty yer tellin me ya don't want to know why

Harry Fogarty a don't need to know why because a already do know – a know my da was a hard workin strict wee man who did the best he could at a time when things here were fucked up – and a don't know about any a this but a do know he wasn't a bad man – ya wanted to do something for yer da – plant some flowers for him – i'll tell ya what to do for him – bury these an say fuck all about

Paul Fogarty i don't like this

Harry Fogarty neither do i – grab a shovel

Paul Fogarty i'm not doin it – i'm not getting involved – fuck it leave them there

Harry Fogarty you do what you want but i know what i've to do (*He lifts a shovel.*) what are ya standin there for go on fuck off

The shop. Betty is behind the counter. She is wearing her new dress. Bop is hesitant about what he is about to do.

Betty Lennon yer the last one – just made it in time – about to close up it's been a long day

Bop Torbett aye

Sammy Lennon (*from upstairs*) this is nearly ready betty

Betty Lennon i've a customer – i'm closin up after that

Sammy Lennon right i'll not put the soup out yet then

Betty Lennon (*to Bop*) think he ran a swanky restaurant to hear him

Bop Torbett this bottle of water (*Hand in his pocket pretending he has a gun.*) don't move – it's a joke right – don't move

Betty Lennon take it easy son – it's alright – ya can take what ya want – don't shoot me

Bop Torbett (*takes his hand out of his pocket*) a don't have anything – look nothing – i'm sorry – a don't know why i'm doin this – i'm sorry

Bop exits.

Sammy Lennon (*from upstairs.*) everything alright down there

Betty Lennon yes – it's alright

Silence. Betty takes the club from under the counter and starts smashing the place up.

ELEVEN

A house. Joe is just home. Maeve is in another room.

Joe Hynes maeve

Maeve Hynes i'm out here

Joe Hynes what's the cot doin here – we can't afford to buy that wee girl a cot

Maeve Hynes a got a lend of it

Joe Hynes what for

   Maeve enters with the baby in her arms.

Maeve Hynes somewhere for this wee man to sleep

Joe Hynes what the fuck

Maeve Hynes before ya say anythin joe just listen

Joe Hynes there's nothin that you can say maeve that's goin to make this . . .

Maeve Hynes it's not what ya think

Joe Hynes it's what a think alright ya crazy bitch

Maeve Hynes don't say that – listen – i know a shouldn't have done this – stealin something isn't right

Joe Hynes isn't right – you'll get fuckin locked up for this

Maeve Hynes a thought if we had somethin of our own to look after for a while

Joe Hynes of our own – you've taken someone else's baby – ya crazy fucker – is it yer cousin's

Maeve Hynes it's not hers

Joe Hynes do ya not see what you've done here

Maeve Hynes do you want me to explain

Joe Hynes no i don't want you to fuckin explain – a want somebody to come and take you away an put ya in a fuckin straitjacket – i've had enough i'm not doin this any more

Maeve Hynes what are ya not doin any more joe

Joe Hynes jesus christ – have children – anybody who would do something like that maeve isn't fit to be a mother – don't think too i'm goin to help ya i'm not – i'll sign any fuckin report or anythin that says yer not right in the head – selfish fuckin bitch

Maeve Hynes what is it yer not goin to do any more joe

Joe Hynes i'm not pretendin – pretendin that our life together isn't a sham – pretendin to be interested in the crap ya talk about our future together – pretendin what a do everyday is worth all this – pretendin a like comin home when a want to be somewhere else – and the big one – pretending yer in some way fuckin normal and that i still love you

Maeve Hynes not normal

Joe Hynes better fuckin believe it's not normal

Maeve lets the baby fall to the floor.

Maeve Hynes it's a dummy joe it's not real – the let mothers-to-be practise on them – i stole one of them because i thought that if you and i could spend a weekend pretending to look after a child of our own that it might make you want one the way i did – that we could both want something together – that's all joe – nothing more than that – nothing crazy just something to bring us together – it felt like that's what we needed – but you have other plans – somewhere else you want to be – to be with someone else

Maeve lifts the baby up and puts it in the cot.

when did it start – it doesn't matter i don't care – no a
do – was it before or after i found out about – my –
difficulty in having a child

Joe Hynes maeve

Maeve Hynes before or after

Joe Hynes before

Maeve Hynes i don't know why but that makes me feel a
bit better

Joe Hynes what are we going to do

Maeve Hynes we – what are we going to do – i'm not
going to do anythin joe – you've just told me what ya
thought of me – what can i do

Joe Hynes a didn't mean things to happen this way

Maeve Hynes what way did ya mean them to happen –
that i would never know and you could go on
pretending – or maybe i was to find somethin in yer
pocket – somethin to give the game away and i was to
confront ya – and somehow it would all turn round that
it's my fault – and although i wasn't happy with the
situation i would feel a bit guilty about it all – so i would
forgive you – and we could go through the rest of our
lives me thinking what's wrong with me – what is it
about me that makes my husband want to fuck other
women – and you thinkin these things happen – that's the
way of the world – is that the way ya meant it to
happen – jesus – a thought just came to me there – i
know who it is – a don't know her but a saw her – kept
lookin at me that whole time i was in the shop – this girl
kept lookin at me then if i caught her eye she'd look
away – she runs the pub or somethin – it's her isn't it

Joe Hynes no

Maeve Hynes doesn't matter – it is though i know it is

Joe Hynes do ya want me to explain

Maeve Hynes don't say a damn thing – i'm not givin ya the chance to justify yerself that's not goin to happen – you hurt me joe an that's it – that's all ya need to understand – funny thing i feel in some way – lighter – when a was up at the hospital today lookin at all those babies i kept thinkin maybe joe an i aren't right for havin children – that was the first time a thought that – i think that's why a brought the doll home – to give us a chance to prove me wrong – ya can take one of the good suitcases – i'll iron some clothes for you

Joe Hynes that mightn't be what a want

Maeve Hynes ya don't have a choice joe – i'm doin my best to maintain what little dignity i have left – if you were to stay here joe i'd only end up havin to cut yer fuckin eyes out – a wouldn't be pretendin either

TWELVE

The pub. Helen is behind the bar. Frank is sitting on his own as is Sharon. Her suitcase is on top of the table. Shanks is at the bar paying for a carryout. Both him and Sharon are drunk.

Shanks O'Neill (*puts all his change on the counter*) if there's anythin left out a that just give me it in tins – (*To Sharon.*) alright there dear

Sharon Lawther aye

Shanks O'Neill ya drink tins don't ya

Sharon Lawther tins aye

Shanks O'Neill (*to Helen*) – out of a shitty poe she'd drink it

Helen Woods ya takin her home

Shanks O'Neill me an her – don't worry she'll be alright – i'll look after her

Helen Woods do that

Shanks O'Neill a will – a will – ya know me – i'm the man for lookin after the women (*To Sharon.*) right come on dear let's hit the road – what's in that suitcase ya have

Sharon Lawther nothin

Shanks O'Neill put the tins in it – easier carried

Puts tins in suitcase.

Sharon Lawther tins in a suitcase – let's go

Shanks O'Neill (*to Frank*) cheers

Frank Coin good luck

Shanks exits.

Sharon Lawther (*to Helen*) ya want a piece of advice dear

Helen Woods what's that

Sharon Lawther all men are a shower a shite

Sharon exits.

Helen Woods think they'll make it

Frank Coin ya wouldn't know – people always seem to find their way home no matter what

Helen Woods it's findin their way back here i'm worried about

Helen pours them both a drink. She sits at the counter and lights a cigarette. She holds the lighter flicking the lid open and closed.

Frank Coin good health

Helen Woods have a few drinks before a close up

Frank Coin it's nearly that time alright – nice lighter

Helen Woods aye (*Hands it to him.*)

Frank Coin used to have one like it myself

Helen Woods didn't know ya smoked

Frank Coin used to – my wife elsie bought it for me

Helen Woods how long's she dead now frank

Frank Coin ten years nearly eleven

Helen Woods long time

Frank Coin feels like no time sometimes and others it's like a lifetime

Helen Woods she smoke did she

Frank Coin the two of us – like chimneys – that's what killed her – a stopped then (*Hands lighter back.*)

Joe is at home sitting at a table. He is smoking a cigarette. He makes a phone call. Helen's mobile rings. Joewalks into the scene. Helen lets the phone ring then she switches it off. Joeexits.

not want to hear what the have to say

Helen Woods no a don't

Frank Coin boyfriend is it

Helen Woods used to be – a realised he wasn't the man for me when he stopped smokin

Frank Coin better off without him – married men can be difficult

Helen Woods what do you mean married men

Frank Coin can't get away with anythin round here – the mightn't say it but nearly everybody knows nearly everythin

Helen Woods people talkin about it were the

Frank Coin sure who'd be talkin to me – i'm either listenin to the radio out walkin or in here – there's days the only voice a hear is my own – there'll be other men for ya

Helen Woods a hope not

Frank Coin it's the company of somebody that puts the smile on yer face

Helen Woods men are all a shower a shite you heard her – thinkin of takin myself off somewhere

Frank Coin on holidays

Helen Woods a don't know – maybe for good

Frank Coin yer young enough to be doin it – don't leave it too long

Helen Woods you lived round here all yer life aye

Frank Coin most of it – come up from the country to work – got married – elsie was from round here so that was that – out where i'm from there's no one left – this is home now – a used to think about movin back when there was ones alive – sure ya think these things but never do them – there's worse places than this

Helen Woods ya want another drink

Frank Coin i'll finish this that's that – enough's plenty

Helen Woods ya ordered yer taxi or do ya want me to do it

Frank Coin i'm goin walk home tonight a think – know what a heard on the radio this mornin – there's goin to be a meteorite storm tonight – light the whole sky up the said – there was another fella sayin that it was the beginnin of the end of the world – people talk a lot of balls don't the

Helen Woods aye – he didn't say when the end was did he

Frank Coin no he did not – that's a more difficult one – the radio's a great thing – there was another fella on – this programme was all about space – he said that when we talk – the sound we make travels up into space and goes on forever – it never goes away

Helen Woods some of the things i've said frank a want them to go away

Frank Coin listenin to it a had this thought y'know – wouldn't it be good to think that if there was somebody ya could no longer talk to – that if ya said somethin to them that yer words would travel up into space and that the might meet up with words that that person had once said to you – wouldn't that be a nice thing

Helen Woods it would frank

Frank Coin right i'll finish this then that's me for the day

Helen Woods you'll be back tomorrow

Frank Coin a will

THIRTEEN

The street. Maggie is standing alone. Bop arrives. They sit on the pavement.

Maggie Lyttle where were you

Bop Torbett nowhere – just walkin about – ya not go to the club

Maggie Lyttle didn't feel like it – what happened round at the shop

Bop Torbett nothin

Maggie Lyttle ya didn't get the skins then

Bop Torbett no

Maggie Lyttle (*produces joint*) have to smoke this then

Bop Torbett where'd ya get that

Maggie Lyttle swiz had skins

   They smoke the joint.

Bop Torbett those two laughin at me for not comin back were the

Maggie Lyttle what the fuck do you care – are swiz an cooper here – no – am i here – yes – this is yer last chance bop

Bop Torbett yer very bossy

Maggie Lyttle i am not

Bop Torbett are so

Maggie Lyttle arsehole

Bop Torbett today was shit ya know that

Maggie Lyttle even the jacuzzi

Bop Torbett what jacuzzi ya kiddin me – she knocked swiz back an then threw the two of us out – a should've went swimmin shouldn't a

Maggie Lyttle yes

Bop Torbett i hate this place

Maggie lies back and looks up at the sky.

we'll go swimmin tomorrow

Maggie Lyttle teach you to be a fish

Frank Coin walks past.

FOURTEEN

Frank stops in the street and looks up at the sky. He is surrounded by noise. A baby crying. A busy road. Loud music. Church bells ringing. Heavy machinery, Police sirens. Gun shots. People arguing. Screaming. Bop Torbett and Maggie Lyttle are lying on the pavement. In the sky there is a meteorite storm. The stage is covered in a brilliant white light. The stage begins to darken and the noise dies.

Frank Coin (*looking up at the sky*) i miss you elsie

The stage darkens to black. A sonar bleep in the night sky.